THE
DEVELOPMENT
OF
HUMAN
RESOURCES

THE
DEVELOPMENT
OF
HUMAN
RESOURCES

ELI
GINZBERG

McGRAW–HILL BOOK COMPANY
NEW YORK
ST. LOUIS
SAN FRANCISCO
TORONTO
LONDON
SYDNEY

Acknowledgments

Except for Chapters 11 and 12 and those noted below, all chapters have been reprinted by permission of the Columbia University Press.

Chapter 7 from *About the Kinsey Report* edited by Donald P. Geddes and Enid Curie reprinted with permission of the New American Library of World Literature, Copyright 1948 by the New American Library of World Literature.

Chapter 9 reprinted with permission of The Macmillan Company from *The Labor Leader* by Eli Ginzberg, Copyright 1948 by Eli Ginzberg.

Chapters 14 and 19 reprinted with permission of Simon and Schuster from *Human Resources: The Wealth of a Nation* by Eli Ginzberg, Copyright 1958 by Eli Ginzberg.

Chapter 16 reprinted with permission of The Free Press from *The American Worker in the Twentieth Century* by Eli Ginzberg and Hyman Berman, Copyright © 1963 by The Free Press of Glencoe.

**THE
DEVELOPMENT
OF
HUMAN
RESOURCES**

Copyright © 1966 by McGraw-Hill, Inc. All Rights Reserved.
Printed in the United States of America. This book, or
parts thereof, may not be reproduced in any form without
permission of the publishers.
Library of Congress Catalog Card Number: 66–26578
1 2 3 4 5 6 7 8 9 0   MP   7 3 2 1 0 6 9 8 7 6

For Columbia University

Through wisdom
is a house builded;
and by understanding
is it established:

And by knowledge
should the chambers be filled
with all precious
and pleasant riches.

A wise man *is* strong;
yea, a man of knowledge
increaseth strength.

PREFACE

This book has been developed for the explicit purpose of providing scholars and students the opportunity of finding in one place the essential results of our efforts, extending over more than three decades, to explore the field of human resources.

The structure of this book can be briefly described. The Foreword and the Afterword seek to set our efforts within the framework of scholarly inquiry and to suggest a few of the links between research and policy. Each of the major sections of the book is preceded by a brief introduction.

The heart of the book is composed of nineteen chapters selected from fifteen of our earlier works. They are reprinted here substantially without change except for the updating of certain statistics in which I was assisted by Mrs. Roberta Handwerger. In some instances the original titles of the chapters have been adapted to our purpose here.

The bibliography lists the volumes from which these selections were drawn and lists the many members of the Conservation of Human Resources project at Columbia University who have been my collaborators in research. The Conservation project and its predecessors have been structured on an interdisciplinary basis, and the current staff includes representatives from the following disciplines: economics, sociology, psychology, history, education, and business.

I should like to note especially my deep indebtedness to my friend and collaborator, John L. Herma, who has played a major role in our work since he first joined us two decades ago, particularly in the design and execution of our several developmental studies.

Acknowledgment is gratefully made to Columbia University Press, Free Press-Macmillan, New American Library of World Literature, Inc., and Simon and Schuster, Inc., for permission to reprint chapters from books on which they hold the copyright.

Eli Ginzberg

August, 1966

CONTENTS

THE
DEVELOPMENT
OF
HUMAN
RESOURCES

FOREWORD:
HUMAN RESOURCES
AS A DISCIPLINE

The ideas that men develop and follow are grounded in the ideas of their predecessors and in the reality which they themselves know or hope to shape. Most ideas, most ways of thought, which emerge are related to an earlier realm of ideas and to the reality of the day.

This introductory chapter will present schematically the combination of forces, intellectual and social, which together help to explain why concern with the human resource factor in economics has moved only recently from a position where it was neglected or elicited only casual interest into the middle of the arena. This chapter will delineate those forces which are turning research in human resources into a discipline.

Our starting point will be to consider briefly the origins and development of economics as a discipline from the specific vantage point of assessing the place of human resources in its evolution. When we have picked out this strand, we can fill in the background by considering briefly the several other major strands, particularly developments in the field of psychology, certain characteristics of advanced technological societies, and the evolution of democratic thought and action. When the significance of each of these four elements is appreciated and the potency of their interaction weighed, we shall be able to understand why we are witnessing the emergence of a new discipline—the discipline of human resources.

A decade hence, we shall note the sesquicentennial of the emergence of economics as a formal discipline: Adam Smith published his great work, *An Inquiry into the Nature and Causes of the Wealth of Nations,* in 1776. Everyone who has even a fleeting acquaintance with this seminal work knows that for Smith, the human factor in economic life was not peripheral but central. In point of fact, he built much of his analysis around the forces governing the acquisition of skill and its effective utilization. According to Smith, it was the skill, dexterity, and competence of individuals which were the basis of individual and national wealth. Although Smith made room in his elaborations for the role of land and capital in the production process, he maintained that land was a form of "expropriated" property and capital was "congealed" labor—the surplus which people had earned through their industry and which they had decided to save rather than consume. Although Smith allowed for three agents of production—land, capital, and labor—it was really in the last that Smith expected to find the basic dynamics of economic development.

Although Malthus called attention to the ceaseless tension created by the rapidly increasing population and the slowly expanding food supply; although Ricardo's *Principles of Political Economy and Taxation* was grounded in a theory of value based on labor cost; although Marx's attack on both the economists and capitalism started with the exploitation of laborers; although Alfred Marshall called attention to the "residuum"—the lowest sixth of the population which cannot escape from poverty, ill health, and illiteracy without special governmental assistance; although Joseph Schumpeter saw the entrepreneur as the prime mover in capitalism; although Thorstein Veblen laid major stress on *The Instinct of Workmanship* as the foundation of all progressive economics and societies; and although J. M. Keynes revolutionized formal theory by focusing on the reasons that the market might be incapable of absorbing large numbers of unemployed persons who want and need to work and earn incomes—despite this evidence of the continuing concern of the great economists with one or another facet of human resources, they did not follow Adam Smith directly. Not one of them centered his attention on the human factor in economic life.

Ricardo, writing in the early days of the Industrial Revolution, saw no reason to be concerned with the availability of labor. There was a great number of rural workers at the doors of the new factories looking for employment. The mills of that day had no difficulty in absorbing illiterate, unskilled workers so long as they were able and willing to submit to discipline. In Ricardo's view the strategic element in the economy was capital. Whether a society would remain on even keel, advance, or retrogress would depend in the first instance on the rate of increase of capital relative to the population that had to be fed and employed.

It is only a slight exaggeration to say that from Ricardo's day to this, most economists have taken "labor" more or less for granted, assuming that the numbers of workers required would be available and that the question of skill would not be a problem, since some workers would make the effort to acquire a higher level of competence in exchange for a potentially higher wage. In short, they saw the working population as passive and responsive to the conditions in the market-place. If employment was scarce in one area and heavy in another, some workers would migrate. If one skill was in surplus and another was short, the information would filter down to those in the education and training pipeline who would incorporate the fact in their plans. If all able-bodied men were employed, the market would begin to draw members from the peripheral labor force—the retired, women, the physically and emotionally handicapped, and members of minority groups.

This is the manner in which the economists elaborated their theories. Some understood more than others the grossness or crudity of their models of workers' behavior. Some early recognized the im-portance of the trade union as an independent influence on equating the demand for and the supply of labor. Others began to question whether the individual worker was as responsive as conventional theory postulated. Many workers did not appear willing to relocate or change their jobs or occupations when a new opportunity appeared on the horizon. Occasionally, an economist began to see important connec-tions in the educational opportunities that government provided, the level of skill and competence of the population, and the vitality of the economy.

If a complete catalog were to be proposed, we could probably find among the economic theories of yesterday an appreciation for each and every facet of the way in which the development and utilization of human resources might be significantly related to the growth and ef-ficiency of the economy. However, with regard to the major drift of eco-nomics, it has been only in very recent years—since the end of World War II—that an increasing number of economists are taking up where Adam Smith left off and considering the human resource factor as the key determinant of economic progress. This is the beginning of a revo-lution in economic thinking that may yet exceed in significance the changes wrought by Keynes.

Every discipline likes to believe that it stands alone and apart and that it can proceed with only a glance now and again at other disci-plines. Frequently it is oblivious of its dependence on other disciplines both with regard to their established doctrines and particularly with regard to their revision and improvement. Economics and psychology have been living together for a long time, in fact since economics drew away from philosophy and set itself up as an independent disci-pline. The conception of man as a calculating individual interested in maximizing his pleasure and minimizing his pain provides the founda-tion of economics from Ricardo's day right down to the dominant con-temporary doctrines. The fact that Veblen, Mitchell, J. M. Clark, and others repeatedly called attention to the inappropriateness of the psy-chological assumptions with which economists worked left its mark, but this criticism did little to bring about fundamental reforms in their ways of thinking and acting. But although the traditional economists acknowledged the validity of much of the criticism, they were not offered a substitute. And without a substitute, they had little option but to continue to use the only psychology they knew.

However, psychology, both as a natural and as a social discipline, has been undergoing revolutionary changes in recent decades, particularly since Freud. Theories of human growth and development have been elaborated and refined. We have come to understand much more than earlier generations about human motives, values, and behavior. Economists have slowly realized that their conception of man must start from the premise that he is not primarily a conscious, rational, calculating, pleasure-seeking animal but is, rather, a complex psychological organism responding simultaneously to internal and external forces which can be differentiated into basic drives, adjustment mechanisms, and value orientations. Moreover, the personalities that people develop are, first, conditioned by their experiences in childhood and, secondly, modified by what happens to them in adolescence and adulthood. Human nature is pliable, and human development must be viewed dynamically. The simpleminded assumption of economists that there is a Scotsman inside of every man is an anachronism.

This revolution in psychology has exercised a major influence on contemporary views about the potentialities of education and training and therefore on the acquisition of skill, talent, and competence. The new psychology has made us realize that all human ability is learned and that the fact that some people become competent and others do not depends much more on the opportunities that they have encountered to become educated and trained than on their genetic potential. Of course, the new psychology does not deny that genetic differences exist and that sometimes they may even be a crucial determinant for later adult performance. But the thrust of the new theory with regard to skill acquisition is that environmental opportunities hold the key.

The new psychology has paved the way for our understanding that the adult's ability to perform useful work depends in the first instance on his opportunities in infancy, childhood, adolescence, and young adulthood—opportunities to develop interests, aspirations, and values and to integrate them into a personality.

The contribution of the new psychology to the deeper understanding of human resources is grounded in its unequivocal stress upon the inherent pliability of human nature and the overriding importance of the environment in determining whether men and women will be able to develop their faculties to the optimum or whether their faculties will atrophy from lack of stimulation and training. Herein lies psychology's great contribution to the emerging discipline of human resources. It has provided the underpinnings for a dynamic approach to the development of skill and talent.

It was not accidental that for so long the economists considered labor a resource of secondary importance in the development of capitalism. The principal demand of the expanding system was for large numbers of able-bodied men, and in most industrializing countries these were available in most locations where an employer sought to start up or expand operations. But each decade saw an increasing division of labor with more specialization. This was true not only of the individual workplace but particularly of the economy and society as a whole. In the early days of the factory system the owner often served as manager, accountant, salesman, as well as engineer and foreman. But as the individual plant and the company grew, these several functions came to be assumed by specialists, some of whom were trained on the job, many of whom qualified by education and training.

Prior to the emergence of the factory system, professional training had been limited to the classic three—theology, medicine, and law. Two of the striking transformations that accompanied the growth of industrialization were the proliferation of the professions and the growth of a large number of technical and skilled jobs for which schools and specialized training institutions provided all or at least a great part of the required preparation. Today, for instance, there are more than twenty specialty boards within medicine alone, and there are over 150 different types of engineers. Or, to come close to home: most universities prescribe five or six areas in which doctoral candidates in economics must pass examinations. The number of recognized fields of concentration in economics, however, is twenty or more.

Without planning it that way, we have become a skill economy. This means that although there still are a considerable number of jobs on the farm, in manufacturing, and in the services which can be filled by persons with little education and less training, the proportion of jobs of which this is true is constantly shrinking, and there is every reason for it to continue to shrink. It is the phenomenon of our contemporary, technologically advanced society—the death knell for an economy preoccupied with capital, one which took labor for granted.

The roots of this transformation were planted in the second half of the nineteenth century: by Oxford and Cambridge graduates' attempts to assure British hegemony on a large part of the globe, by the scientists' enlarged role in the spurt of German industry, and by the spread of general and vocational education and training through the system of land-grant colleges and the subsequent gains of American agriculture and industry. Since we are still in the middle of the process of transforming our economy from one based on brawn to one based on brains, it is difficult to see clearly how far we have come and impossible to foretell where the process will end. But we have a clue or two. In some parts of the United States about half of all eighteen-year-olds enter college; in many other parts junior-college graduation will soon be the norm. And increasingly leaders of opinion point out that education and training will soon be no longer a one-time process undertaken early in life but a continuing involvement that will take place throughout the whole of an individual's life.

It is this transformation, more than any other, that lies at the root of the new concern with human resources. When formal education for the majority of the population was limited to their acquiring the three R's and little more, when only a small minority went on to complete high school and even less to college or professional school, the development of human resources appeared to be a relatively simple matter. A society could discharge its responsibilities by providing a limited amount of free education and assuring that through philanthropy, government, or proprietary sources a select minority could prepare for their chosen professions. But we have increasingly come to realize that our society and our welfare as well as the rate of our economic progress depend more upon the availability of a population that is educated and broadly trained than upon any other factor. It is this recognition that has given the major stimulus to the development of the new discipline of human resources.

The developments outlined above—the anachronism of an economics that was centered on capital to the neglect of the human factor in production; the emergence of the new psychology with its illumination of the dynamic facets of human growth and development, including the growth of intellect and skill; and the transformation of the economy from a dependence on unskilled, physically strong laborers to one in which both output and distribution depend increasingly on men of general and specialized education and skill—these three major occurrences have left their mark on the basic political structure within which these transformations took place. Although a full recital would have to consider not only what transpired in the democracies of the West but also the changes in the more authoritarian systems of Soviet Russia and Japan, the present account will be restricted to the changes at home. As we became a more affluent people, we began to redefine the roles of private and public responsibility. Workers who were injured received compensation; those who lost their jobs had access to unemployment insurance; when people became too old to work, they received Social Security benefits; and most recently the older members of the population have general access to a wide range of medical services.

These changes reflected a continuing reinterpretation of the nature of our democratic society and a willingness to act on our new perception and insights. As we acted to reduce or eradicate blemishes and defects that we had come to recognize, we began to transform the very structure and functioning of our democratic system. Nowhere were these transformations greater than in the broadening and deepening of the opportunities that are essential if individuals are to be able to develop their latent potentialities. In one realm after another society acted to broaden opportunities: in health, education, and welfare.

In the early days of industrial capitalism, Ricardo warned about the dangers of general impoverishment if a society used the savings of the rich to feed the poor. The only outcome of such a program, he said, would be universal poverty. Some among us have not been able to quell all the doubts about the elaborate welfare system which we have installed. But nobody—including the most acrimonious critics of recent innovations—any longer fears the impoverishment of the larger society. Doubts are more restricted and limited. They question whether the industrious and the self-disciplined should do so much for the indolent and the incompetent.

But most of us, though we may still harbor doubts, have a much more positive stand toward the new. We approve what has been added to democracy's house, convinced that most people will make constructive use of their broadened opportunities. In fact, the public has caught the essence of the new commitment, which is that an affluent democratic society can grow from strength to strength if it has the wisdom and the courage to invest in the development of its people. As with other types of sound investments, the sums spent on improving the terms of life will be repaid, with margins to spare, through the broadening and deepening of people's capabilities and skills. Not only will we have a better society, but we will also have a more productive economy.

And so, after a muting of the theme for almost two centuries, the importance of the human resource factor is increasingly stressed in the halls of academe, in the management of industry, and in the political arena. The long period of neglect is now over. But it will be some time before the theories are elaborated, the facts assembled, and the analyses made which will provide the foundation that this new discipline requires to grow and flourish.

During the last quarter century and more we have been engaged in developing theories, assembling facts, and undertaking analyses of selected facets of the development and utilization of human resources. We know the immense gap between what exists and what is required to provide a sound foundation for this new discipline. But disciplines do not emerge full-blown from the inspiration of any man, even an Adam Smith. The building blocks must be shaped and assembled, one at a time.

WORK AND FREEDOM

The three following chapters are an exercise in perspective. The first sketches the life of the laboring poor at the time of Adam Smith that is, at the birth of industrial capitalism. It illustrates the ways in which the worker was constricted and oppressed in the days before the factory system was established.

Chapters 2 and 3 set out the goals that workers have attempted to achieve in an expanding capitalism. First, and most important, the workers refused to accept the teachings of the economists which held that the competitive market would result in the greatest good for the greatest number. They knew better. They therefore set about to increase their power in order to influence the operations of the marketplace both directly through bargaining collectively with employers and indirectly through government action.

Increases in wages and decreases in hours have long been important targets at which workers have aimed. However, Chapter 3 calls attention to what has perhaps been their primary goal, at least in the United States. Workers have sought to gain control over their jobs. A man who can be summarily discharged is only half a man, for he must bend to the demands and the whims of those who employ him; else his family and he may starve. But a man who is secure in his job as long as he performs satisfactorily can face the future without fear. The freedom that the workingman won in the political arena is the freedom that he is now seeking to win in the job arena. Economics is much less the study of the production of goods and services than it is the study of how human beings seek to use their capacities and energies to make a better life for themselves and their children.

1. THE LABORING POOR

The Bible recommended the care of the poor; Solon enacted legislation in favor of the oppressed debtors; the Roman senate provided bread and circuses for the urban proletariat. The records of the past, however, do not deal in great detail with the life and the activities of the vast masses of the laboring poor. The wisdom of Solomon, the oratory of Pericles, the conquests of Caesar were considered more worthy of description than the struggles of the common people. The rulers of the state despised the populace, and, except in times of crisis when manpower became important, ignored it completely. During normal periods the commonalty had to labor hard, pay high taxes, and behave itself. Art, politics, and learning were the vested interests of the rich and the powerful.

The poverty of the Middle Ages was appalling. All were poor. After the fall of the Roman Empire the gulf which separated the common people from the nobility narrowed greatly. The church-state had to be most circumspect in dealing with the laboring poor, for they formed almost the only group in medieval society. After many centuries of want and deprivation the economic horizon commenced to brighten. The disintegration of feudalism, the increases in foreign trade during the period of exploration, and the breakdown of the autocratic power of the Church, did much to pull Europe out of its long depression. The satins of the East and the exotic fruits of the West became well known. A rich class reappeared. The cleavage between the courtiers and the peasants broadened. Money once again became the mark of a man, and he who was poor was ignoble.

From the reign of Elizabeth until the outbreak of the French Revolution, British statecraft worked hard to increase the power and wealth of the country. The programs of national aggrandizement did not fail to include the working population, although no unanimity of opinion existed as to the proper role of this group. Would increasing their numbers be a boon to British prosperity? Would limitations upon their freedom be of value to English manufacturers? These and similar questions perplexed the rulers of England. However, at no time was the discussion primarily concerned with the welfare and happiness of the laboring poor. Peasants and artisans had not been created by a wise Providence in order that they might live happily and contentedly. Theirs was a higher destiny.

The eighteenth century revolted against many ideas and institutions of earlier times. One of the most startling insurrections in the realm of thought was the new approach to the study of man. For the first time in history, philosophers became vitally interested in the welfare of the populace. The Professor of Moral Philosophy at Glasgow was pleased by this change; in fact, he helped to bring it about.

Adam Smith was not the first to advance the theory that all wealth is derived from labor. A medieval churchman and a seventeenth-century philosopher had developed a labor theory of value. Smith, however, broke new ground in building a complete system of economic thought around the concept of productive labor. The opening lines of the *Wealth of Nations* illustrate the importance of his approach. He believes that the annual labor of every nation originally supplies it with all the necessaries and conveniences of life. The earlier writers in analyzing the economic order had woefully underestimated the significance of the laboring man. They were too concerned with the activities of the manufacturer, the merchant, and the farmer to pay much attention to the simple artisan. In Smith's treatise the laboring poor occupy a position of primary importance.

The labor expended upon the manufacture of a commodity establishes its value. The quantity and quality of the country's total production is in large measure determined by the ability and dexterity of the working population. All techniques and institutions which affect the skill of the laboring groups are therefore most important because they directly influence the wealth of a nation.

Smith's emphasis upon the hitherto most neglected stratum of society was most radical, and it is not surprising that he ran into difficulties in developing his thesis. In the past, land had been viewed as a productive force in the national economy; capital had likewise not been considered sterile. Smith's presentation of labor's claim conflicted with the vested rights of land and capital. It soon became clear that some compromise would have to be established, because the entrenched position of the older claimants was very strong. Even as attorney for the plaintiff, Smith had great respect for the defendants. Their prestige rather overawed him. Although he at first contended that labor was the sole determinant of value, it was not long before he admitted that rent and profits might also influence value. This compromise contained many implicit contradictions, which Karl Marx almost a century later devoted some time to eradicate. He succeeded, but only to a limited extent, for though he strengthened the weak links in Smith's chain of reasoning, he added new ones which proved none too strong.

Adam Smith, however, wrote a very interesting brief, despite its deficiencies in logic. The history of the world was in his opinion the history of the increasing efficiency of labor. The absence of specialization in antiquity accounts for the poverty of that period. The agriculturist could improve the yield of his crops only if he were able to make intensive use of the land. He was, however, forced to spend a considerable part of his time in securing food, shelter, and clothing for himself and his family, and was therefore unable to devote his entire energies to the care of his plants. Some members of the community showed great talents in the chase, while others proved to be expert house builders. After many millennia of development it became clear that the entire group would benefit if each member engaged in that activity for which he was best fitted. A hunter could kill within a very short time more deer than he could possibly use for his personal needs. A thatcher was able to put his own dwelling into condition by two weeks' concentrated effort. A farmer, working on fertile land, could raise more than he could consume. The several specialists commenced to exchange their surplus commodities and labor power, and soon the wealth of the community increased. An economic society could be most efficiently organized upon the basis of specialization and exchange.

The first book of the *Wealth of Nations* is devoted almost entirely to an analysis of those forces which facilitated the division of labor among men. The treatment afforded the working population becomes highly significant in an approach which considers national progress to be largely determined by improvements in the specialization of labor. Merchants had maintained that English prosperity was due to their trading activities. The farming population had contended, although less frequently, that they formed the backbone of the national economy. Adam Smith, however, asserted that the welfare of all countries, at all periods in the world's history, depended upon the status of labor and the development of the industrial arts.

The theorists before Smith had not viewed the workingman as an important element in the national economy. True, traders were forced to employ sales clerks; manufacturers could not get along without factory hands; and wealthy landowners needed men to work their fields. Former generations, however, considered the laborer important only because he aided the merchant, the manufacturer, and the farmer in fulfilling their economic functions. Their attitude toward labor was not only narrow but actually perverse. The older writers, reflecting the opinion of the ruling class, maintained that a state could be powerful and wealthy only if the laboring population were kept under strict control.

During the sixteenth, seventeenth, and eighteenth centuries English laborers were greatly oppressed by the apprenticeship laws which the masters strictly enforced. The parishes, in a vain attempt to keep the poor rates down, added to the tribulations of the workingman by holding him prisoner in the town of his birth. The state did its bit to make the laboring poor completely unhappy by heavily taxing the commodities which they used. It was deemed good policy to deal with the working population in a high-handed fashion. The fortunes of the rich depended upon the penury of the poor. From the days of Queen Elizabeth, Parliament did little to improve the status of the impoverished and docile working population. In the fifth year of the reign of her Majesty the Statute of Apprenticeship was passed. It provided that no one could ply a trade unless he underwent a seven-year period of training. The avowed purpose of this act was to insure the purchaser against shoddy and imperfect goods for clearly no artisan would lack skill after so long a tutelage. The legislators further believed that the statute would form young people to industry.

Corporations with exclusive privileges were established better to enforce the apprenticeship regulations. A society of master artificers obtained from the government an exclusive right to engage in trade or manufacturing within a specific area. The masters were frequently permitted to establish rules and regulations for the conduct of their business. In most cases the charter members of a corporation limited the number of people who might engage in their trade. This procedure insured their special privileges.

In the middle of the eighteenth century there were twelve important corporations in the city of London. Only a member of one of these companies could be elected Lord Mayor. In addition, there existed seventy-nine other corporations each possessed of privileges of lesser significance. It was customary for a youth, after obtaining the consent of his parents, to bind himself for a period of seven years to a master in one of these ninety-one corporations. If, perchance, his employer were indifferent, the young man might pass his entire time in drudgery, acquiring no skill whatever in his craft. Not a few masters drove their apprentices like slaves, exploiting them to the utmost. Some few concealed the secrets of their business in order to keep their pupils in a state of dependence.

Novices, upon the payment of an entrance fee, received free board and lodging in return for fourteen hours' work per day. They were likely to waste their time and cheat their masters at every turn for they received no wages and therefore had little reason to be interested in their work. The conscientious hireling was promised the protection and assistance of Divine Providence but unfortunately he would not be rewarded until the hereafter. An apprentice, after seven years of service, became a journeyman. He then received wages for his labor and secured a modicum of independence. In theory but not in practice, a journeyman might become a master after several years' additional service. Without wealthy relatives one could never hope to become the head of a trade for often a capital of several hundred or even thousand pounds was required. But money was not always a trustworthy sesame; at times even it was unable to unlock the powerful doors which the old masters had built to keep out newcomers.

The apprenticeship regulations were undoubtedly a great boon to the masters, for it enabled them to secure much free labor, and enhanced the prices of their commodities by reducing competition. Parliament refused to alter radically the Elizabethan legislation because in its opinion the public was not oppressed by these measures. It likewise denied that the restrictions upon the workingman violated the rights of English citizens. The government viewed with favor the apprenticeship and corporation laws for it believed that the public benefited from the regularization of industry. However, it really was an impertinent affectation to maintain that any good could result from legislative measures which trampled upon the most sacred property of man—his labor.

People of enlightened views deprecated the restraints upon the workingman not only on political but also on economic grounds. They scoffed at the pragmatic defense which the advocates of regulation attempted to establish. The claims of the mercantilists that the apprenticeship regulation inclined young people to work could not be substantiated. Man would never exert himself were it not for the rewards which industry promised. Apprentices who received no wages were therefore lazy and indifferent. The lengthy period of service which the apprentice was forced to undergo was entirely unjustifiable, because a young man of average intelligence could be taught the tricks of any trade within a few months. Many maintained that corporations raised the quality of workmanship but this was most doubtful. The best check upon fraud and negligence would be to offer the consumer an opportunity to deal with competing groups. Unfortunately, under existing conditions the monopolistic privileges of the corporations forced the buyer to purchase his goods from a specific individual, at a definite price, irrespective of the quality of the merchandise. It was often necessary to go into the suburbs to have a piece of work tolerably well executed. Corporations were urban institutions, but they did possess the right to exclude competing goods from their territory. Smuggling was therefore not uncommon.

The Statute of Apprenticeship was probably less baneful to the working population than were the other restrictions upon labor. Corporate monopolies not only raised the rate of profits but also enhanced the wages of certain laborers. The increase in wages, however, was not sufficient to compensate for the disabilities of apprentices, especially for their enforced period of free service. The laboring poor would gain greatly from the repeal of this statute. A liberal, despite his general distrust of all repressive measures, might have tolerated the apprenticeship laws if they had benefited the wage toilers. One could have disliked bounties and yet not have attacked them, if the poor were directly aided by their enactment. The payment of public monies to those engaged in the herring trade might have been endorsed if the price of fish had thereby been reduced, for the poor could then have purchased their food more cheaply. A noble end might have justified the use of ignoble means. But the act passed in the fifth year of Elizabeth's reign regulating the conditions of labor did not show a net balance after a careful audit. Hence liquidation was in order.

The apprenticeship laws doubtless obstructed the free circulation of labor and were therefore detrimental to the true interests of the working population. The Settlement Acts were even more injurious. During the sixteenth century the relief of the poor was in a most chaotic condition, and toward the end of Elizabeth's reign a law was passed with the aim of establishing some semblance of order in the dispensation of public charity. Local responsibility was established, and henceforth each parish would be forced to care for its own indigent members. Each municipality therefore studied means of preventing the numbers of its poor from increasing. The law provided that a parish did not have to assume responsibility unless the individual could prove that he had resided therein for forty consecutive days. The village overseers were in effect transformed into detectives whose primary duty was to discover potential charges. The justices of the peace could be petitioned to remove a newcomer unless the latter were able to rent a house for ten pounds a year or give security to the amount of thirty pounds. Those citizens of the British Isles who were so shortsighted as to have chosen parents without means became for all practical purposes prisoners for life in the town of their birth. The few who refused to suffer the consequences of their bad judgment were not likely to improve their condition by bold action. They might trek the highways, but their fate was far from enviable. If they succeeded in hiding the place of their birth they would be sent from parish to parish, for each village would desire to relieve itself of responsibility as quickly as possible. The venturous souls were not at all certain that they could remain outside the clutches of the law, for their poverty marked them as potential criminals. At any time they might be haled before a justice of the peace and, if unable to account for their past and their present, be convicted of poverty and sentenced to be transported. The penalties for this serious crime had been modified as the legal code became more humane. In former years, the indigent poor were liable to whipping, ear-piercing, branding, and decapitation with and without benefit of clergy. The enlightened eighteenth century retained corporal punishment, but evidenced its progressiveness by substituting transportation for the more barbaric penalties of old. The judge, if in an indulgent mood, might show the vagrant extreme kindness and not order him to be transported, but press him instead into the army or the navy. Regular gangs abetted the magistrate in the performance of his judicial duties. These ruffians would overwhelm a poor man and hale him into court. If he failed to give a satisfactory account of himself he would be ordered to board a man-of-war or to enlist as a common soldier.

The life of the docile poor was not much happier than that of the vagrants. A child whose parents had either died or disappeared was most unfortunate. The community would hand the youngster over to anyone who would offer room and board, in exchange for his labor. One lad relates that at the age of five he was working ten hours a day for his meat and drink. His master, fearing that he might run away, confined him to the house and the yard before the door. Upon his employer's death this happy existence came to an end. The boy was then forced to shift for himself, eating when he found employment, starving when he had none. The rich did everything in their power to enforce the biblical injunction that he who does not work shall not eat. If the poor, seeking employment and finding none, asked charity, they were whipped as sturdy beggars; if they stole in order to feed themselves and had the misfortune to be caught, they were hanged for thievery.

Most people agreed that a large population was the best criterion of a country's prosperity. The number of England's inhabitants was doubtless increasing during the seventeenth and the eighteenth centuries. There was one serious drawback to the nation's progress: her poor were augmented with every increase in her general population. During the second decade of the eighteenth century one estimate placed the number of unprofitable poor at a million and a half. As only a very small fraction could be transported, the vast majority had to be supported at home by the landed and the commercial interests. The care of the poor developed into England's most important industry. The burden was especially severe upon the landowners. The land tax was very high. Parish officers did everything in their power to ease the situation, even committing murder in the interest of their economy program. Nor did they hesitate to defy the king's court in order to save their fellow taxpayers and themselves some paltry shillings.

During the reign of George I the Settlement Acts were amended. Several communities felt that the cost of poor relief could be reduced by rationalizing the outmoded techniques, and therefore petitioned Parliament to permit the erection of workhouses. The poor were to be housed in dormitories and forced to work for their food and lodging. The parish officers hoped that great economies would result from institutionalizing the indigent. But the erection of workhouses required large amounts of capital, and though many were established the reform was not generally adopted. The great increase of robberies which took place during the middle of the century could be explained only by the desperate condition of the poor. One writer believed that workhouses offered the only solution and suggested that they be erected with private funds, if state monies were not forthcoming.

After a century and a half of experimentation the methods of poor relief were still most unsatisfactory. The liberties of Englishmen had been severely curtailed in an attempt to solve this perplexing problem. The law ordered people to starve at home though they might find suitable employment abroad. The various regulations violated natural liberty and justice without achieving any practical results. Unfortunately the common man, after suffering from these oppressions for more than a hundred years, had not yet rebelled. His docility is all the more remarkable when one remembers that "there is scarce a poor man in England of forty years of age . . . who has not in some part of his life felt himself most cruelly oppressed by this ill-contrived law of settlements."

The state never hesitated to pass the most drastic labor legislation. The Settlement and Apprenticeship Acts interfered with both the supply of laborers and the conditions of labor. At an early period the government usurped control over the very heart of the labor contract by legislating on wages. The Black Plague radically reduced the size of England's working population. Parliament, fearing a rise in wages, outlawed all private bargaining between employers and employees. Those seeking work were ordered to present themselves in the market square on an established date, at which time the officers of the crown would announce the scale of wages. In most cases a maximum rate was stipulated and it was illegal to pay or to receive more than this amount.

During the many centuries that the magistrates fixed the hire of laborers, wages were kept low. Though in Adam Smith's time the judges no longer exercised this prerogative, the legislature did establish a maximum rate of wages for workers in the garment trade. Governmental regulation was however not customary.

The attempt of Parliament to settle disputes between masters and workers usually results in a decision favorable to the former, for the wealthy and powerful classes counsel the government. Therefore, whenever a law enhances the welfare of laborers, it is just and equitable. For instance, Parliament in prohibiting employers from paying their workmen in kind rather than in money, acted most honorably, for it prevented unscrupulous masters from exploiting their laborers.

The laws of conspiracy prove, however, that the legislature has not always acted chivalrously. Workmen cannot form combinations to raise wages or to improve working conditions, though employers are not prohibited from operating in concert. The law reinforces the economic disabilities of the weaker class, because master manufacturers can organize so much more easily than their employees. In fact, the former are always in a constant and uniform combination to insure their rights and advantages, and social ostracism is visited upon the employer who acts independently. In case of struggle, the workingmen are always in an inferior position, and therefore use either violence or outrage; they must frighten their masters into an immediate compliance with their demands. A landlord, a master manufacturer, or a merchant can live for a year or two upon his accumulated stocks, but the savings of the laboring poor are not sufficient to prevent them from starving to death within a week. Despite these odds in favor of the wealthy and powerful groups the state throws the weight of its authority against the weaker party. Masters demand and obtain the rigorous execution of the severe anti-combination laws. Were the state to act impartially, it would likewise prosecute masters for conspiracy, but unfortunately government is always class government.

Labor legislation was not the only scourge of the working class. The taxation system was certain to have important, though indirect, repercussions upon its welfare. Mercantilism had perverted the true principles of public finance by employing taxation not only for revenue but also for monopoly. Parliament was unable to levy the most equitable and efficacious taxes because it was constantly preoccupied with the establishment and the furtherance of monopolies. The government utilized all the means at its disposal to aid British merchants and manufacturers, and occasionally the pursuit of this design injured the laborers. However, the hurt which it inflicted was superficial. Without governmental aid, English commerce and manufacturing might languish, with the result that labor could have neither work nor food. The class interest of the parliamentary legislation could not always be disguised behind protestations of concern for the very people who were the subject of attack. The government deliberately attempted to whittle down the standard of living of the laborers, hoping to satisfy the manufacturing group by placing at its disposal a cheap and docile working force.

The cry had often been raised that the laboring population of England was indolent and slothful, and that a worker who earned enough by three days' labor to keep him for a week would spend the rest of his time in riotous dissipation. The payment of low wages would put an end to this nonsense, and force the laborer to be industrious. A project was discussed which contemplated importing a large number of German workmen in order more successfully to reduce the wages of native employees. It was abandoned only after the evidence proved that Germans ate and drank at least as much as the English. Many observers of British culture were shocked by the prevalent use of luxuries, for every poor family drank tea at least once a day, and ate wheaten bread instead of loaves made from rye and barley. The self-appointed defenders of English civilization begged Parliament to stem these decadent tendencies, and the government strained itself to accede to their requests.

Excises were levied on many commodities which the poor consumed: soap, salt, candles, leather, fermented liquors were all subject to tax. To increase the cost of these products would force the working population to lead more simple and frugal existences. There would be no funds for debauchery, no time for licentiousness. Laborers would have to work six days in the week to earn enough to keep themselves alive. One of the keenest critics of English society was certain that the laboring population would never become industrious until the cost of living was raised.

Adam Smith had not the least sympathy with the philosophers of this school. He deprecated the heavy taxation of necessities; future generations would suffer if the poor were unable to give their children a proper upbringing. If the laborers' wages were lowered their offspring would probably suffer from malnutrition and exposure. Taxes which fall on a necessitous person are always cruel and oppressive; the worst taxes are those which bear more heavily on the poor than on the rich. For instance the window levy was most unjust, for the poor could no longer afford to have either light or ventilation in their homes.

The taxation of the poor cannot be supported even by mercantilistic arguments. A careful analysis proves that taxes upon labor or upon commodities used by labor are certain to be paid by their superiors. If the subsistence of wage earners were reduced their efficiency would be impaired and manufacturers would suffer. The latter, in order to protect themselves, would probably raise wages. In either case the middle and upper classes would be forced to bear the burden.

The policy of England was to keep the laboring population servile and industrious. Merchants and manufacturers, fearful that they would have to foot the bill if the laborers improved their condition, attempted to stifle all social reform. No respectable member of English society would have advocated raising the standards of living of the laboring poor. Adam Smith, however, was Scottish and was therefore not oppressed by the taboos which prevailed south of the Midlands. He did not hesitate to emphasize the facts that rent and profits eat up wages, and that the two superior orders of people usually oppress the inferior one. Furthermore, he pointed out that unless circumstances force them, the wealthier classes never act generously or humanely in their dealings with their less fortunate brethren. Manufacturers loudly bemoan the high wages which they pay their workmen, but remain silent when profits are discussed. If the public complains about the dearness of commodities, the shrewd business men lose no time in placing the blame upon the high rewards of labor, forgetting to mention that their own rate of return might possibly influence prices.

During the seventeenth and eighteenth centuries the vast majority of English statesmen exerted themselves to keep wages as low as possible in order to encourage trade and industry. But they were only partially successful. The laboring population were receiving more than a bare minimum, though their wages were seldom so high as their enemies maintained. The leaders of English society bemoaned their inability to prevent the improvement in the condition of the working class. Educated people were depressed by this progress, for clearly it could come to no good end. There was, however, a singular philosopher who believed that the group which fed, clothed, and lodged the whole body of the people, had a right to be tolerably well fed, clothed, and lodged itself. But he was a queer academician. Men of affairs knew that the laborers had no rights, although they ought upon occasion to be pitied and patronized.

It was fantastic to fear high wages, for whatever improves the general welfare of the greater part of the community can never be considered an inconvenience to the whole. Poverty is a great social liability. An able laboring population is possible only if workers receive ample remuneration for their efforts; hence to complain of the liberal rewards to labor is to lament the effect and the cause of the greatest public prosperity. As wealth increases, wages increase, and therefore population increases, all of which is for the good of the commonwealth.

The effect of high wages upon the laborer has never been properly studied. Workingmen are more active, diligent, and expeditious in countries where they receive large rather than small rewards. The contention that high wages make for riotous living is without foundation; men do not work four days a week in order to spend the remaining three days in the pub. It is the strain of their work which forces them to take prolonged and frequent rest. Masters might well listen to the dictates of reason and humanity, and moderate rather than intensify the application of their workmen. Disorders generally prevail in the economy of the rich, but in the homes of the poor, workmen frequently ruin their health by excessive diligence. When piecework is well rewarded, laborers frequently overstrain themselves in their desire to improve their position. Many men have a working life of less than ten active years.

Industry has been carried on for the benefit of the rich and the powerful, to the neglect and oppression of the poor and the indigent. Civil government, so far as it is instituted for the security of property, defends the rich. Adam Smith hoped that the government would eventually exert itself in behalf of the poor, and make it unnecessary in the future for them to pray daily to the

Gracious Lord God, who has opened thy hand and satisfied us with good; who hast clothed the naked, filled the hungry, and gathered the poor who were scattered and solitary into one house; affect our hearts with a deep sense of this thy goodness towards us; And mercifully grant that always being exercised in good works and not cherishing sin with the bread of idleness we may use thy liberality to thy glory, and walk worthy of so great benefits in sobriety of life, in the obedience to our Governors, in brotherly love one towards another, and in constant obedience to thy word. Pour down thy blessings on this whole parish; and grant, we beseech Thee, that as our necessities are daily relieved out of their abundance so their wants may be supplied out of thy riches; for Jesus Christ his sake, our blessed Lord and Savior. Amen.

WHAT WORKERS WANT

For two thousand years and more, religious leaders have preached the doctrine of human dignity and respect for the individual but their preachings and teachings in this regard went largely unheeded because, among other reasons, the struggle for survival was so intense. Most men had to struggle from sunup to sundown to earn enough to feed their families and themselves. In time of war or national calamity, many were unable to secure even the minimum required for survival and died a speedy or a slow death.

Only those who were able to command the labor of others could escape from the treadmill of incessant work and grinding poverty. Since men had never willingly parted with the fruits of their labor, it usually required the exercise of power to effect such transfers from the hapless many to the fortunate few. In a recent senatorial campaign in Massachusetts, a worker challenged Mr. Ted Kennedy during a factory tour with the statement, "I understand you've never worked a day in your life," and, while the startled candidate mumbled an inaudible reply, the worker added, "Well, let me tell you, you haven't missed a thing."

While the margins above mere subsistence increased in Western Europe in the two centuries before the French Revolution as a result of the extension of the market and the improvements in technology, political freedom and economic well-being were still restricted to a small minority. The vast majority, in England as well as on the continent, had neither.

Without a vision of a better future, men must reconcile themselves to the realities of the present, no matter how dreary, deadly, and dangerous these realities may be. In the face of overwhelming power, they have even reconciled themselves to the galley and the concentration camp.

The American and French revolutions provided the vision of a better future, not for the few, or even the many—but for all. These revolutions held forth a promise of freedom for the individual. No longer would man be subject at worst to the pleasure or the whim of authority, or, at best, to the *noblesse oblige* of the king or viceroy. Henceforth, they themselves would be party to deciding on the limitations of their own freedom.

While the elimination of arbitrary political power is a necessary condition for the establishment of freedom, it is not sufficient to assure freedom. For if men must barter themselves or their wives and children in order to secure the essentials for living or if they must barter their labor during most of their waking hours in order to acquire these essentials, their freedom is severely limited. They can enjoy it mostly when they sleep.

The English laboring man in the early days of industrial capitalism had a considerable number of rights and privileges—many more than had workers in other countries. But he was not a full-fledged citizen who participated directly in the political process. He had no direct part in determining the laws and regulations that governed his life and work. And, at the very time that government began to remove its heavy hand, he found that another weighed increasingly upon him.

Forced to barter his labor for a wage, he found himself for twelve hours of the day under the authority of his employer. Since more people were looking for jobs than there were jobs available, he not only had to agree to whatever wage his employer was willing to pay him but he had to endure chastisements and fines for breaches of rules of conduct and discipline.

Moreover, he had to strain his body and muscles to match the pace of the employer's machines; he could not absent himself from the bench—even to take care of his urgent needs—without the permission of his supervisor. And, in all ways, large and small, he was, in Marx's terminology, an industrial slave who might at any moment be discharged, no matter how long or how faithfully he had worked.

There was a gap between the revolutionary promises of a better life for all and the stark realities of the laboring man's existence. His only chance of making the promise come true, short of working towards the destruction of his society through revolution, was to exert pressure on two fronts—the political and the industrial—in the hope that he could eventually secure a major voice in determining the conditions governing the way in which he lived and worked.

There was an important difference, as well as many similarities, in the struggles of British and American workers. The former found it much more difficult to establish their rights to full citizenship. It was not until the latter years of the nineteenth century that the British worker without property was permitted to vote. Even more important was the much harder struggle engaged in by the British worker before he was recognized as an individual entitled to be treated with personal dignity—irrespective of his social origin, uncouth speech, and limited education. In a class-conscious society, every man is not as good as every other; just the opposite. The best men were those who belonged to the upper classes. And workingmen were at the bottom of the ladder.

The American constitution had laid the groundwork for the full-fledged political freedom for all except the slave population. Free land and relative shortages of labor enabled most Americans to escape from the extreme economic duress that characterized the British worker during the early decades of industrialization. Since this nation did not have a true aristocracy of blood, status, or wealth, the American with limited means might be pitied but not despised. For many of the leaders of society had only recently left poverty behind.

But important as those initial differences were—and they left their mark on all that has transpired since—by the turn of this century, there were many striking parallels between the two countries. The working population in both countries had the right to vote but the prevailing ethos in both societies was to limit the role of government in the operation of the economy. Labor, through its unions, had succeeded in exerting more pressure on employers, but the balance of power remained very much with the owners of capital.

There were small groups of workers in England and the United States who argued that the long-delayed realization of a better day for the mass of mankind could be achieved only through the overturn of the capitalistic system. The mass of British labor looked forward, however, to substantial but less radical reforms in the ownership structure. American labor, in contrast, openly professed its support for the system of free enterprise. It wanted changes but these changes related to the way in which the system functioned—not to its basic structure and objectives. Gompers's statement is relevant. When asked what American labor wanted, he said, "More, more, more." He also insisted that the most unforgivable crime that a businessman could commit was to fail to make a profit.

Most people assumed, and quite correctly, that Gompers's "more" referred to wages. But they did not appreciate—and Gompers himself may have been unclear about the matter—that the workers wanted not only more wages but also more of all the desirable things of life: more job security, more leisure, more freedom from the employer's arbitrary actions, more opportunity to be trained and promoted, more protection in their old age, more assurance that their skill and training would not be made obsolescent by the installation of a new machine, more freedom to speak their minds both on and off the job, more consideration by the employer for their health and safety, more rest periods, more equitable work schedules, more vacations—in fact, and this was most significant, the list was without end for as opportunity offered, new objectives could be added. While the economists of an earlier day were undoubtedly right in arguing that man's desires were unlimited, it was a vulgar error on their part, and on the part of all those who subscribed to their doctrine, to see these desires solely in terms of material goods. Men will not fight, much less die, for a second suit of clothes or even for a second car.

Recognizing that there was little likelihood of obtaining the good things in life, material and otherwise, through the intervention of government since the mood of the country precluded the government's interfering directly with regard to the conditions under which people worked or the rewards which they received, the nascent trade union movement pragmatically addressed itself to the task of strengthening its bargaining power to secure its most important objectives from the employer. It had no alternative.

The major thrust of labor's effort was directed towards achieving a trinity composed of organization, higher wages, and job security. Organization was by far the most important of the three for once achieved, it would provide the fulcrum with which to force the employer to bargain with the union about the terms of employment. No longer would he be in a position to determine unilaterally—subject only to the pressures of the competitive market—what he would pay, whom he would hire, whom he would promote, whom he would discharge, how fast he would operate his machines, whether he would install safety devices—and the myriad of other decisions important to him because of their effect on his costs and therefore on his competitive position; and important to the men and women who worked for him because these factors determined to such a large extent the quality of their lives, on and off the job.

Although American labor leaders repeatedly testified before Congressional committees and other public bodies that they staunchly supported the capitalistic system, they saw no incongruity in pressing the employer group as hard as possible for improvements in wages, hours, and working conditions. Labor's admiration for the competitive system never went so far as to inhibit it from pressing its claims for more. The workers heard spokesmen for capitalism argue that no worthwhile and surely no permanent gains could be achieved except through the mechanism of the free market, but they were not impressed by these contentions.

The same employers who beat a direct path to Congress for tariff protection argued that it was impossible for them to grant their workers higher wages because they were already paying very much more than employers overseas. Trade unionists challenged this contention because, despite the fact that the United States had always had a level of wages far above that prevailing in other countries, American businessmen were usually able to make large profits. The relation between the wages that employers paid, their labor costs, and their profits was much less direct than the conservative interpreters of capitalism pretended. Since the domestic market was protected from foreign competition by the costs of transportation and a tariff wall, and since exports accounted for only a small percent of total sales, American labor concluded early that it had little to lose if wages were raised. Trade union efforts would have to be very successful indeed before they could jeopardize the future of the enterprises for which their members worked. Here was still another fundamental difference between American and British labor, for the latter learned early from the dependence of Great Britain on foreign trade that their wages did have a direct bearing on the competitive position of the enterprise for which they worked and therefore on the future of their own jobs.

Despite its pragmatic objectives, American labor found it difficult to organize and to press its claims. A major obstacle to labor's efforts was the fact that employers could usually count on the might of government and the law. There were additional deterrents such as the constant inflow of the large number of immigrants who were willing to take whatever jobs were available, even if the condiitons were hazardous and the wages low. In addition, of course, the ablest people— those who might otherwise have risen to positions of leadership—left the ranks of labor as opportunities opened up. Nevertheless, despite these and other difficulties, labor made substantial strides in organizing the crafts as well as other sectors of the industrial economy—such as mining, clothing, and railroading—where the pattern of work or the characteristics of the workers, or both, established a predisposition toward trade unions.

The establishment of a union implies not only that employers and employees must develop mechanisms for adjusting their differences but also that the union must strive for the establishment of rules and regulations that will allocate equitably the available jobs among its members, for a union is a voluntary organization whose strength depends in the first instance on the loyalty and support of its members. And the overriding interest of the union member is his job, particularly in holding it as he grows older and his strength and vitality begin to diminish.

The struggle between the generations is characteristic of all peoples at all times but the American labor market at the turn of this century was unique in that the numbers of its young people were being swelled by the large-scale inflow from abroad. Small wonder, therefore, that American trade unions placed major stress on seniority which alone could protect the older worker. In fact, the impetus to the establishment of craft unions was to protect a group of established workers against competition from newcomers.

Seniority—an orderly system of advancement, layoff, and recall based on length of service—is not an easy policy to establish and maintain. Employers will almost always fight its introduction because it restricts their ability to hire, promote, and fire. They fear that a seniority system will force them to favor the less capable man with the result that their labor costs will rise. Some of their fears are justified but the continued profitability of many concerns with strong seniority is presumptive evidence that employers' fears have often been exaggerated. What is more, a seniority system frequently prevents many troublesome personnel issues from arising.

But the establishment of a seniority system is a beginning, not an end. The system cannot be self-operating. Through contract and arbitration, answers must be found as to the unit within which seniority prevails; the conditions under which the employer is permitted to disregard seniority in selecting workers for training or promotion; whether seniority with respect to layoff or discharge must follow exactly the same pattern as in the case of recall or the allocation of overtime. How are seniority rights handled when a particular unit is discontinued and its work is parcelled out among other units? What happens when a man selected for supervision fails to make the grade and returns to the bench? Or when another, who made the grade and served as a supervisor for a decade or more, finds that his position is eliminated and he must return to worker status? If the job is crucial to the worker, then these questions and many more like them assume an urgency and importance that transcends all other facets of the employment relation. It was in this arena that American trade unions early made a significant contribution to their members. In the decades before the establishment of private pension systems and social security benefits, seniority was the worker's basic security; and, even today, it continues to have the most pronounced and direct influence on his employment status.

Unions have failed to attract large numbers of white collar and women workers mainly because these groups have less concern with seniority. White collar employment has been much more stable than blue collar, and the majority of women workers have tended to move in and out of the labor market. The efforts of the trade union movement to organize these groups will probably continue to be particularly difficult unless the attachment of women to the labor market becomes more regular or white collar employment becomes more unstable. Both are likely to occur and may already be under way.

The slow but steady growth of American trade unions after the early years of the century was accelerated by the tight labor market of World War I, but organized labor lost some of its position during the "New Era" when manufacturing employment grew slowly; industrialists pursued elaborate welfare policies to thwart the growth of unions; and the mood of the country was reflected in the successive elections of Harding, Coolidge, and Hoover with their pronounced bias in favor of big business, small government, and their conservative attitudes toward the expansion of human rights.

The Great Depression of 1929–1933, which brought the economy to the verge of collapse and the society to the brink of upheaval, left an indelible mark on American labor. In the absence of jobs, seniority had little value. The depression proved beyond a shadow of a doubt that the employer could not assure the workingman a job. And so labor, which had for so long put most of its energies into extracting gains from the employer group, shifted its attention increasingly to seeking benefits from government. And, in the years that followed, it got much from government: assistance in organizing, friendly tribunals before which to plead its cases of conflict with employers, unemployment insurance, and old age and survivors' benefits—and much more. It had a new opportunity to fill out its ranks, regroup, and reenter the fray of bargaining with the employer in a much strengthened position.

The spectacular recovery of the economy as a result of World War II pushed wages up very rapidly but it also laid the basis for certain additional labor gains. As the war progressed it became public policy to try to hold the line on wages and prices; as a result the War Labor Board looked with favor on agreements between management and labor that stressed deferred benefits, such as the employer's payment of premiums for health and hospital insurance, vacations with pay, additional holidays, pensions. Moreover, management and labor agreed to many new work rules which had the double-barrelled objective of speeding output and at the same time increasing the earnings of labor.

The level of the economy since the end of World War II contributed to further improvement in the welfare of the laboring population: average weekly earnings in manufacturing rose in 1965 to over $107. (in contrast to about $25. at the beginning of World War II). Even after allowing for inflation and higher taxes, the real disposable income of a married worker with three dependents increased by more than one-half during this period. And, currently, most workers are employed in establishments where both office and plant personnel receive 7 or 8 paid holidays in the year; up to 3 weeks paid vacations; and where they have life insurance, hospital insurance, surgical and medical insurance, sickness and accident insurance, and retirement pensions. Moreover, the basic work week has been reduced to forty hours or less.

In recent years, labor has found that the employer is once again a good source of additional gains. His profits have been sufficiently high and sufficiently sustained to enable him to agree to many substantial improvements in the employment contract. Many students have questioned the basis for these managerial concessions for they believe that when business agrees to a wage increase it turns right around and raises prices, thereby establishing the circuit for a continuing inflation. There has even been some uneasiness in the ranks of labor that this may be the case and that what workers gain in higher wages they lose in higher prices. But, in the face of high profits, no labor leader could long survive if he did not succeed in getting more for his members. There is much more basic democracy in unions than most critics realize. This is not to say either that there are no differences in objectives between trade union management and the members nor that all trade unions are operated solely for the benefit of the members. One need not stretch the analogy very far to recognize that not all businesses are run for the benefit of stockholders.

But, again, union members are interested in much more than their wage rate. They want more money now but they also want more money in the future—when they are sick, or unemployed, or retired. The several governmental programs are good but they are not good enough. Hence, the renewed pressure on the employer. Too few business leaders have understood the necessity of determining whether it is better from their point of view to have industry or the community carry the cost of new social benefits. Management must sensibly anticipate that labor will be successful in an expanding economy in improving its rewards. The only issue is the locus of such gains. Here, management has scope for influencing the outcome. Management cannot successfully oppose improving the state unemployment system without running the risk of having a strong union bargain successfully for supplementary unemployment benefits. After pensions were introduced in the steel industry, management lobbied for a rise in social security benefits.

A new trend appears on the horizon. The combined value of unemployment insurance and supplementary unemployment benefits are resulting in some unions considering clauses which would give the worker with seniority the right to first layoff. More broadly, the worker is concerned about what the contract affords him when wages and leisure are both kept in purview.

Workers also want more leisure. They want to work less so that they will have more opportunity to enjoy the good things which their higher wages have now brought within their scope. But they have also begun to advocate a further reduction in the work week because they are restive about the signs which indicate what the acceleration in technological change may do to their jobs. They recall the recent serious redundancy of labor in mining, steel, automobiles, meat packing, and other sectors. Over the years, the gains in productivity have been divided into about three-fifths in the form of more goods and two-fifths in the form of more leisure. With vastly more emphasis now than previously on research and development, the threat to jobs from technological advances is much greater and labor has consequently begun to advocate, if not press for, a shorter work week.

Over the years, then, the American worker has been able to improve substantially the quality of his life off the job by virtue of the reduction in hours and increases in wages which he has been able to obtain, plus a considerable number of fringe benefits. All of these gains, he has secured from his employer. In addition, he has secured important gains from government that have helped to raise his standard of living.

The substantial and continuing gains that he has made and that have been enhanced in many families by the fact that his wife is also a wage earner, have tended to shift his focus increasingly to the conditions under which he works—the eight hours or so that he spends every day, five days a week, in earning the money which enables him to support his family.

The conditions under which he works have also vastly improved; no longer is he exposed to dangerous machinery or to health hazards; no longer is he exhausted at the end of the day so that all that he wants is to find oblivion in drink or in sleep; no longer is he bullied by the foreman. Despite these and other substantial gains, he is not satisfied. From the time he enters the plant until the quitting whistle, he is not in control of himself. His body, his mind, even his soul belong in some degree to those who are paying him. He is under their authority. They tell him what to do and what not to do. They even tell him how to do it. They set the pace and determine the rest periods. In fact, almost every decision of importance has been made by others who supervise him.

This subordination is not a condition of servitude because he is free to get up and leave. But how free is he when his major option is to enter upon a similar arrangement with another employer who will exercise the same order of authority and control over him?

It does not follow necessarily from the fact that American workers today have much better work conditions than did employees at the turn of the century that their feelings reflect those objective facts. For feelings are determined only in part by reality. They also depend on more subjective considerations. Even on the objective side, one trend has been adverse. Advances in technology and in the theory and practice of management have led to a much tighter scheduling of work and a much more elaborate system of articulating the work of different groups. The result has been more and tighter supervision, or at least more dependence of workers on the flow of work set by others. The new technology may be reversing this trend. The more rapid increase in non-production jobs is operating to make tight controls much more difficult.

But what of the man himself? How has he changed? A significant proportion of the industrial work force early in the century were immigrants or the children of immigrants. Most of these immigrants came from countries where power and property had long been concentrated in the hands of the few. They had known neither freedom nor comfort. They had emigrated to the United States either because they had no option or because they looked forward to making a better life for themselves and their children in the New World. These people were used to very little, expected very little, and were satisfied with very little—at least, until they learned that many others had much more and that they too, with work and luck, might achieve much more.

The American worker today is likely to be native-born; in fact, most American workers had grandparents who were born here. During his formative years, the worker is indoctrinated with ideas of equality and freedom—with the belief that every man is as good as every other man. Further, he is taught that all distinctions based on education, wealth, family, or other social criteria have little importance, since a man should be judged by what he does, not by his parents or by the schools which he attends.

And he knows that four times within three decades his father and he were called to arms to make secure the freedom and liberties which give meaning to the American dream.

Nurtured on this heady drink of freedom and equality, of liberty and justice, he cannot fail to become restive, disturbed, antagonistic by what he finds in the employment situation. From the moment the starting whistle blows, his freedom is in suspense; justice is in jeopardy; one man is clearly the superior of another; power and authority permeate the work place.

Philosophers and lawyers earn their livelihood by making distinctions, refined and subtle. They can explain to their own satisfaction and to the satisfaction of the owners of capital and their representatives who manage their enterprises for them that there is no contradiction between the practice of democracy in the political arena and the presence of autocracy in the world of work.

The average man is neither philosopher nor lawyer, but he is a man who sees his life as a whole. He cannot live without tension by one set of values in the hours during which he works and live by an entirely different set of values during the hours when he is off the job.

The lessons of democracy which have been drilled into him tend to become the touchstone for all of his actions. Experience has taught him that he need no longer fear for bread; in fact, he can afford cake. Much of what he has struggled for, he has gained.

But, in the arena of work itself where he spends so much of life and energy, he is mocked. Small wonder, therefore, that it is here that he is seeking to realize the democratic values which he holds dear.

3. THE JOB BELONGS TO THE WORKER

The classical economists, whatever their strengths and weaknesses, were responsible for an amazing piece of historical generalization when they described the competitive market as the natural way to organize an economy and society. It may have been a preferred way but it surely was not the accustomed way. Right up to the beginning of the nineteenth century, England had many of the hallmarks of a society based, in Sir Henry Maine's words, on status rather than contract.

Status certainly governed the relationships of the vast majority of the citizenry who still lived and worked on the land of their employers. Most farmers were tenants. They paid a set or variable rent in money or in kind or in a combination of both. Occasionally, they also had to work for their landlord for a stipulated number of days in the year. But the employment relationship was not limited to specific obligations. It was much broader. Most landowners, especially those with large estates and whose family had been landowners for many generations, possibly centuries, assumed that they had a continuing obligation to take care of "their" families in bad years as in good, in sickness as in health. Landowner and tenant farmer had a long-term understanding. It was not subject to sudden dissolution.

This pattern still prevails today in many parts of the world, including even the United States, in a few areas below the Mason-Dixon line. In some underdeveloped economies, then, even if the farm population conventionally lives at a very low level, they enjoy a type of social security. They may not be able to eat properly or obtain proper medical care but they do have a modicum of security by virtue of free use of a house, land for farming, and, in an emergency, seed or food.

The growth of modern industrialism especially in capitalistic societies dissolved the ties that bound workers and their employers to each other. Thereafter, individuals were on their own—to drive the best bargain they could but with no claims beyond those growing out of the employment contract. The early economists thought highly of the potentialities of the new system, for they correctly perceived that it would contribute to speeding the rate of growth of the economy far beyond that achieved by an agricultural society based on status. But they failed to note, or at least to delineate, the sizable risks that workers soon had to confront since they no longer could look to their employer for even the minimum requirements for survival. While the new industrialization certainly opened up many opportunities for capitalists and workers alike to improve their circumstances, it greatly increased the costs to those who were unable to keep pace or who were victimized by it.

Under the decisions of the courts, a man's property came to be viewed as an extension of himself and, therefore, subject to very wide-ranging protections. The leitmotiv of the nineteenth century and the early part of the twentieth, especially in Anglo-American countries, was the broadening and deepening of the scope and scale of action reserved to the individual. But the worker was generally a man without property. Unless he was able to find a man of property who needed to have work done, he might go hungry. He had first to sell his labor to an employer who wanted to hire him and then he could purchase the essentials for survival—food, clothing, housing.

The only "right" he had was the right to sell his labor and in the exercise thereof many initially contended that it was illegal and immoral for the state to interfere even to the extent of setting minimum conditions that sought to protect his health and life. But government was slowly but surely forced to become more active. Legislation finally shifted from the shoulders of the individual workingman to the employer or to the community responsibility for covering some of the most serious risks faced by workingmen. Compensation was provided for work accidents or injuries, and later on benefits were provided for unemployed or retired workers.

More important transformations occurred within the free market itself. This was the direct result of the efforts of groups of workers who succeeded in altering the range of freedom available to the employer in contracting for labor. The efforts of workers to establish unions for a long time ran afoul of the law which judged such efforts to be criminal and later civil conspiracies aimed at the destruction of the employer's property. Efforts at unionization were also thwarted or slowed by employers' throwing into the conflict all resources at their command—from the manipulation of public opinion, through bribery of officials, to the use of force.

But labor persevered and eventually broke the stranglehold that employers for so long had over the major organs of society—press, courts, political parties, law enforcement agencies. In the United States, this was done during major emergencies. The first was the entrance of this country into World War I; the second followed the public's disenchantment with the prevailing economic system after the blistering depression of the early 1930s which paved the way for the radical legislation of the New Deal.

The continuing pressure exercised by many segments of the laboring population to gain a voice in the determination of the employment contract was much more than the work of professional agitators who saw an opportunity to rise on the shoulders of the masses. There was deep and widespread conviction among workers of every description and circumstance that they had a great deal to gain from influencing the conditions governing the terms of their employment. Although the conventional interpretation of trade union activity stresses the prominent place of higher wages and shorter hours on the agenda of labor, these were only two of the priority objectives. Equally important—and, in many cases, even more important—was the workingman's interest in establishing limits on the employer's right to discipline and on his right to disregard seniority in making determinations about promotions, layoffs, and discharges.

In seeking to place these continuing efforts of labor into perspective, we must consider several crucial developments in the larger society which provide considerable illumination both of labor's targets and its relentless efforts to achieve them.

Despite the contributions of the self-regulating market to increasing the standard of living and speeding economic growth for the population as a whole, the workingman found that it had many drawbacks and shortcomings as far as his role as a supplier of labor was concerned. He could not be indifferent to such matters as to the bankruptcy of his employer, one way in which the market squeezed out high cost producers; or to the ebb and flow of business activity, fluctuations appeared to be of the essence of capitalistic enterprise; or to technological change, the driving force on which economic expansion and cost reductions were based; or to unrestricted immigration, which in the United States supplied the great accretions of labor required for the industrialization of the country. For the efficient businessman or the scholar who helped to interpret the structure and mechanisms of a business society, these adaptations had much to commend them at least in the long run. But for the worker who faced the continuing necessity of getting and holding a job and who, as Keynes said, would be dead in the long run, these regulatory devices in the market place were a bane. His intellect and his emotions told him that in an economy and society in which depression, bankruptcy, obsolescence were imbedded, his self-interest demanded that he seek to moderate the influence and impact of these untoward forces on his job. The fact that he was accused by businessman and professor alike of violating the dictates of laissez-faire impressed the worker not at all. He noted that employers always were engaged in restricting their output whenever it served to increase profits.

His vulnerability was not limited even to these general economic trends. He also had to cope with the exigencies resulting from personal misfortune which might reduce his ability to earn a living as well as with the arbitrary exercise of power of his employer who could discharge him without cause or for minor infractions of rules and thereby destroy the advantages which he had slowly gained over the years as a result of faithful work, faithfully performed.

In its efforts to reduce and if possible, eliminate, much of its vulnerabilities, labor received reinforcement from the fact that as managers replaced owners as the executives of large enterprises, they quickly set about establishing elaborate benefit systems to reward executives who devoted their lives to the corporation. With this model before them, labor redoubled its efforts to secure similar considerations for those who worked at jobs below the executive level.

There was a further spill-over. Trends in the political arena were operating to give increasing meaning to the core elements in our democratic tradition. More and more of the gross differences among citizens were being eliminated or modified. It was not possible for democratic values, principles, and practices to gain strength in the political arena without exercising some impact on the world of industry. Too much of a man's life was tied up with his job to permit him to be indifferent about its impact on the totality of his life. Changes in either area affected the other.

Other forces further encouraged workers to seek to influence the terms on which they sold their labor and performed their work. In the early days of industrial capitalism, the worker who acquired skill had the opportunity to exploit it. His knowledge and his competence were part of him. If and when he changed jobs, he took his specialized capital—his skill—with him. But the advent of extreme specialization has altered the nature of skill. Many workmen develop a know-how and a high order of competence that is very valuable, but only to their present employer. If they were to shift jobs, their special competence might be of little or no value to another employer.

A closely related development has been the acceleration in the obsolescence of skills because of the greater investments that society and industry are making in research and development which, in turn, are resulting in more speedy changes in technology.

In the face of these developments affecting the role of skill, it is scarcely surprising that workers have become even more interested in reducing the possibilities of their being summarily discharged or removed from preferred jobs where they have been able to earn higher wages. The emphasis which the unions have long placed on seniority has thus been further reinforced. To round out this picture, it should be noted that the acquisition of skill in the United States has come to depend increasingly on job progression and in-service training rather than on formal apprenticeship. This helps to explain why unions have pressed so strongly for seniority to govern bidding for jobs and training when they become available.

So much for the broad picture. The heart of the matter lies in the fact that labor knows that if employers have a free hand in matters of discipline, promotion, layoff, and recall, then the worker has no protection other than that afforded him by the competitive market. The market has seldom been able to assure employment for all who seek work. Workers have therefore sought to limit, confine, and restrict the power of the employer to determine the terms of employment.

Effective influence on the terms of employment led to renewed and intensified efforts of labor to have a voice in the manner in which work is carried on within the shop. As long as the employer retained the exclusive power to set work norms and rest periods, to discipline, and to make other basic determinations about the way in which work was to be performed, workers would indeed be not his contractual equals but his factotums. Here, then, is one of the most important arenas where the workingman seeks to have his vote count. Important as is the wage that he earns and the hours that he must devote to earning it so are the conditions and circumstances under which he labors.

This dimension of the employment situation inevitably gains in importance as the economy becomes more affluent and the question of a living wage and reasonable hours of work fade more into the background. Next in importance to earning a living wage is a satisfactory working relationship. One of the strengths of a democratic society is the opportunity it offers all citizens to improve the condition of their lives. Small wonder that the workingman is utilizing this freedom to seek to improve the conditions under which he spends so much of his time and his energy.

The efforts of labor have been directed toward improving basic facets of the employment relationship. In the first place, workers sought to protect their jobs. Second, they have sought a voice in the determination of the amount of effort that they were required to expend in their work. And third, they have sought to increase the rewards which accrue to them by virtue of their work.

The conventional collective bargaining agreement specifies the major conditions under which workers agree to work and in turn commits the employer to provide these conditions. Even in the face of an agreement, no employer is under any compulsion to keep his plant operating and his workers employed if business falls off, a strike prevents his receiving essential components, a breakdown occurs in his machinery, or if any other of the multiple exigencies of production or marketing interferes with his profitable operation. But the contract does bind him not to initiate actions aimed at eliminating jobs or reducing wages through innovations that are not necessitated by either a change in technology or a dislocation in the market place. Of course, the contract does not prevent him from consulting with the union's representatives to determine jointly whether changes might be introduced that would contribute to the economic viability of the company without loss to the worker. The contract simply limits the scope of unilateral action. In a literal sense, his managerial prerogatives have been restricted. However, a collective bargaining agreement—or contract—like every mutual undertaking represents the exchange of a quid for a quo. While the employer's freedom of action has been narrowed in some respects, so too has that of the workers. For instance, they usually relinquish the right to strike during the course of the contract; they forego seeking changes in the terms of the agreement; and they pledge to cooperate in furthering the aims of the enterprise.

Since job security is the core of the worker's interest in the agreement, arbitrators usually hold management to a rather strict interpretation of the contract when it comes to taking actions which will result in the elimination of jobs. They usually uphold management only if there has been an unequivocal change in technology, product line, or market or if other substantial alterations have occurred which necessitate effecting economies in the work force.

But even when management is upheld by the arbitrator in reducing or changing jobs, it must adhere strictly to the prevailing rules of seniority. It cannot simply dismiss those directly affected by the change. Management must follow the contract's provisions with respect to seniority, which may mean the reassignment of a considerable number of workers so that those with the greatest claim on a job retain theirs. In a labor force reduction and bumping process, management must absorb the costs involved in letting trained workers go and providing proper training for the older workers who are then being placed in new jobs. It often is not enough to offer a worker with seniority just one new job and training opportunity and, if he fails, to discharge him. More likely, management must offer him a series of opportunities before it can conclude that there is no suitable work that he can learn to perform satisfactorily.

In the event, that, because of age or other reasons, a worker can no longer meet the demands of his job, he cannot be summarily dismissed as happened to thousands and even millions of men prior to the establishment of collective bargaining agreements. In earlier years, it was entirely within the province of the employer to decide whether or not he would attempt to find alternative employment for a man who had served him long and faithfully but who was no longer capable of meeting the demands of his job. Today, most employers are under contractual obligation to make a conscientious effort to reassign such a worker. Only after such an effort has been made and has failed will action to discharge be upheld.

Much of the insecurity that workers experience results not from the elimination of their jobs or their inability to continue to meet acceptable performance standards but from seasonal and cyclical fluctuations in employment which may put them out of work for a week, a month, or, in the advent of a serious recession, for many months or even years.

Among the most valued aspects of security to the worker are the rules which the employer must follow in determining who should be laid off first and who should be recalled first. Except in periods of severe depression or when a company is faced with a long term decline in its work force, employees of fifteen or more years' service are not likely to be exposed to market fluctuations in the demand for labor. This represents the most valuable type of insurance against unemployment.

The second area in which workers have sought through collective bargaining to play a significant role in determining the conditions under which they work is the setting of work standards. No employer is required to keep an inefficient worker on his payroll, but the arbitrators have made it clear that the simple finding that an employee is not performing satisfactorily is not of and by itself ground for discharge—especially if the employee has many years of service. One of the questions that the arbitrators insist on exploring is whether the worker has had competent supervision. The efficiency of the worker is considered not solely in terms of his competence but in the broader context of the work situation including the competence of the managers themselves. Management must manage; it must provide direction, support, and guidance for its work force. If it fails to do this either because of lack of interest, competence, or training, it has the responsibility for any later shortfall in the quantity or quality of the work performed by its employees.

As indicated earlier, management also has an obligation to provide adequate training opportunities. Many contracts contain explicit provisions about the number of hours of training required for different types of jobs, and, in the absence of objective criteria, the arbitrator will usually be sympathetic to grievances claiming that training was too short or otherwise unsatisfactory. When a worker is discharged, he loses not only his job but all the valuable rights that he has accumulated as a result of seniority. This must, in fairness, be the result only of shortcomings on the part of the worker. If management neglects to take any one of the multiple actions that might prevent such failure, it will not be permitted to discharge the worker.

Poor performance, especially if adequate warnings have been given, will of course lead to discharge. But the steady accretion of benefits that workers with long service enjoy have led arbitrators to exercise great caution before they will uphold the discharge of senior workers. The arbitrator usually assumes that long service is proof that the worker has been efficient and otherwise satisfactory.

The arbitrator also assumes that a worker with substantial seniority appreciates the importance of doing his job satisfactorily so as not to jeopardize his valuable rights. Therefore, if such a worker begins to slacken off, the arbitrator is likely to look beneath the surface in order to ferret out any special circumstances. If he discovers that the worker is under special types of personal stress or that the fall-off in work followed a recent transfer within the plant, or that the worker is in constant conflict with the foreman, or the existence of some other "extenuating circumstance," the arbitrator is likely to recommend discipline short of discharge. He surmises, and in most instances the future proves him right, that a worker's poor performance for a few weeks, following upon a long record of satisfactory or superior performance, reflects some special rather than chronic incapacity. He usually decides that it is an implicit obligation of management to take this into account and to give the worker another chance. The way in which management goes about the task of assessing a worker's performance weighs heavily with the arbitrator in determining whether or not to uphold a decision to discharge. A major and continuing effort of trade unions has been to reduce, restrict, and eliminate management's scope for arbitrary action. This grows out of its long experience which taught it that through arbitrary action management could reward employees who were friendly to it and punish those who were active on behalf of the union. The very survival of trade unions requires vigilance, for there are always managements that would welcome an opportunity to escape from continuing their relationship with a union. The charge of poor workmanship, unless subject to check and review, could provide management with an easy way of getting rid of the more active union members. But once a system has been introduced to protect the few, it is likely to serve as an umbrella for the many. Thus, many workers, whose performance was held by management as unsatisfactory and were discharged, were reinstated because the arbitrators were dissatisfied with the criteria used by management to reach a conclusion about poor workmanship. Arbitrators usually insist that the standards be objective, that they be objectively applied, and that they be applied to all workers alike. Then, and only then, are they likely to uphold management in its decision to discharge a worker for inefficiency.

We have so far considered how workers, through collective bargaining agreements and through grievances processed under them, have sought to protect themselves from the loss of jobs. A related facet of the employment relationship has likewise been the source of considerable negotiation and arbitration; these are the issues that arise out of clauses and interpretations involving earnings and other benefits. From the worker's point of view, there is, of course, a close relation between the amount of effort required of him and the rewards to which he is entitled. Many cases, therefore, have arisen about the setting and, even more, about the changing of work norms and pay schedules. Since the contract between the union and the employer usually covers both conditions of work and pay, disagreements usually arise if management seeks to alter either the work load or the way in which earnings are calculated. Even if management has hired a consulting firm to undertake a time and motion study before it moves to introduce changes, it may not satisfy the arbitrator. Arbitrators have learned that there is a wide gap between the employment of scientific gadgets or gadgeteers and the emergence of valid results. In general, they will accept results where the union has been party to such a study. In many cases, where this has not been the case, they will appoint their own experts.

The same logic which requires management to negotiate with the union in changing work norms and pay rates also covers working rules. These practices of the shop and the trade play a large role in determining how employees work and what they are able to earn. The origin of many of these work rules is often shrouded in the past but while their legitimacy is sometimes questionable they are for the most part clearly understood by both management and labor. Consequently they are generally protected by the agreement. Therefore, they cannot be altered unilaterally.

In recent years, more and more managements—in steel, railroading, theatrical enterprises, trucking—have complained about the way in which work rules interfere with efficient and economical operations. They tend to slide over the fact that in previous negotiations many of these work rules were proposed and accepted by employers or workers. They represent valuable assets and are not likely to be given away except for equivalent consideration. Harry Bridges bargained the work rules on stevedoring on the West Coast for approximately $25 million. His members had secured these rules through earlier agreements, and like good businessmen, they were now willing to sell their "property" for an appropriate consideration.

In addition to the fact that workers place high value on the local practices of the trade because they are used to them and consider them an integral part of the job, they understand that any change may result in their having to work longer or harder, or that they will earn less for the same amount of effort. Work rules can be changed but the changes must be bargained for; no employer can hope to get rid of onerous rules just because they are onerous any more than any union can contemplate establishing a new rule without proving that it will cost management nothing or that management will gain an equivalent compensation.

While the major advantage of seniority relates to job security, it is also an important determinant of extra earnings. Overtime is an essential element in efficient operations. It provides management with flexibility to meet fluctuating work loads. With overtime pay calculated at time and a half or double the base rate, the amount of overtime pay that a worker is able to earn can mean the difference between a modest and a comfortable standard of living. Therefore, the rules governing the allocation of overtime work are an important part of most collective bargaining agreements. Not every worker who is offered the opportunity to work overtime will want to. But it is his right to have the opportunity in accordance with the terms of the agreement. Arbitrators are careful to protect this right for they know that many men decide between jobs on the basis of prospective overtime. Any unilateral change which threatens their ability to earn overtime is likely to be viewed by the arbitrator as a violation of an agreement similar to management action to reduce wage rates.

Since workers increasingly are guaranteed certain holidays with pay and vacations of usually two to three weeks under the same contract that establishes their base pay and the conditions for overtime, arbitrators are careful to insure that all of these benefits are protected and that in granting one the employer does not eliminate another. The greatest difficulties arise with respect to vacations, for many contracts stipulate that the worker's preference as to when he goes on vacation will be considered; however, management must likewise be in a position to schedule vacations so as to avoid undue disruption of its production schedules. To complicate this matter, a high proportion of all workers prefer to take their vacations during the summer months. In the face of a clause in the contract which stipulates that workers' preferences as to the time of their vacation will be given consideration, arbitrators will hesitate to uphold a plant shut-down during a slack season as meeting the requirement of choice. It may be more efficient for management to plan for a shut-down but it is not more beneficial for workers to be deprived of choice as to the timing of their vacations.

Arbitrators have come to realize that one of the major satisfactions that workers seek is to be able to plan and order their lives off the job. Many fringe benefits, such as holidays and vacations, contribute substantially to expanding the opportunities of workers to obtain greater satisfactions from the use of their time off the job but they must be able to plan ahead. Hence most arbitrators are willing to agree to protecting their freedom of choice in timing their vacations. On balance, collective bargaining has tended not only to regularize the demands made on a worker at work; it has also gone far to protect his time off the job from arbitrary incursions by his employer.

We have briefly reviewed the many ways in which the worker has gained an increasing role in determining the conditions under which he works and the rewards which he receives. What is the overall impact of these developments? The time is long past when management can deal with labor as with other resources and unilaterally introduce changes with an aim of increasing productivity in disregard of rights of the workers. The existence of a collective bargaining agreement explicitly or implicitly provides that most changes involving workers must be jointly agreed to by management and the union. While management frequently considers consultation and negotiation as a restriction of its ability to manage, it often stands to gain by such actions. Workers know a great deal about what goes on in the shop and surely know better than others what they want. It may be that management is still at an early stage of learning how to profit from the advantages inherent in a consultative process but there are advantages, as well as disadvantages. Arbitrators repeatedly point out to management the gains that they might have made had they taken the trouble to seek the opinion and the help of the union before they initiated or altered a particular policy.

Management has found it difficult to share power. Its inclination is to go it alone. And, yet, it has much to gain from learning how to work cooperatively with labor, not only because it must but because of the potential contributions that labor can make to the heightened efficiency and profitability of the company.

The last decades have witnessed not only a shift in power but a shift in the division of the profits between management and labor. The power of organized labor, supported by a friendly government and public, has been sufficient to alter the way in which costs are calculated and earnings are divided. Many of the real costs that the individual laborer formerly was forced to absorb have now been transferred to the employer's account or to the account of the community. Nor is there any end to this process in sight. The latest development has been that arbitrators and the courts have recognized that a worker has a property right in his job by virtue of years of faithful service and the many benefits that attach thereto. The employer cannot escape responsibility by the simple device of relocating his plant. This may look like a radical innovation in legal philosophy but in point of fact it is simply an extension of a straight line trend. Employers have recognized that men who have served them long and faithfully are entitled to various types of deferred benefits—particularly pensions, separation wages, paid-up insurance. Nothing is more valuable to a worker than the right to his job and the protection of his seniority. Those who sit in judgment about the changing equities of the worker and management have sought to limit the opportunities of management to destroy such valuable rights.

The multiple developments reviewed in this chapter must appear to those concerned solely with managerial rights and employers' costs as actions which can only have a severely limiting effect on the performance of the free market. It is easy to jump from this conclusion to the generalization that these limitations will be reflected in higher prices, lower profits, and slower growth.

And well they may. But there is no certainty that they will. The American economy has long been characterized by relatively high wages but these have not stood in the way of many companies competing successfully in the markets of the world. The crucial issue always is the response of management and labor to new constraints and new opportunities. There is overwhelming evidence from our history that improved conditions of work are a stimulus, not a deterrent, to economic progress.

In any one industry or in any short period of time, costs that have come to be assessed against management as a result of the expanding control exercised by labor over work may not be fully compensated for by increases in productivity. But a society in which workers are freed from many insecurities incident to employment, where they have acquired dignity and freedom, and where they have gained the right to play a significant role in determining the conditions of their employment is a better society than one in which they are fully exposed to the vagaries of the free market.

Within the purview of the larger sweep of history, the current transformations are easy to understand. That stage of industrial capitalism in which workers lost all control over their jobs was unique. There was no counterpart in any prior society and it is unlikely that any future society will provide a parallel. Jobs have always been to a considerable degree under the control of those who filled them. This is likely to continue to be the pattern in the future.

2.

CAREER PLANS

Life changes, frequently radically, long before students and scholars become aware that it has. This is spectacularly illustrated in the field of occupational choice and career development. Although the average American now spends over twelve years in school and another two to three years in the armed services before he starts to work, the ways in which he acts and reacts to this long period of preparation have been the subject of little research. Occupational studies, especially those with a developmental orientation, are still few and far between. If one seeks a reason, it may be found in the fact that such studies do not fall within any single discipline, such as economics, sociology, or psychology, but cut across all three.

Another barrier to systematic studies is that social science research, especially in the United States, has gone number mad. What cannot be quantified is shunned. But numbers to be meaningful require a framework. Speculation continues to have an important role in all scientific work, in the natural sciences, and especially in the social sciences.

The three chapters that follow indicate our conviction that the development of theory must precede statistical inquiries and the testing of hypotheses. Chapter 4 presents a schematic framework for assessing the ways in which individuals go about clarifying the type of work that they will pursue as adults, making tentative choices, and testing them along the way. Note is taken of the differences in options of the well-to-do and the poor, of the differences between young men and young women.

Chapter 5 delineates three distinctive patterns of career development. Although these patterns emerged from a study of a group of highly educated men who entered upon professional or managerial careers, we hope that they can be adapted to the entire labor force.

In Chapter 6 the individual, rather than his career, usurps the center of the stage. We find that different individuals seek different values in work: some place a high value on autonomy; a minority seeks position of leadership; others prefer a congenial social environment; and a few are dedicated to furthering ideological goals.

The three chapters together indicate that the work that people do is never solely dictated by the circumstances in which they find themselves any more than it can reflect completely their wishes and desires. The shaping of a man's work always represents a compromise between his interests and the opportunities which he confronts. Some men have many opportunities; others only a few; but in an affluent democracy every man has at least some scope for self-determination.

THE THEORY OF OCCUPATIONAL CHOICE

The outstanding conclusion from our findings is that occupational choice is a developmental process: it is not a single decision, but a series of decisions made over a period of years. Each step in the process has a meaningful relation to those which precede and follow it.

From this primary finding, there follows a second important generalization: the process is largely irreversible. This is a result of the fact that each decision made during the process is dependent on the chronological age and development of the individual. Time cannot be relived; basic education and other exposures can only be experienced once. Of course, the individual can shift even after he has tentatively committed himself to a particular choice. But the entire process of decision-making cannot be repeated and later decisions are limited by previous decisions.

The primary finding that occupational choice is a process leads to a further generalization: the process ends in a compromise. Throughout the years of his development the individual has been trying to learn enough about his interests, capacities, and values and about the opportunities and limitations in the real world, to make an occupational choice that will yield him maximum satisfaction. If he could base his choice on but one element, such as his interests or capacities, without regard for the job market, the income structure, and the social prestige which attaches to different kinds of work, his choice should be simple and direct. However, a series of factors, both internal and external, affect his decision. He must renounce to some degree the satisfactions which he might derive if he based his choice exclusively on a strong interest, a marked capacity, or a realistic opportunity. He must find a balance among the major elements. Hence, the compromise aspect of every occupational choice.

The basic elements in our theory of occupational choice, then, are three: *it is a process; the process is largely irreversible; compromise is an essential aspect of every choice.* In reviewing the evidence which supports these basic elements, we will indicate the areas in which further research must be undertaken before our tentative formulations can be validated.

We found that the process of occupational decision-making could be analyzed in terms of three periods—fantasy, tentative, and realistic choices. These can be differentiated by the way in which the individual "translates" his impulses and needs into an occupational choice. In the fantasy period the youngster thinks about an occupation in terms of his wish to be an adult. He cannot assess his capacities or the opportunities and limitations of reality. He believes that he can be whatever he wants to be. His translations are arbitrary.

The tentative period is characterized by the individual's recognition of the problem of deciding on a future occupation. The solution must be sought in terms of probable future satisfactions rather than in terms of current satisfactions. During this period, however, the translation is still almost exclusively in terms of subjective factors: interests, capacities, and values. In fact, as most individuals reach the end of this period, they recognize that their approach has been too subjective. They, therefore, consider their choices tentative, for they realize that an effective resolution requires the incorporation of reality considerations and this will be possible only on the basis of additional experience.

During the realistic period, the translation is so heavily weighted by reality considerations that a synthesis is difficult. The individual recognizes that he must work out a compromise between what he wants and the opportunities which are available to him.

These gross distinctions between the three periods seem valid. But there are many important aspects of the problem which warrant more detailed study than we have been able to undertake. We determined, for instance, from retrospective material that all three groups had made fantasy choices, but the entire period of fantasy choices invites systematic appraisal. The outstanding characteristic of this period is that the choices are arbitrary and are made without reference to reality, though the content differs according to the environment to which children are exposed.

The period of realistic choices, characterized by the impact of reality considerations on the decision-making process, is also greatly affected by the sex and educational status of young adults. But the differences rather than the parallels between the groups were notable. Since actual work experience is the final test, it would be desirable for future investigators to explore its impact on the definitive vocational decisions of the individual.

Another important area of future research would be a systematic analysis of the relation between the period of fantasy choices and the later periods. The important link appears to be in play activities and attitudes toward work rather than in the specific occupational choices which youngsters verbalize. During the early period essential attitudes and values first appear, such as, "I do not want to work too hard"; "I don't like to do things where I get dirty"; "I love machines"; "I like to do things by myself."

The period of tentative choices was divided into the interest, capacity, value, and transition stages. Without exception, all of our case materials point to the fact that both boys and girls in the pubescent age group first approach their occupational choice in terms of their interests; this would be expected since interests are, after all, most directly related to the wishes of the fantasy period.

The capacity stage is amorphous. Even children in the interest stage say, "I want to find a job that I am suited for"—an early indication of awareness of the "capacity" factor. But during the capacity stage, the question is formulated as: "What am I suited for?" or "Am I suited for this or that?" This step from the recognition of the capacity factor to an effort at self-evaluation may have one of two consequences. It can help the individual to discard "wrong" choices, based on interest only, by showing him that he is not suited for certain types of work; or it may reinforce his interest-oriented choice by increasing the satisfaction derived from the successful performance of an "interesting" activity. The school with its emphasis on grades helps the individual to recognize his capacities and his weaknesses. The limitations of the marking system in this respect, however, are many; to mention only one, the youngsters themselves realize that there are at least two relevant factors that control achievement—endowment and effort.

In outlining the value stage, greater clarity is possible. All individuals, except those who are obviously retarded, become aware during their early adolescence that their various interests and values may be incompatible. They love to spend their afternoons playing ball, but they are also anxious to do well in school. Boys in the lower income group are eager to find a part-time job so that it will not be necessary for their parents to give them spending money, but if they do take a job, their time for play is greatly reduced. Many would like to continue in school in order to have the satisfaction and advantages which come with a high school diploma, but on the other hand they want to become "a man" as quickly as possible, which means among other things, a full-time job and a good weekly wage. The system of values serves as a means of resolving conflicts between incompatible objectives by establishing some kind of order among them. It is during the value stage that the boys in the upper income classes begin to think more seriously about the difference in income in various jobs; about the length of time that they are willing to stay in school; whether they prefer to live in the city or in the country; whether the satisfactions to be derived from work itself are to be considered more important than monetary returns.

The last stage in the tentative period—the transition stage—has two characteristics: a general calming, which reflects the end of the turmoil of early adolescence, and an increasing awareness of reality factors. At this time the girls we interviewed seemed to have adjusted their value scheme to incorporate a future role as wife and mother. While up to this point their approach to occupational choice was similar to the boys', at this stage the girls become oriented to marriage rather than to work.

In the exploration stage—the first in the reality period—the young adult is striving to link his decision-making to reality. This is in contrast to the preceding period when his preoccupation was largely with subjective elements. But our case materials suggest that even though his behavior during the exploration stage is increasingly "reality-oriented," the individual now makes a final attempt to link his choice effectively with his basic interests and values. The emphasis which college educators place on exposing freshmen and sophomores to various courses and fields of endeavor, and the eagerness with which many students look forward to this opportunity, reflects their intense desire, almost their need, to test their interests and values.

Although we did not study the counterpart to this exploration stage among boys from the lower income families, we know from the work of other investigators that these young people also test their interests and values during their early working years. Among the girls from upper income families, the parallel is limited to those who are primarily career-oriented and, to a lesser degree, to those who look forward to a future in which work will play a significant, if not predominant, part.

An essential characteristic of the next stage, crystallization, is the quality of acceptance, which stands in contrast to the confused or vague activity, almost hyperactivity, of the exploration stage. Most individuals have now committed themselves to a vocational objective, at least to the extent of being able to direct their efforts henceforth to further their choice, even though they remain uncertain about the details. Crystallization is the culmination of the entire process. The prior stages contributed to effecting the crystallization; the final stage contributes to refinement.

The final stage in the realistic period is specification, which involves specialization and planning within the area of choice. Our study included a few persons who were sufficiently advanced in formal education or who had had enough experience in the Army or in industry to be specific even in the details of their choice. This does not mean that an individual must delay specification until he has acquired considerable training or experience, but simply that he is likely to do so. We also noted that some individuals became so dissatisfied with work in their chosen field that they found it necessary to return to school and seek a new field. It appeared, however, that the choices of these particular individuals had never been really crystallized. Hence, it required a relatively small amount of external pressure to upset the prior decision. However, some persons respond to work experience by reopening what had been a truly crystallized choice. This problem offers another challenge for future research.

Before concluding this summary of the choice process in terms of periods and stages, we will indicate the range around each of the norms. Our estimates are supported not only by our limited case materials but also by data drawn from the vast body of knowledge accumulated by developmental psychology. Our materials suggest that the onset of the tentative period occurs within a range of about two years. Bright children with certain kinds of experiences begin to consider an occupational choice by ten; others, whose intellectual and emotional development is somewhat slower, remain in the fantasy period until twelve. But the variability would be contained within this range, at least for the groups which we have considered. Perhaps even such a different group as the sons of poor farmers might still fall within this range, because the transition from the period of fantasy to tentative choices appears to be dependent on general intellectual and emotional maturation which, in puberty, is closely related to chronological age. But a definitive answer to this would require further research.

The period of realistic choices starts near the end of the seventeenth year. Our materials again suggest that the variation around this norm is contained within two years. One boy from the lower income group crystallized his choice at sixteen, and one or two college freshmen, aged eighteen, did not yet seem to be actively engaged in an exploratory process (the first stage of the period of realistic choices). But by and large, a two-year range is a reasonably close approximation. Crystallization, the most important of all the stages, may have a wider range, though it is probable that the majority reach it between the ages of nineteen and twenty-one.

Variability is also represented in our analysis of choice patterns, such as the range of alternatives considered during the period of tentative choices. There is, for instance, the youngster who, for whatever precipitating reason, decided early in life to become a doctor. His courses in mathematics and the sciences prove to him that he possesses the essential capacities to complete the formal education. His choice is compatible with the values held important by his family and the class to which he belongs; moreover, his family can support him during his long period of studies. This boy will probably not give any consideration to other vocations. His pattern represents a narrow range.

The pattern which we have just outlined is found frequently among engineers. The future engineer is a boy who can test his interests at an early age by his ability to spend long hours at mechanical or related activities; he can also test his capacities by taking courses in high school which are basic for the work which engineers actually do. When boys who make an early decision about engineering later find it unsatisfactory, it is usually because of a shift in values or a belated recognition of other proclivities, which had remained hidden as a result of the premature commitment to engineering. A considerable number of young men, after going through engineering school, find that they would prefer to work more directly with people than with materials.

The more typical pattern consists of a gradual narrowing of the range from an initially broad area of interest to a specific choice. For instance, many individuals know early in the tentative period that they would never want to work in the sciences, although they are drawn to the social sciences. It may take a number of years before they learn enough about themselves and reality to crystallize a specific choice such as economics or law.

In contrast, there are children who at the beginning of the tentative period have multiple interests and capacities of about equal strength in several fields. They have not yet developed a scheme of values, and actual opportunities and limitations of reality are still obscure to them. The task of evolving an effective translation of their present interests is particularly complicated. A studious boy of thirteen or fourteen with an inquiring mind cannot know very much about the occupational opportunities open to "reserach workers." Nor is it easy for another, who likes to serve as the captain of his baseball team and does it well, to recognize that this interest and capacity may eventually enable him to pursue a successful career as an administrator or a personnel specialist. These translations can only come later.

Still another type of variability in choice patterns can be found in the age range within which persons succeed in crystallizing their choice. For a few, this happens at sixteen or seventeen, as soon as emerging values reaffirm the tentative choice. Probably, the majority tends to commit itself within the period around twenty; but there are a number who, for a variety of reasons, fail to reach a firm decision before the age of twenty-three or twenty-four. Thus crystallization may take place within a range of eight years.

Some individuals require still more time. Others fail completely to reach a decision; but according to our analysis, this is considered not as a variation but as a deviation of the choice process. In general, inability to crystallize a choice indicates a rather serious emotional disturbance. But although this is usually the major reason, defects may arise also from major interferences from reality—for example, calamitous developments such as the death of a parent, the loss of familial income, permanent personal injury.

We have discussed two important variations; those related to norms and to choice patterns. A word must be added as to how generally applicable our theoretical formulations are. Our analysis must be viewed in terms of a "tentative formulation." To gain a first impression of the applicability of this structure, we undertook small studies of two different groups, boys from lower income families and girls. We found, as was to be expected, striking differences in the *content* of the choices of these two groups when compared to those of the boys in the upper income families. But we also found that with respect to the *form* of the process of decision-making, these three groups have much in common.

One of the important steps for future research should be controlled studies of different social groups; of boys and girls of different economic backgrounds living in urban centers; and of such radically different groups as sons of farmers or of the economically and socially handicapped, such as Negroes. Major environmental pressures will undoubtedly tend to distort not only the type of choices that are made but the form of the process of decision-making. Stunting in the development of the choice process, brought about by premature termination of schooling, may have an important bearing on the later work adjustment of these groups. Comparative studies of the kind we have just recommended should not only contribute to an advance in the theoretical formulations, but should also provide important insights into similarities and differences among various groups.

It would be desirable to refine the analysis of the stages, primarily in the tentative period. This could be achieved by a continuing study of a group of individuals throughout the entire period of the decision-making process. This recommendation is made despite the cost and other difficulties of carrying it out and despite the fact that the individual's awareness of the study might affect the result. There are also serious shortcomings to accumulating a large number of cases for the purpose of analyzing "retrospective" materials, the recollections of people about their various approaches during the decision-making process. There is no doubt that people can readily recall much of this material, and they will usually present it without significant distortion. But they will be unable to recall the relevant factors at any particular stage and they will be unable to report on the subtleties which were unknown to them but which might have had a determining influence on their decision-making.

In view of these limitations, the refinement of the analysis of stages can probably best be furthered by expanding the approach which we employed. Many more cases are required, and much additional work must be devoted to refining the qualitative analysis and the criteria. Once firm criteria have been developed, it should be possible to undertake extensive studies which will permit the emergence of statistically valid differentiations among the stages and the determination of their variability.

We noted early in the chapter that one important correlative of the fact that occupational choice is a developmental process rather than a unique decision is its irreversibility. This irreversibility should be the subject of further research. What is the essential resource that becomes committed during the period of occupational choice determination? The answer is time. In our society, families recognize an obligation to support and educate their children for varying lengths of time, depending primarily upon economic circumstances. But there is a minimum period written into law which obtains even for the poor, and there is a maximum period which is not customarily exceeded even by the rich. During puberty and early adolescence, all youngsters are preparing for their role as adults; for the middle and upper income groups, this period is frequently prolonged to include late adolescence and early adulthood. But regardless of the length of the period, it is a unique segment in the life of every individual. During this relatively short period, the individual is forced to make a series of decisions which relate primarily to his education but which also have basic significance for his occupational future.

What are some of these important decisions? On entering high school, the student is confronted with a choice of pursuing an academic course leading to entrance into college, or a self-contained high school course. Upon graduation from high school, those who have prepared themselves for college must weigh the advantages of a further four years of education. And even those who do not go to college often have the option of continuing with a year or two of specialized training before starting work. The college student must soon select a major subject or a field of specialization, and the end of college brings the necessity of deciding whether to stop there or to enter a professional school.

Early decisions exercise a very real influence on later options. In large part this results from the reality situation: students will be admitted to good colleges and professional schools only if they have creditably fulfilled certain formal requirements. Therefore, individuals select certain subjects and neglect others; they spend long hours in preparing for examinations. As they proceed they increasingly commit themselves; they attempt to accomplish certain goals in the hope of preparing themselves for a certain type of life. And as they proceed, they must affirm their tentative choice to themselves and, increasingly, to their family and friends.

Because of his investment in educational preparation for work, an individual hesitates to disrupt his plan, especially after he has pursued it for some period of time. A shift in late adolescence or young adulthood will force him to acknowledge, first, that he was in error in some of his prior planning; secondly, that at least part of the effort devoted to overcoming specific educational hurdles was misplaced; and, finally, that certain values are probably not so important as he had previously thought—an admission which he must be willing to make to himself and at least to his intimates.

The irreversibility of the process, then, is inherent in the reality pressures which introduce major obstacles to alterations in one's planning; further, psychological barriers stand in the way of a shift because a shift too easily takes on the quality of failure, and therefore presents a threat to self-esteem. There are further elements which tend to strengthen the irreversibility of the process. During the early stages of preparation, plans can be changed without serious loss of time; at a later stage an individual may fear to alter his approach, feeling that he has repeatedly reaffirmed his tentative choice. It is true that during the exploratory stage of the realistic period, when he is under real pressure internally and externally to commit himself, he may suddenly become aware of considerable uncertainty. But at that point he also becomes aware, usually for the first time, of important pressures which urge an early rather than a late termination of his formal preparation. He is now on the threshold of young adulthood and, therefore, increasingly aware of the desirability of soon securing at least some economic security so that he can contemplate marriage. Many of our cases illustrate the fact that crystallization of choice can occur despite the persistence of uncertainty if one has a desire to marry in the near future. Anticipating the satisfaction of many deep needs and the attainment of many important values through marriage, these young people do not permit residual uncertainties to delay the completion of their preparation for work. Moreover, some realize that a major shift in planning does not guarantee the elimination of their present uncertainties. After all, a substantial element of uncertainty is inherent in all planning. Doubtless many cling to their chosen path because the advantages of a change may not outweigh the disadvantages.

It might be contended that this discussion of irreversibility has limited applicability because those from the lower income classes make such a small "investment," and those in the upper income classes —the college group—retain considerable flexibility irrespective of the type of education which they pursue. But it is important whether boys from lower income families pursue academic or vocational courses in high school; on this hinges their continuance in school, their ability to enter college, and their level of work adjustment, including possibilities for advancement. And although large numbers of the college group will enter business regardless of their major subject, and many others who pursue professional training may eventually find work in other fields, there are important implications to following one type of collegiate training rather than another. Many individuals whose work is not specifically related to their occupational planning and educational preparation succeed in deriving considerable work satisfaction. But for most individuals work satisfaction will be influenced by their occupational preparation which, as we have seen, propels the choice process in the direction of irreversibility.

We have noted that a second important correlative of the process of choice determination is that it inevitably results in a compromise. We have seen that the individual gradually gains insight about and control over himself as he gains knowledge about the external reality, particularly the world of work. At the age of eleven he cannot effectively consider an occupational choice, since he knows that he himself will change in the future and will reevaluate the various elements. During adolescence, the individual becomes increasingly aware of himself, and his approach to a future occupation is largely in terms of subjective factors. His interests provide him with the initial differentiating criterion by which to formulate a tentative choice, but he soon discovers that the basis of choice must be broadened to include an appraisal of his capacities. Somewhat later, in his fifteenth or sixteenth year, his tentative choice must be assessed in terms of an emerging value scheme. In short, throughout adolescence the individual adds to the subjective factors in his considerations.

But throughout this period, during which he is primarily subjectively oriented, he is also becoming aware more and more of the complex structure of reality with its job hierarchy, variety of working conditions, specific conditions for entrance into occupations, various income and security factors, and the host of allied elements which are part of the working world. As he learns about all this, he recognizes more clearly the relationship between his school curriculum and his eventual occupational status. For example, a decision in high school not to take courses required for entrance to college may cut him off from future opportunities. Similarly, in college, his decisions about curricula will have a significant influence—positive or negative—on his occupational future.

This summary of the choice process points to the inevitability of compromise in crystallizing an occupational choice. We have noted how the individual works to establish a balance—a compromise—among his interests, capacities, and values, during the tentative period. We have further noted that during this period he must take care to pursue at least the minimum number of courses required to qualify himself for the later stage of his occupational preparation. Irrespective of whether he is interested in, or has the capacity for, or even believes that he will have much use for intermediate algebra, he will include this subject in his high school program if it is required for admission to college, when college is his next objective. Regardless of his great interest in English literature, or how important he considers it for a general education, he will limit his courses in it if his major objective is admission to medical school, for he must find room in his program for a large number of courses in the sciences.

But the role of compromise in the occupational choice process is considerably more important than is suggested by these examples of compromise among subjective factors or between subjective factors and educational options. At the age of about seventeen, reality considerations which were on the periphery of consciousness, move into a more central position. In large part this shift reflects the fact that the values which an individual hopes to realize through work are deeply embedded in the social and economic structure to which he must adjust himself. He will not be able to realize his major values except by meeting and resolving the host of problems and overcoming barriers which are part of the world of reality.

The decision concerning an occupational choice is, in the last analysis, a compromise whereby an individual hopes to gain the maximum degree of satisfaction out of his working life by pursuing a career in which he can make as much use as possible of his interests and capacities, in a situation which will satisfy as many of his values and goals as possible. In seeking an appropriate choice, he must weigh the actual opportunities and limitations and the extent to which they will contribute to or detract from maximum work satisfaction. A person with real talent in music may still hesitate to venture upon a musical career when he discovers that successful musicians are few and the failures many. Despite his real desire, he may decide against a musical career, lest it jeopardize many other values, particularly economic security. And so he may decide, as many people do, to pursue a career more likely to yield a steady income, hoping to satisfy his musical interests through avocational activity.

We saw that crystallization of an occupational choice is not likely to occur until young adulthood, for, prior to that time, the individual rarely has the necessary knowledge about himself and reality. But at twenty, he knows that his formal period of preparation is coming to an end and he also knows that a commitment cannot be long postponed.

This, then, is our general theory. First, occupational choice is a process which takes place over a minimum of six or seven years, and more typically, over ten years or more. Secondly, since each decision during adolescence is related to one's experience up to that point, and in turn has an influence on the future, the process of decision-making is basically irreversible. Finally, since occupational choice involves the balancing of a series of subjective elements with the opportunities and limitations of reality, the crystallization of occupational choice inevitably has the quality of a compromise.

5.

PATTERNS OF
CAREER DEVELOPMENT

Much more is known about the way in which young people prepare themselves for work than about their experiences after they begin to work. There are, however, several pieces of information concerning career development which are in the common domain. A very high proportion of certain groups such as physicians, who have pursued a long period of training, are likely to remain in their professions throughout the whole of their working lives, while others who have also pursued professional or technical training such as lawyers, engineers, clergymen, scientists, often shift out of the field for which they were originally trained. Some may even never enter their chosen field, such as the lawyer who goes into an administrative post in government upon graduation from law school, or the chemist who upon receiving his master's degree accepts a position with the marketing division of a large corporation.

Although considerable data have been assembled about the occupational mobility of those who have had advanced education, the information is usually gross and reflects shifts among occupations or jobs. Very little information is available about the more subtle but important changes within the same field, such as when a physician shifts his role in a hospital from therapist to administrator, or when he changes the nature of his employment and leaves his own practice to work for an industrial firm or a government agency. Moreover, since most occupational studies are limited to reporting job changes, they do not consider the interaction of forces within the individual and within the world of work that lead some to continue in the same work and others to make moderate or even radical changes in their careers.

This chapter will attempt to describe systematically the first ten to fifteen years in the work history of our group of 342 male graduate fellowship holders at Columbia University (1945–51) and determine the varying degrees of continuity, shift, and change that occurred in their occupational development. In developing this description attention will be devoted to three dimensions of the process: the direction, progression, and continuity of the individual's work history.

With respect to *direction*, the question is the relationship between the individual's present work and his original occupational goals. Are the two identical or closely related or was the individual deflected from the route on which he had set out so that it can be said that he changed direction?

Since jobs are hierarchically ordered and since even very able and well-prepared persons usually begin at or close to the bottom rung of the ladder, an important axis of occupational analysis is the extent to which the individual moves up the ladder over a period of years. Is his career development characterized by an element of *progression?*

A third facet of the way in which men enter into and make their way in the world of work relates to the number and degree of interruptions that they experience. Some move from their entrance job straight ahead while others may be deflected because of military service, family demands, or a decision to return to school. The element of *continuity* is a third important dimension of career development.

We will now attempt to order the occupational experiences of the members of the group in a manner that will reveal parallels and differences in the direction, progression, and continuity of job experiences. Our aim is to develop a limited number of discrete patterns of occupational development.

The likelihood that we will uncover career patterns is increased by the fact that many sectors of the world of work are rather rigidly structured. The conditions for employment and advancement are more or less explicit, and the hierarchy of positions is generally known. Although the conditions governing promotion may vary from one institution to another and even within the same institution, most of those who enter upon and engage in the competition for better jobs are likely to acquire early a reasonably clear idea of the performance required of them if they are to advance.

There are some sectors in the world of work which are not rigidly structured. Advancement in such professions as architecture, journalism, engineering, and many others is relatively open. There is even less structure in some sectors of business, government, and self-employment. But here too there are discernible tracks. However, individuals may be deflected and therefore we cannot know in advance which individuals or how many in a particular group will reach the higher levels in the occupational hierarchy. At best the patterns can provide the framework within which to study the differential work history of individuals.

While the environment within which the members of our group made their decisions contributed to the establishment of certain occupational patterns, the heart of these patterns is imbedded in the cumulative decisions which the individual makes about the successive alternatives that he confronts. It must be emphasized again that as a result of their excellent preparation and the favorable economic conditions during the period when they were starting out on their careers the members of our group had a wide range of options.

The number of discrete patterns that we could delineate would depend both on the variability of the career development of the group and on the analytical use that was to be made of the patterns after they had been elaborated. In view of the basic character of the study, which was exploratory and would seek to open up key questions rather than to provide exhaustive answers, we decided to limit ourselves to three basic patterns.

The first characterizes those individuals whose career development follows a more or less straight path; after they have crystallized and specified their occupational choice, they enter and remain in one field and continue to perform essentially the same type of work. Among those who follow this pattern is the young man who selects chemistry as a major in college, goes on to earn his doctorate in chemistry, and then enters an industrial laboratory, where he remains; or the individual who in college chooses journalism as a career, becomes the editor of the college newspaper, attends a graduate school of journalism, and then takes a job as a reporter and continues to hold down positions as a working journalist. We define this type of career development as a *straight pattern*.

Related, but clearly distinguishable from those in a straight pattern are individuals whose career development reveals that they have shifted their field or have moved to perform a different function within the same field or have made both changes. The key word that describes this group is "shift." Their new field or the new functions that they perform in the same field are more or less logically related to what they had been doing before. There is no sharp break between the new activity and the old. The type of shifts involved suggests that these individuals have broadened their occupational horizons by extending and expanding the range of their interests and activities.

Among those who fall within this second pattern is the young man who earns a doctorate in economics and starts his career as a college teacher, but leaves this position after a few years to become the economist for a bank where he thereafter is concerned primarily with economic research and writing; or the engineer who on graduation accepts a job in industry but after a few years returns to the university to take a doctorate in physics. He then joins the faculty of a school of applied science where he teaches and conducts research in advanced electrical engineering. Those whose careers are characterized by such proliferation and shifts are said to follow a *broad pattern*.

The occupational histories of those who fall into the third group, which we have designated as the *variant pattern*, are quite different from the other patterns and differ among themselves. First, they contain individuals who have made one or more radical changes in their field of activity, such as the geologist in our group who after a few years of college teaching went into a retail business. Those whose careers are marked by such radical changes resemble to some degree those who fall within the broad pattern, except that their careers contained radical changes rather than moderate shifts both in direction and continuity.

The other major subgroup that falls within the variant pattern is composed of individuals who have not altered the direction or continuity of their work but whose careers reflect a lack of progression. They have advanced not at all or very little. They are related to those in the straight pattern except for this lack of reasonable progress. This group includes, for instance, the young classicist who ten years after earning his doctorate is still an assistant professor, a position which he has held for eight years. Although he has moved from one institution to another he has not moved up the academic ladder. Another example of those who follow the variant pattern is the talented young man who takes a job as a high school teacher to support himself while he attempts to write a novel. But the novel remains unfinished and he remains in this position.

Since the occupational development of the group was characterized by directedness and persistency, it is not surprising that 58 percent of the group falls into the straight pattern. However, the proportion comprising the broad pattern is surprising. In view of the favorable intellectual endowment and advanced education of the group and the favorable employment situation, we might have anticipated that the proportion which fell into the broad pattern, which was 29 percent, would have been higher. Of course time is a factor here. If this group were reappraised a decade hence, it is likely that the proportion in the straight pattern would be smaller, that in the broad pattern larger.

The relatively small size of the variant pattern, 13 percent, might have been expected. Since one criterion for this classification was a lack of progression in their career development, it is not surprising that only a minority of these able people followed this pattern.

Our classification scheme could be applied to a wide range of occupations as well as to those represented by the members of this group. For instance it would be feasible and probably illuminating to study the occupational histories of a group of skilled workers or a group of clerical or sales workers in terms of these three patterns. But while the schema might have broad applicability, the distributions which we found to prevail in the present study might not apply to other groups. Members of our group had a long time to try out and test their interests and capacities; they had to make a great many decisions about their education and training such as whether they were willing to invest time, effort, and money in preparing for particular careers. They were therefore much more likely to be deeply committed to their choices than would a group of clerical or sales workers whose education and training has been much less extensive and who had not made corresponding sacrifices and commitments for the accomplishment of a specific career goal. Moreover the members of our group were in a better position to shift or change their career goals because of their superior endowment and training than occupational groups with less training who would have been more limited in their alternatives.

The following extracts from the questionnaires indicate the criteria that we used to distribute the respondents among the three career patterns. A member of the American foreign service used language identical to our own to describe his career development and he is thus the prototype of those who fall within the straight pattern. "I have followed a more or less straight line since my senior year in college as regards choice of career and pursuit of it. . . . The fact that I chose active employment with the federal government is a consequence of the opportunity following college to have an introduction to a career along these lines. . . . I derive great personal satisfaction from my work. Let us say simply that I chose the right career for me and am happy with my work and the future it offers."

An attorney on the West Coast also hewed to a straight path. "My choice of profession has always been the law. It has been a very rewarding and absorbing profession. I have thoroughly enjoyed my training for and the practice of my profession, as well as the associations and opportunities it presents." Not even five years of military service deflected him!

A professor of music reported the stages of his career development as follows: "At 7 introduced to music through piano lessons. After reaching a decision at 12 to become a composer my parents and the schools which I attended made possible lessons in piano, theory, history of music through 'released time.' Good choice of a university (with School of Music) helped. A small legacy at the end of the conservatory years made it possible for me to come to New York and then pursue studies with [a major contemporary composer]. . . . So far as the 'compositional career' rather than the academic career is concerned, fellowships . . . made it possible to get away from teaching at intervals and obviated the necessity to teach summer school."

An assistant professor of classical languages dates his career development from high school: "Foreign languages, especially Greek and Latin, have greatly interested me from secondary school days. I majored in Latin and Greek at B——— College . . . with a view to becoming a college teacher. I continued my work in classics at Columbia University where I received the A.M. and Ph.D. degrees. Since leaving Columbia, I have embarked on a career in college teaching."

These cases illustrate the type of career development followed by those whom we included within the straight pattern. They are individuals who usually were headed in a particular direction by the end of college if not before, and they moved along the same track through graduate school and work, from one decade to the next.

The special quality of their occupational development that we sought to capture through the use of the word "straight" is further illustrated when we contrast them with those whose careers fall within the broad pattern. This second group includes an international consultant in mining resources. His early employment was in engineering in connection with various mining enterprises. He returned for two years of graduate study in mineral economics because his job experience had pointed to the significance of this field. During the next five years he was employed as a mineral economist by corporate and governmental agencies. He then became the executive vice president of a uranium company but left shortly thereafter as a result of a disagreement with the president. He then became a consultant for both private companies and governments. Five years ago he accepted a position with an international agency in which he is presently employed. This man's career development is the result of a broadening of interests, capacity, and responsibility. Each step in his occupational history is meaningfully related to his previous experience and in turn lays the foundation for the next step.

A group leader in statistical analysis in a research and development laboratory on the West Coast got his first job after high school in 1942. "Though I had taken a college entrance course, finances did not indicate a college education. Our small school did not promote scholarships. . . . I did take a science talent exam and received honorable mention. Incidentally, though I was interested in civil engineering I wrote an essay on guided missiles and rockets, not dreaming that one day I would be working on the design of moon and planetary space craft. My mother pushed me to enter college . . . and by part time work in a cheese factory (3 to 7 a.m.) . . . plus my mother's sacrifice I received a B.A. in civil engineering in February 1946." After he was awarded a fellowship by Columbia, "the direction of my career was altered upward. I turned down a position to stay at Columbia after receiving my M.S. in favor of returning to [my undergraduate college]. Had I stayed at Columbia my career would undoubtedly have been different. After teaching until 1952, I married. I knew I needed experience or a Ph.D.—I had turned down the latter opportunity by not staying at Columbia. Since my wife had asthma and I wanted aircraft experience, the logical location was California."

He became a stress engineer at a major aircraft company but soon was dissatisfied. "Through a friend who worked in a space laboratory I learned of a possible opening. I applied with no immediate indication of success. A month later, however, I received a job offer. Thus I arrived at the laboratory and the present level of my career."

Here is a case of very considerable broadening. At first college was beyond his horizon; then graduate school seemed outside his purview. But in each case the leap was made. While he did not earn his doctorate, he was able to secure first a teaching position at the college level and later a research position in a space laboratory. From arsenal worker to development engineer represents a substantial broadening!

A young veteran with a liberal arts degree had an opportunity to join the staff of the prosecutor at the war-crimes trials that were held some years after World War II. After several years on this staff, he left to pursue graduate work at Columbia. From 1950 to 1955 he held a position as an instructor in government at a good college. After securing his doctorate, he joined the Department of State as Intelligence Research Specialist. Again the several stages of a career are related to each other and this respondent's present work is the natural outgrowth and extension of both his education and his earlier work experience.

In contrast to those in the straight pattern who are on a single track, those in broad pattern tend to move away from their original locus or focus. However, the direction towards which they move is related to their previous work. It is an outgrowth of earlier experience. The past, present, and future are organically connected. They frequently manifest an element of venturesomeness or eagerness for the new in their approach to their work.

Even though the number of the respondents who fell into the variant pattern is relatively small, they represent a particularly interesting group because of the difficulties that they experienced in getting launched on their careers despite their substantial ability and superior education. An illustration of this group is a highly successful member of the bar, a partner of a firm that carries his name, who noted that "after being a working newspaperman for four and a half years I wanted a more permanent and financially remunerative way of life . . . therefore I went through law school and became an attorney. I have found now both the permanence and the remuneration that I sought."

Another respondent had also started work as a journalist and continued somewhat longer before he changed to another field. He had been a newspaper writer for four years and then became the editor of a trade association magazine. As an outgrowth of this job he "found an opportunity to increase income through a marketing practice" and established himself as an independent marketing consultant. He then took a further step and became a part-time lecturer in marketing at a large university. At the time he replied to the questionnaire he had been promoted to associate professor, but his teaching was still limited to a part-time schedule. In this case we can see how the change came about. Through his editorial work the respondent became acquainted with a new field. From journalism to marketing and teaching represented a complete change rather than a broadening of occupational goals, since his new occupation had no similarity or relation to his former one.

A radical change in field and function but not in employer characterizes the career development of a research chemist who became a patent expert. After graduate work in chemistry he accepted a position with a large industrial corporation in laboratory research. At the time he replied to the questionnaire he was working in the patent department. In the interim he had moved from a city in up-state New York to New York City which both he and his wife greatly preferred. After relocating he had attended law school at night and graduated. This change in his career "required considerable thought." The considerations that led him to it were: "1) In industrial laboratories, research projects in physical chemistry tend to be ancillary to primary projects in organic chemistry or physics; 2) In the lab, the opportunities for supervisory experience was very limited—lab technicians were seldom available to research chemists with less than five years' experience; 3) Major interests and abilities . . . did not favor a shift in emphasis to research in organic chemistry; 4) While working in the laboratory I found my ability to analyze and write up research results were above average. This is important in patent work."

In the foregoing instances, the respondents made radical changes in their careers and landed on their feet; in fact, they improved their circumstances and prospects. Of course they might have been in a better position had they earlier had a clearer perception of their needs and desires and of the realities of the world of work. But confronting work situations that were unsatisfactory relative to alternatives which they had not previously known about or had not considered, these men were able to mount the considerable effort of making a radical change and are doing well in their new careers.

Others who made changes, however, did not really solve their career problems. They continued to find considerable dissatisfaction in their work. For instance, a respondent who is currently a self-employed lawyer reported a modest income of between $5,000 and $7,500 annually. His original training had been in chemical engineering, and he had been employed for several years in this field. This is how he summarized the change in his career: "Interest in chemical engineering work was my own. However, after having been released twice due primarily to economic factors, I was a proper subject for the influence of an uncle who was a practicing attorney. As a result, I obtained my law degree. . . . Occasionally I feel a sense of longing and nostalgia for the engineering field, but I feel it is getting too late in life for any further changes."

One of our respondents had been a radio announcer for several different stations for four years. Then, for a brief period, he became the associate editor of a fairly successful new monthly magazine. He left this job and returned to radio announcing. He then tried high school teaching for one year but did not like that. In 1960 he joined a West Coast paper as a feature writer. He reported a salary of $5,800 per year and stated that he expects to stay with the paper until retirement. Here is a case of much movement but little progress.

The common characteristic of this group within the variant pattern is a belated or unsuccessful resolution of occupational choice. While some are able to crystallize or change their choice by making special efforts later in their lives and do not suffer serious set-backs, others are not able to make such an effort or cannot do so successfully. In many instances where such a difficulty exists it appears that an underlying personality problem is finding expression in the occupational area.

Our attempt to order the work histories into a few basic patterns pointed up the continuity and consistency characteristic of the occupational development of most of the group. In general, even those who did not stay with their original choices entered fields which were organically related to their previous experience rather than grasping an accidental opportunity.

We cannot expect to understand what might account for these differences in the career development of our respondents by looking for a single factor. The case materials have suggested a great variety of determinants in the choices and decisions that the respondents have made about their work. In looking for the differentiating characteristics our first line of inquiry is to search the preparatory process. Were there significant differences in the age at which they crystallized their occupational choice? The answer is an unequivocal yes: there were differences and they were pronounced. Over three-fourths of those in the straight pattern had determined on their occupational goal before college graduation, while only two-thirds of those in the broad pattern and just over half of those in the variant pattern had crystallized their choices by this time. At the conclusion of their graduate studies only 2 percent in the straight pattern, 4 percent in the broad pattern, and 24 percent in the variant pattern had not reached a resolution of their occupational choice.

An inspection of the grades which the respondents received in graduate school was also revealing. The largest proportion of the graduate students with the best grades (A and A+) were found in the straight pattern, the smallest proportion in the variant pattern. Correspondingly, those with the lowest marks in graduate school were more likely to be in the variant pattern than in the straight pattern.

There was one rather subtle matter with respect to grades that warrants mention. Slightly over one-third of those in both the straight and broad patterns had pursued fields of specialization in graduate school in which the departments did not grade routinely. Doctorates were awarded on the basis of oral and written examinations alone. But the percentage of those in the variant pattern who followed courses of study for which grades were not given rose to 57. There is a possibility that the relatively unstructured nature of their graduate education intensified the problems connected with crystallizing career objectives for those who later fell into the variant pattern. However, it is also possible (at least we cannot exclude the possibility) that their choice of these fields of study itself reflects some element of uncertainty, hesitancy, or doubt about occupational plans.

Another important differentiating characteristic of the respondents within these patterns turned out to be the earning of a doctorate and the age at which it was received. More than 3 out of 4 of those in the straight pattern achieved this degree; 69 percent of those in the broad pattern, but only slightly over half of those in the variant pattern, received the doctorate. With respect to age, those in the straight pattern were more likely to receive their degree relatively early, and those in the variant pattern were concentrated among those who received it late.

The explanation of these findings remains somewhat equivocal; we cannot be sure whether the speed with which those in the straight pattern acquired their doctorate helped to anchor them occupationally or whether the early clarification of their goals enabled them to pursue their doctorate aggressively. There are also alternative lines of explanation for those in the variant pattern: was it their uncertainty about their occupational goals that reduced the proportion of those who acquired a doctorate or delayed those who acquired it; or did the lack of this degree handicap their later occupational development? While our data do not enable us to select the correct hypothesis it is possible that these alternatives are not mutually exclusive.

To what extent does a period of military service and the length of service help to differentiate among those in the three patterns? Sixty-five and 62 percent respectively of those in the straight and broad patterns served on active duty, and a somewhat smaller percent (53) of those in the variant pattern saw military service. Possibly more of the variant group were rejected for military service on psychological grounds. While approximately one-quarter of those in the straight and broad patterns served for less than two years, only about one-tenth of those in the variant pattern served for such a short period. This longer military service of those in the variant pattern may have had an adverse effect on their career development.

An interesting finding about length of service is that the highest proportion serving four or more years was found among the broad pattern. There is a strong presumption that during such a lengthy interruption, many men reappraised their original plans and considered how to make use of their military service so as not to "lose" four or more years. Apparently a considerable proportion found the answer by broadening their careers in a manner which enabled them to make constructive use of what they had learned in the military.

A third line of inquiry about the career patterns involved such differentiating characteristics as the fields, functions, and institutional settings in which the respondents worked. Among the questions to be explored were these: were there subtle ties between each pattern and the field or functions in which the respondents worked, in that some fields and functions helped to lock people in and therefore kept them in a straight pattern, while other types of work facilitated broadening their development? Are the career patterns perhaps no more than a disguise for these basic determinants?

With respect to fields, those with careers in the natural sciences are overrepresented in the straight pattern, and those in the humanities and business are overrepresented in the variant pattern. With regard to the broad pattern, the fields are fairly evenly represented except for a slight overproportion of those in engineering. A few speculations can be ventured although definitive answers cannot be provided. The relatively high proportion of those in the straight pattern found in the natural sciences can be explained by the fact that without a high degree of directedness and perseverance one is not able to qualify for a specialized career in science; a high proportion of those who pursued their education to the doctorate in a scientific field were likely to be strongly attracted to this type of work, and the opportunity to be well rewarded in science probably encouraged many to stay with it.

The high proportion of those in the variant pattern who were following careers in the humanities or business may reflect the difficulty for one trained in the humanities to find a satisfactory alternative if he becomes dissatisfied with his original choice and the appeal of business for those who do not have or cannot maintain strong professional interests.

The relatively greater proportion of those with a broad pattern who had studied engineering may reflect the fact that engineers in large profit-making organizations often have a good opportunity to move over into general management where the financial emoluments are greater. The choice of engineering in college often reflects a mixture of scientific and economic interests, and this may explain why many engineers later broaden their occupational horizons.

With regard to the relations between the functions performed by the respondents and their career patterns, the following emerged: there was overrepresentation of those in the variant pattern in teaching alone, of those in the straight pattern in teaching and research combined, and of those in the broad pattern in administration. As might be expected, the following underrepresentation emerged: the broad in teaching alone, the broad and variant in teaching combined with research, and the variant in research and research administration.

A few comments on the foregoing: teaching alone seems to have been too restricted for those who sought to broaden their occupational goals, while it helped to provide a refuge for those still in search of a final resolution of their career problems. Teaching combined with research, which is usually a preferred university position, was secured most readily by those who had developed excellence in a particular discipline. Research and research-administration were beyond the range of those in the variant pattern, who had not acquired sufficient depth in a particular discipline. Administration was a magnet for those who wanted to broaden their careers, and it offered an escape for some who had initially floundered.

A few interesting findings emerge from a consideration of the career patterns and the institutional settings within which the respondents worked. There was overrepresentation of the straight pattern in academic life, of the broad in corporate enterprise, and of the variant among the self-employed. These findings are easy to interpret. A high proportion of graduate students start their careers as teachers in the subject of their specialization. Many in the straight pattern started in academic life and continued in it. Those in the broad pattern, however, sought to expand beyond their starting point and found preferred opportunities in corporate enterprise. Some started in business with the intention of broadening out if and when the opportunity offered.

The overrepresentation of the variant among the self-employed is probably a composite result: some who were uncertain about their future sought to avoid an institutional commitment for as long as possible, others had tried and failed to fit themselves into a hierarchical structure, and a few were pursuing lines of work such as writing or composing in which they could be on their own.

We see then that the career patterns are to some degree characterized by the field, functions, and institutions of the work of the respondents; but since the statistical differences are not very pronounced, other factors are unquestionably present and operative.

There is one more piece of evidence at hand. This derives from the answer to whether the patterns can be distinguished in terms of the average number of employers worked for by the members of the group. The findings are surprising. Almost 3 out of 5 in the straight pattern had worked for only one or two employers; this was true of 26 percent of the broad and only 19 percent of the variant. Most of those in the broad pattern had had three or four employers. Almost half of those with a variant pattern had had five or more employers while only 9 percent of those in the straight pattern had had this many. From the explanations they offered about job changes we know that those in the broad pattern used employment opportunities that opened up to expand their occupational horizons and goals. The frequent job changes of the variant indicated that these people did not like what they were doing and hoped that they would fare better if they shifted to a different field or function or institution. The infrequent job changes of those in the straight pattern do not in general reflect absence of opportunity but rather a disinclination to make a change which might deflect them from long-run career objectives.

The data presented above about the preparatory cycle and several facets of the work experience of the members of the group suggest that the career pattern scheme, although it was developed on the basis of gross occupational behavior, was actually associated with the personal characteristics and probably with the total personality structure of the respondents. Otherwise the many connections which we found between the patterns and the other factors in their career development could not be explained. It may be helpful to pull together what we have learned about these factors which appear to be associated with the career patterns.

Those in the straight pattern appear to have a stronger commitment to their occupation than those in the other patterns. For the most part they resolve their occupational choice early, and once they enter full-time work they tend to remain set. They stay with one employer or make only a few shifts. They convey the impression of having a good capacity for work. Many had very good grades in graduate school and a high proportion secured their doctorates.

Those in the broad pattern appear to be less committed to a specific field. They take a somewhat longer time to decide on their occupational choice and, having decided, they seem less firmly bound to it. Their somewhat looser interest in a particular field of work is probably reflected as early as graduate school where their marks tend to be less good than those received by individuals in the straight pattern. They were apparently able to adjust to long military service, sometimes even to build on it. They tend to work for more employers and generally seem more fluid with respect to their career development. As a group, they convey the impression of being in search of a goal beyond a particular job, i.e., they are more readily deflected from their original course. Additional data suggest that they may also be more responsive to outside influences.

The most conspicuous characteristic of those in the variant pattern is that they experienced difficulties in resolving their occupational choice. Some crystallize a choice only to find after a time that they are dissatisfied with it and that they must tackle the problem anew. Others are simply stymied from the start and struggle for a long time to find a satisfactory resolution without much success. They do less well in graduate school, and a considerable proportion of them are not accepted for military service. A high proportion do not acquire a doctorate. When they go to work, many take up teaching as interim employment; others prefer to be self-employed. Those who work for others change employers frequently, apparently in the hope that their next job will prove more satisfactory than their last. The variant pattern conveys the impression of many able people who have experienced difficulty in coping with the world of work, possibly because they cannot meet these demands and at the same time cope with the other demands that are made on young adults. But included in the variant pattern are others who have considerable strength. They realize, usually fairly early in their careers, that they have made an initial mistake in the determination of an occupational choice. But they face up to this and make the necessary adjustments. Many do much better the second time around.

The career patterns thus turn out to have significance on several distinct levels. Descriptively, they tell us about the occupational history of our group. If we compared the patterns of our respondents with those of another sample—graduate students of lesser ability or people who stopped their education earlier, it is probable that significant differences would be found in the career development of the two groups. The patterns also have value as an analytic tool which enables us to explore connections between the career development of individuals and various forces in the occupational world that influence and affect them. They also provide a basis for precipitating an analysis of certain personal characteristics that find expression in the occupational area.

For our purposes the career patterns have provided us with a first opportunity to order the diversified materials which reflect the occupational experience of this talented group during the early years of their careers. We can say that the patterns of career development tell us something about the groups of individuals within them. At this point we do not know what a pattern can reveal about a particular individual, since it is a gross category reflecting only broad tendencies.

Finally, of the three constituent elements—direction, continuity, and progression—the patterns are most revelatory about the first two. Only in the variant pattern, and then only with respect to some of the group, was the lack of progression a key characteristic. The role of progression in a career still remains to be examined in its own right.

6. VALUE ORIENTATIONS IN WORK

The preceding chapter on career development enabled us to organize and evaluate the behavioristic materials which describe the successive stages in occupational development. But an analytical framework must make room for the individual. For the individual is not passive in the structuring of his career however much he may be buffeted by forces beyond his control. While external forces may overshadow the self-directing efforts of people who do simple work for which they need little specific training, this cannot be assumed with regard to our group who spent over twenty years preparing for work. While we cannot hope to encompass all aspects of the individual's personality, we must at least elucidate the basic preference systems that underlie the choices which he makes with respect to his work and career.

The major elements of an individual's preference system can be described in terms of his needs, goals, and values. A word about each. Every individual has needs, wishes and desires, and some are so powerful that he must seek to gratify them directly and quickly. But no adult is restricted to or bound completely by his immediate needs. He has other goals, long-range objectives which he has set for himself. Their particular quality is that they have a time dimension and cannot possibly be achieved immediately. Hence they provide a link between the present and the future; the future goals determine the behavior in the present which is directed toward their realization. We make a distinction between needs and goals because individuals must frequently defer the satisfaction of some of their needs in favor of accomplishing some long-range goal.

Values, the third constituent of the individual's preference system, may demand postponement or renunciation of the search for satisfaction of various needs; sometimes they are actually at variance with some of his needs. On the other hand, values have the power of needs in determining an individual's behavior. Values are evolved during the course of the individual's development as he accepts some and rejects others from among those which are strongly held by persons close to him and by the society in which he lives. It is this dual origin of the adult's value scheme which accounts for the fact that it may be at variance with the dominant values of his society. Another source of variability is the diversity of value orientations held by various sub-groups in the larger society.

Values are the generalized principles to which the individual has committed himself; in turn these help him to choose and order the alternatives that he encounters in any number of life situations. Since individuals hold more than one value, there are frequently pulls and counterpulls among them. The individual then must organize his values into some type of system, loose or tight, by arranging them into some sort of hierarchy. The elaboration and organization of such an ordered system of values is a major developmental task of the individual during adolescence and early adulthood. When he has established such an order, he can handle more readily any situation involving choices in terms of values which are more important and others that are less important to him.

Different individuals evolve significant differences in attitudes towards work. An artist may spend months on one painting, while a businessman may devote evenings and week ends to working out a merger. Although they both devote their major energies to their careers, neither has much understanding of the values of the other. Each may even look with suspicion on the work of the other.

We need not consider such sharply contrasting careers to illustrate the wide differences in attitudes towards work. They also show up among individuals who appear to be pursuing much the same type of work. Take the college science teacher and the research scientist. The teacher is likely to find his major satisfactions in the classroom, in his relationships with his students whose horizons he seeks to broaden and whose competences and interests he hopes to deepen. He is engaged in an ongoing exchange with a group of young people whose intellects and personalities are still in the process of development, a process that he seeks to direct and influence.

The research scientist may find his greatest peace and contentment in his laboratory, alone with his chemicals and apparatus. One of his major needs and desires may be to establish a wide no-man's-land between himself and others, for he does his best work and derives his greatest satisfactions when he can think uninterruptedly in abstract terms and then test whether he is on the right track.

The individual's preference system which is, as we have seen, composed of his needs, goals, and values, determines his choices in all aspects of his life, including the choices which he makes initially, and then again and again in the area of his work. Since out of the complexity of their endowment and life's experiences, individuals develop different preference systems, and since as a result of their educational and employment experiences, they confront a wide range of work situations, it is inevitable that wide differences exist among people in what they seek from their work and their careers. This diversity, embedded in the differences among people and within the range of opportunities that prevail in the world of work, is increased by changes that are inevitably introduced with the passage of time—as the individual grows older and as the economy and society are altered.

The large number of different attitudes that prevail toward work and career in a modern industrial society confronts the investigator with the challenge of developing a system of classification that is both valid and practical. The way in which people approach their work, their career objectives, the satisfactions that they seek to derive from their work—in short, the whole web of their occupational objectives—do not stand alone. They are part of a larger nexus which encompasses what the individual hopes to get out of life itself—his total life values and goals. The underlying preference systems are the spine which give structure to these larger dimensions.

It was difficult to develop a category scheme that would enable us to assess the role of values in work and career. First, a quantitative approach would not allow for interaction among values; second, each individual's value hierarchy is to some extent unique; and third, we wanted to relate an individual's principal values to other aspects of his life. We resolved these difficulties by deciding on a highly simplified approach. We evaluated each case in terms of what appeared to us to be his dominant value orientation, disregarding subsidiary aspects of his value scheme as well as the sometimes highly personal coloring that it might assume in any given instance. Finally, we focused our attention primarily on those values which had a direct bearing upon work.

In reviewing our cases we were struck by the fact that several respondents saw their occupational development largely in terms of resolving acute value conflicts. Such was the young man with a socialist background who after earning his doctorate in philosophy sought to make his living by working with his hands. But he also wanted to make use of his education and training. For many years he was torn between these two values. He finally resolved his conflict by reconciling his intellectual interests and ambitions with his equally strong desire to make a humble contribution to the welfare of others. The latter could be considered his dominant value orientation. In most of our cases, however, there were no such conflicts, and we were able to discern without difficulty the dominant value orientations that appeared to have a guiding influence on the individual's attitudes and decisions concerning his work.

We developed a fourfold system of classification. We considered individuals who had a distinctive value orientation toward work as belonging to one or another "type," but our categories were arrived at empirically and do not reflect any preconceived social or psychological theory.

The first and most striking value orientation is held by people whose attitudes and behavior towards their work are characterized by a strong desire to structure their own activities and to be as free as possible from any pressure or interference from others. Underlying this attitude is a deep-seated desire to pursue their own interests. These individuals also want to make optimal use of their capacities in their work. They want to be in a position where they are free to set and change the objectives which they pursue. They want to set their own pace at work. They desire as much freedom as possible to determine their relations to their collaborators and their colleagues. Above all, they want to be free from directional dictation.

The common denominator in these attitudes is the strength of their need or demand for a high degree of autonomy in their work. This is the all-pervasive factor. When such a person is confronted by a choice, the consideration that looms highest is how his decision may affect the degree of autonomy that he exercises in his work. Because his behavior with respect to his work is so much under the dictate of this search for individual autonomy, we have called a member of this group the *individualistic type.*

The orientation of the second group towards work is focused on their relations to others in the work situation rather than, as in the case of the individualistic type, on subject matter or on materials. Those in the second group are much more heavily involved in the organization or structure within which work is carried out, and even more specifically in their hierarchical relationship to the many other individuals and groups who play a part in the work process.

Among the needs and desires that the members of this second group display in their attitudes and behavior towards their work is a strong drive to direct and guide the work of others. They share with the individualistic type a strong aversion to being directed and guided by others. But their response is quite different. They do not flee from people, but they do not want to take orders from others. They seek a leadership role and they feel comfortable and happy when they are in a position to encourage others, in one fashion or another, to follow the directions which they have established. In broad, their objective is to control others and their work. Some of this group are content with a supervisory role where they serve as the source of information, encouragement, and correction; they do not want to control minutely the work of others. They want those who work for them to recognize that they are the source of authority and power, but they do not need to demonstrate constantly to those under them that they do in fact possess such authority and power. Some of this group, however, are not content unless they can demonstrate repeatedly that they are dominant.

The keynote to the behavior of this group is their desire for authority over others, not, as with the individualistic type, autonomy for themselves. Achievement for these people is to arrive at a position of dominance over others. They can be, and frequently are, just as deeply committed to their work as the individualistic type. But their efforts are directed towards securing, holding, and expanding their positions of influence or dominance over others. They are in search of positions of leadership, and for this reason we decided to call them the *leadership type*.

The third type is concerned neither with optimizing their freedom of choice nor with dominating others and aggrandizing their own power. Their basic orientation is to gain, hold, and increase acceptance by other members of their work group. Among their main characteristics is their desire for security and satisfaction which they derive from membership in a work group or larger organization. They find satisfaction in being able to meet the demands and expectations of the group to which they belong. It is the esteem and approval of the group that is at the heart of what they want from their work activities. They are group- or community-minded persons. They feel good about being a member of "the team." They have a tendency to conform to the mores and attitudes of the group, an orientation that has been subsumed under the caption of "the man in the grey flannel suit." These people are more at ease if they do not have to work alone. They have no objection if another person issues orders and supervises their work; in fact they may prefer it that way.

This type stands in sharp contrast to the individualistic type; they freely and willingly give up the "autonomy" which the others prize so highly. They also differ from the leadership type who seek separation from the rest of the work group in order to dominate it. The group-oriented individual seeks to lose himself in the group. The fulcrum of his relationship to his work is the magnetism that the group exerts on him and his desire to be bound more closely to it. Hence, we have called him the *social type*.

The outstanding characteristic of the members of the fourth group is their dedication to a system of social, religious, or political ideas and ideals. While they may be interested in and involved with groups in their work, they are primarily concerned with ideas or ideals which they seek to propagate and advance. Their goals are to serve a higher value—higher in that it transcends their own needs and wishes. They seek the acceptance, sometimes by small numbers, more frequently by many, of a set of ideas and ideals which they hold to be true and worthy of dedication. Their own needs and wishes tend to get pushed into the background, as they become enmeshed and involved in furthering their causes. Their work takes on the quality of a "calling" as they attempt to proselytize for a religion, a revolutionary political doctrine, or some other overriding end. Most, though not all, of these individuals tend to make a commitment to a cause early in life, and they often, though again not always, stay with it for the rest of their lives. Since their work is directed by an overriding commitment to a set of ideals or ideas, we have designated these individuals as the *ideological type*.

The ideological type frequently shares one aspect of the orientation of each of the other types, but differs from them in others. For instance, the ideological type frequently seeks autonomy, but his search for autonomy is not for himself but for the cause for which he is working. Ideological types are frequently engaged in leadership struggles, but they want power over others not for itself but because they sincerely believe that power is essential to furthering their cause.

While the ideological like the social type is concerned with relations to the group, there is an important difference. If a conflict should arise between loyalty to the group and loyalty to the ideology, the ideological type has no difficulty in turning his back on the group and remaining faithful to his ideology. Even during the Nazi holocaust which showed all too clearly the power of the group to command the allegiance of its members even at the cost of their having to betray previously held values, the power of conviction enabled ideologically oriented individuals to resist group pressures. Those who hold deep political, religious, or moral convictions and commitments may become exiles, members of a resistance movement, or even sacrifice their lives. For centuries, believing Jews, offered the choice between conversion and death—a choice which Hitler did not offer—chose death. Such was the depth of their religious commitment.

The ideological type may think that the individualistic type is too concerned with private matters, that the leadership type is too concerned with power for its own sake, and that the social type overvalues the group *qua* group because he does not concern himself with the ends that the group seeks or represents.

These four types are not of course as mutually exclusive as our schematic description might suggest. Some individuals have many of the characteristics of the individualistic type and still have elements of the leadership, social, or ideological types. This is true of each group. Nevertheless, while it was difficult to classify certain respondents we were able finally to subsume each of them under one of our four types.

The following quotations indicate how the respondents were classified according to the dominant value orientations which were reflected in their work and career development.

First is a profile of an individualistic type who is currently an associate professor of geology and senior research scientist.

I did not get along too well with my father and this gave me a drive to get ahead on my own. I am an only son and I spurned my father's good-income business ($25,000) to work on my own for much less money.

I decided not to marry because the personal responsibility might have forced me to leave my chosen work.

[Under what conditions would you leave your present position?]

Those providing an opportunity in change of living and working conditions or if political pressures would become too unbearable here.

[What is the least gratifying aspect of your work?]

In part editorial work, but mostly personnel management and relationships with petty officials, self-appointed dictators, and supersensitive colleagues.

I used to work every day and every evening. I now often relax on Sundays and don't work more than two nights a week.

[What do you plan to do after retirement?]

Continue with my research, perhaps write or rewrite a textbook.

A successful government research scientist, also classified as an individualistic type, added the following comment to his questionnaire: "You are interested in the conservation of human resources. Well, the greatest conservation measures you can devise is to foster a climate in which creative people are free to pursue their own goals, untrammeled by stricture of money, institutional rigidities, red tape, pedantics, choking critics, and group conformity. I accept limits, of course, but where are they?"

A quite different outlook towards work is suggested by the following two summaries of the careers of men who were classified as the leadership type. The first is a general manager of a subsidiary of a large chemical company. He left his previous position because of an "interest in broad management responsibility," and he accepted his present job because of his "interest in being associated with a well-financed, research-oriented, progressive company." He would leave his job if an "opportunity to totally manage a technically oriented larger new business arose." He explained that he had "changed from research to research management and general management in an effort to exert overall control on outcome and fate of my own work." He anticipates over the next decade that "additional responsibility will come with probable rapid growth of the area of business responsibility." He finds most gratifying "the task of organizing new activities with capable, intelligent workers and associates." His additional activities include "professional society, Junior Chamber of Commerce, Kiwanis," and all sorts of manual and skilled crafts, which he describes as an "excellent change of pace leading to more effective human performance." He contemplates that after he retires he will do "consulting work or start [my] own business." In assessing the factors affecting his career development, he notes as "interfering" factors: "1) disinterest in people; 2) impatience with co-workers."

The second example of the leadership type is a professional man who had recently shifted from the successful practice of the law to a senior position with a large lumber concern with gross sales of over $35 million annually. He explained his shift in these terms: "In the course of my practice . . . I began to feel frustrated because the power of decision always rested with the client, as well as the rewards (or other consequences) of the cause of action selected." As the most gratifying aspects of his present work he referred to "being in the line of command rather than in an advisory position as a lawyer." He shortly expects to "assume complete responsibility for the operation of my present company as it becomes the wholly owned subsidiary of a larger corporation." He expects that in ten years he will be "president of a major corporation" and in twenty years "chairman of a major corporation."

The chief design engineer of an important durable goods manufacturing concern typifies the social type. Among the situations which might lead him to leave his job, he listed "an adverse change in my superiors that would lead to unpleasant human relations." In looking back over his earlier jobs he concluded that his "development was not systematically planned and executed by my superiors." Contemplating his future progress he said, "I do not know the specific nature of that advancement but it is at least five years away and management will make the decision according to the needs of the company." Among the least satisfying aspects of his current job, he singled out, "not enjoying consistently full confidence of my superior." He listed among his additional activities: "homeowners' association, gardening, home maintenance, contributing to children's education." The first factor he cited as interfering with the growth of his career was "lack of guidance from superiors." In an additional comment he laid further stress on the strategic role of his superiors in his development: "The greatest disappointment in my professional career was the realization . . . that most fruitful knowledge comes from doing rather than from being taught by others. I found most superiors either consciously withholding information or technically too weak to educate others, or just not caring."

Another example of the social type is an associate professor of English who listed the following explanations for taking a series of academic positions:

Eastern University: Opportunity to serve my teaching apprenticeship at a first-rate eastern university.

Southern College: Opportunity to teach interesting courses in a quality institution in a colorful city.

Preparatory School: I liked teaching in a first-rate preparatory school in New York City.

Chairman, High School English Department in A⎯⎯⎯⎯: I felt drawn by the challenge of working to help a small "typical" community.

The following is his listing of the most gratifying aspects of his work: "1) The satisfaction of working with young people at a malleable, responsible age; 2) The pleasure of working alongside congenial colleagues in a congenial intellectual atmosphere; 3) A sympathetic department head who seems to understand and appreciate my special interests and abilities." His additional activities included playing the organ in church at Sunday services, other church work, serving on committees, as an usher, playing the piano, interior decoration. His father had been an influential Methodist clergyman in the South and the respondent said that he expected to retire at 65 after which "I should like to take a house in London and live among the English for the rest of my life."

Illustrative of the ideological type is the philosopher, mentioned earlier, who wanted to work with his hands. He is now an associate professor of philosophy, a position he reached only after a detour of about ten years. In the middle of his graduate studies in philosophy, he left the university to live and work "among the people" as a machinist, artist, teacher, and in still other occupations. In 1957, he returned to the university to complete his work for the doctorate and to pursue his academic career which he had interrupted on ideological grounds.

"I was torn between intense and sincere interest in philosophy and the notion that my social and political commitments required more direct involvement in life (with a big L) than academic life afforded. Philosophy, I believe, had to be functional, and ethical and social values needed more than philosophical analysis; they needed functional fulfillment. Dewey and Marx convinced me, as did a radical upbringing. I must add that my years in the art field, and as a machinist, were not frustrating with regard to the work I was doing. . . . I enjoyed working at a machine, I enjoyed working as an artist. It was not intrinsic dissatisfaction with the work that led me to make a major change back to academic life. It certainly wasn't money, which I have always been weak-minded about. But it was a positive sense of waste, and an intellectual frustration—I *needed* students and colleagues— contrary to the post-graduate notion that I could be a nonacademic philosopher that led to the decision. My point here is that it is *not* particularly frustrating for *this* Ph.D. to do manual or technical work for a living . . . The absence of fulfillment of one's training rather than the promise of attractive kinds of work" held the key to this respondent's dissatisfaction. He saw "two apparently mutually exclusive considerations: 1) self-fulfillment in terms of a major early investment in direction of work; 2) social (or other) obligations which preclude this self-fulfillment. The resolution is to discover that they are not mutually exclusive . . . but they need to be constantly and continually reviewed, Aye, there's the rub."

In explaining why he had taken certain types of work, he indicated he "wanted to do manual labor, prospective union activity (idealistic?)." His additional activities included "cultural and political organizations . . . these activities in some cases contributed to my sense of social obligation, my interpretation of the role of a teacher in society."

There were others who had less difficulty in resolving a conflict between an ideological commitment and a choice of a field of work. Included in the ideological group were several missionaries, one of whom had responsibility for supervising a very large school system in the Congo; another had worked in the Far East among the Japanese. There were several Catholic priests pursuing careers as college instructors and a Protestant minister with an urban church. Still another example of an ideological type was a foreign service officer who said, "I decided early that, for me, satisfaction from my work . . . would be derived from the feeling of importance which could be attached to my work. . . . World War II and its aftermath . . . led me inevitably to focus upon foreign policy as the area of greatest importance. . . . I am, I suppose, what can be described as an 'idealist'."

We had no difficulty in assigning any of the foregoing into one of the four types that we had established to differentiate among value orientations as they relate to work. It was more difficult to assign a classification to those who had conflicting values. For instance, there was a physician on the staff of a government hospital who is currently the head of the metabolic unit on the medical service. "I think that the main problem facing me at this crossroads is a materialistic one— living at the level which is 'expected' of a maturing physician, providing security for young children, maintaining a home—in general, providing all the 'goodies' of a materialistic society on a $15,000 income. Society pays substantially for services, not much for thought, teaching, research, or government work. If one's chief goals and pleasures lie in these areas one must reconcile oneself with falling behind in the economic competition. While one can easily make the decision for oneself, the dictates of family responsibility make the choice much more difficult."

An associate professor of physics who "had contemplated dimly the idea of the ministry" while on a fellowship at Cambridge, England, wrote that "this idea has recurred from time to time, stimulated by a desire to commit my life wholly to the service of Christ (the logical inescapable consequence of becoming a Christian) and balanced by a feeling that this service lay in academic life as a layman, rather than in the ministry. Despite my enjoyment of, and satisfaction in, the work, both teaching and research, and despite what seems to me to be a fair talent in this line, I have been feeling more and more dissatisfaction with it both in terms of the demands it makes on the physicist's life and in terms of the irrelevance to man's major needs. . . . The primary motivation for pure research is at the root of its curiosity, and the pursuit of it seems like self-indulgence, at least in the present day, when the scientific and technical advances we have already made have been so little applied to meeting the world's needs. These general considerations then . . . have led me to consider such a change. It seems to be impossible now, but it is nonetheless much on my mind."

There were others who were caught between conflicting values, but rarely did the conflict cut so deeply and the resolution loom so difficult as for the two described above. We classified the physician as an individualistic type, for though he fretted about his relatively small earnings he continued to pursue the type of work he preferred. We included the physicist with the ideological types because even though he had continued to work in physics, his concern with finding a way of practicing his faith appeared to be compelling in the shaping of his life.

Although the types we delineated were developed on the basis of the case material in this study—that is, they were constructed from the value orientations of highly endowed and educated individuals, they appear to have wider applicability. For instance, we could easily find people of the individualistic type among those who pursue such disparate careers as farmers, truck-drivers, storekeepers, skilled workers, handymen, taxi drivers, and still others.

The leadership type is likely to be in many fields besides corporate enterprise. Wherever power is concentrated at the top of a hierarchical structure such as in politics, trade unions, the Armed Forces, even in the church, the universities, hospitals, men with the characteristics of the leadership type will be competing for power. However, the nature of competition in closed institutions results in a rapid thinning of the ranks of the leadership type near the top. Many who start are unable to tolerate the adjustments they must make in order to advance and at the same time to avoid drawing the hostility and the opposition of competitors on themselves. Only those with very deep leadership needs and a range of capacities are likely to reach the top or near the top.

In the work force at large, the greatest number are probably the social type. Work to them is a mixture of the good and the bad; they enjoy it but they also resent it. Much of their work satisfactions derive from the social context within which their work is carried out. They make friends at work and enjoy the companionship of many with whom they are less closely tied. They do not intend to become a boss and they have no desire to be their own boss. They see their work as a key part of their lives but they see it primarily as a job that yields income. We pointed out years ago in *The Unemployed* (1943) that the major deprivation attendant on losing one's job and not finding another is the cost of social disenfranchisement. The unemployed man has no place to go in the morning, no place to spend the hours of the day, nothing to return home with at the end of the day.

The ideological type may be more rare in an affluent society than in other societies. For instance, the Catholic Church has long found it necessary to recruit manpower from abroad to run its schools, hospitals, and other basic institutions in the United States. It cannot attract the numbers it requires from among native-born Americans, who, faced with many attractive alternatives, are less inclined to enter the service of the Church. And for most of our recent history, the tensions in politics have not been such as to attract and hold a large number whose lives are dedicated to public service. But in every generation some have been willing to devote their lives to causes: to missionary work among the heathen; to the improvement of the handicapped at home; to the eradication of racial conflict; to the organization of workers; to the elimination of war; to radical reform of society; to the propagation of a new religion or the strengthening of an established one.

The types of work pursued by those who belong to the ideological type indicate that these individuals differ from the run of mankind. They are likely to be much more complex people who are able to set themselves off from the rest of the community in the goals that they seek, in the efforts they make, and in the risks that they are willing to run. An extreme example is the martyr.

But not all who have ideological commitments, even deep commitments, can or must work them out in their occupational lives. In our society jobs have come to take only a part of a man's energies, and many with strong commitments can find opportunities for realizing them in other sectors of their lives. As we know, a great many do just that. We need refer only to the lay leaders of many social welfare organizations and the activists in political parties. In fact, there can be congruence or conflict between a man's working life and his life off the job. For example, a captain of industry who is interested in better race relations and who devotes much of his free time to this end has an opportunity to live by his commitments in his business by helping to open opportunities to those who have been discriminated against. But a staff specialist who is a Negro and devotes most of his time off the job to race relations may find himself in a working environment where he must tolerate negative attitudes and prejudice on the part of his associates which inhibit him from pressing the social goals which mean so much to him.

We see then that the four types that we have developed in connection with our study of educated men pursuing professional or scientific careers do have applicability to a much broader band of people. We limited ourselves to four types, among other reasons to avoid undue complications in the analysis. However, a study which is focused on a more diversified group might have to introduce several additional types to capture adequately the variability in value orientations that exist towards work in our society.

The classification of people in terms of a dominant value orientation towards their work, however much it may be rationalized, did result in severe constrictions. For this reason we will introduce here two additional conceptions that will enable us to broaden and deepen the analysis. The first relates to the distinction between the work and nonwork areas of life. Increasingly, people are able to seek and find satisfactions not only through their jobs but also through the purposeful activities that they engage in off their jobs. The second point has to do with the relationship between the two: people can follow one of three patterns which relate their activities off the job to their career concerns. Their nonwork activities can reinforce, complement, or compensate for their activities at work.

This larger framework makes it possible to take account of a wider play of values and more diversified behavior. A lawyer who misses the opportunity to play a leadership role in his work may become active in community affairs. He can thus realize a value which is important to him—leadership—in his nonwork activities. Or a businessman who has not been as successful as he had hoped may throw himself into church and social welfare activities from which he derives some compensation for the disappointments in his work.

The following table presents the distribution of our group among the four value types.

Value orientation	Percent
Individualistic	50
Leadership	18
Social	27
Ideological	5
Total	100

That half of our group were classified as the individualistic type is noteworthy but not too surprising in light of its special characteristics. These men had made a substantial investment of time and effort in finding the type of work they preferred. They wanted to be masters of themselves, and they wanted to dictate their own patterns of working. It is this orientation that may explain at least in part why they were willing to make such a big investment in preparing for work.

In view of the outstanding ability of the respondents, the relatively small number who were classified as the leadership type might at first appear surprising, since we could expect those with superior ability to seek and gain power. The small proportion who fall into this category may reflect the fact that the key sector of contemporary life in which men can find an outlet for leadership proclivities is in corporate enterprise. But people heading for top positions in business do not have to pursue graduate or professional education; this was surely so in the early postwar years. Therefore our selection produced a group with a smaller number of individuals with leadership orientation than might be found in another group with superior ability.

The proportion of social types can at one and the same time be considered large and small. It is relatively large in view of the long period of preparation for work undertaken by our group. We might have thought that such people would be more strongly directed to find work in which they would be masters of their own destiny, and to be less concerned about relationships with superiors and colleagues. On the other hand the proportion is relatively small considering the emphasis placed on social adjustment in our society.

We might have expected that only a small percent would be characterized as the ideological type since those with this kind of value commitment are unlikely to pursue their education beyond college.

Before concluding this analysis of value orientations, let us see in what manner this axis is related, if at all, to the two other axes which deal with career patterns and levels of achievement. The following table sets forth the relationships between the value types and career patterns.

| Career pattern | Value orientation | | | |
	Individ-ualistic	Leader-ship	Social	Ideo-logical
Straight	67	56	49	53
Broad	22	34	33	27
Variant	11	10	18	20
Total	100	100	100	100

The first point to note is that the relationships are somewhat tenuous. Nevertheless, a few formulations may be ventured. Compared to the leadership and social types, a relatively higher proportion of the individualistic type is found in the straight pattern and a relatively smaller proportion in the broad pattern. This probably reflects the tendency of those who place a premium on autonomy in their work to remain in the same field if their first job meets this dominant need.

The finding that the leadership type was rather prominently represented in the broad pattern may reflect the process of accumulating power in our society which usually forces a man to branch out beyond his original field of activity. The relatively higher proportion of the social type in the variant pattern may reflect their inability to move as directly as many in the straight pattern from an interest in an area to a field or function. Perhaps the goal they were seeking in their work was elusive because they did not know quite what they were seeking. Hence they were more likely to experience delays and changes in getting into an occupational groove.

The very small numbers who comprise the ideological type make even a tentative formulation questionable. There is, however, a suggestion that a higher than average proportion of this type may also be engaged in a prolonged and uncertain search before they find their occupational objectives.

The other major relationship to explore is that between the value types and achievement levels. These are set out below.

| Achievement level | Value orientation | | | |
	Individ-ualistic	Leader-ship	Social	Ideo-logical
Upper	32	36	28	33
Intermediate	38	44	29	27
Lower	30	20	43	40
Total	100	100	100	100

There was no reason to expect a pronounced concentration of the individualistic type in any achievement level and that is what in fact the table revealed. And we might have anticipated the tendency of the leadership type to land in the higher achievement levels, perhaps even more than in fact occurred. Since we have learned of the delays that many in the social type experienced in getting started on their careers, a drift towards the lower achievement level for this group was to have been expected.

The most important aspect of the relationships presented in the last two tables is the support which they offer our hypothesis that value orientations are key elements in occupational development and deserve to rank with career patterns and achievement levels as a major analytical axis.

3.

PERSONALITY
AND PERFORMANCE

The founders of economics had little difficulty in building a bridge between psychology and economics. They postulated that every man wanted to maximize his own position—to work as little as possible and to earn as much as possible. In adopting this simple view of human behavior they did not understand that it rested on a basic assumption that work is irksome and to be avoided and shunned. Thorstein Veblen upended classical economic theory on this basic issue, but most economists went on as if he had never written.

Another link between economics and psychology is considered in the first of the essays which follow, the link between economics and sex. Both Malthus and Ricardo assumed that men were the prisoners of their need and desire to satisfy their sexual urges. They felt that this simple fact had the most pervasive influence on the quality of their lives and on the structure and functioning of society. They went further to distinguish between the small number of educated men whose behavior was controlled by their future goals and the vast majority who were unable to "postpone." In making this distinction they laid the groundwork for a much more sophisticated approach to human motivation by recognizing the influence of developmental experiences on the structuring of the individual's behavior and by making allowance for income and class factors in the molding of personality.

A hundred years had to pass before psychology fully grasped the challenge of developing a theory of human growth and development. Sigmund Freud did most of the work for the breakthrough. In Chapter 8 an attempt is made to set out the significance of this dynamic psychology and its impact on the development of human potential, together with a consideration of the dangers of faulty understanding and application.

Chapter 9 is an effort to demonstrate the importance of singling out for special study those individuals who succeed in rising to the top and the interactions between them and the institutions within which they make their way. Here is an arena which has long been recognized to be important but where research is still at the takeoff stage.

Chapter 10 presents the major theoretical findings that emerged from our large-scale study of manpower in World War II, published in a series of volumes including the three-volume *The Ineffective Soldier: Lessons for Management and the Nation* (1959). This summary demonstrates that performance can be studied and evaluated only within a matrix that makes place for such key determinants as the strengths of the individual, organizational policy, and environmental supports and stresses and their interactions. We have learned that no monistic theory of performance can be supported or validated.

7.

SEX AND
CLASS BEHAVIOR

In the absence of facts, social scientists inevitably rely upon impressions, hunches, and introspection, as a foundation for their general theories. The fewer the facts, the more elaborate the superstructure; that seems to be the "law of compensation" in the social sciences. For a century and a half, economists have been guessing about the facts of sex. All students of social behavior are therefore in Kinsey's debt for the wealth of factual information about the sex habits of the American male which he has collected and organized. A more comprehensive and valid theory of group behavior can now be developed by utilizing this information.

"We need to know more than we do, and vastly more than economics has generally permitted itself to know, about the human material of which a community must be built; about its motives, reactions, capacities, and needs." That is the considered judgment of Professor J. M. Clark, one of the outstanding economists of our day.

Kinsey has made a major contribution to the enhancement of our knowledge of the "human material" with which economics and the other social sciences must deal. Kinsey has made a host of significant facts available—those which highlight the incidence and frequency of the outlet of the sexual drive; those which prove that the sex drive reaches maximum intensity in late adolescence; and facts which emphasize the class differences in the sexual pattern. Economists have a particular interest in the materials which bear on class differences, for they have long surmised that as a man regulates his sex life, the rest of his life is regulated accordingly.

With the facts that are now available can economics improve its theoretical framework? And, in turn, can economics possibly contribute to the better understanding of the newly uncovered facts? The answer to both questions is yes.

This can be illustrated by reviewing Kinsey's data on the differences in the sexual behavior of the "upper" and "lower" classes. His figures show that the group of laborers with grade-school education has a rate of regular premarital intercourse approximately seven times greater than that of the college population. Here assuredly is proof of a significant class difference. (Nor is the quality of the difference substantially affected by recalling that the college group has a much higher rate for masturbation, nocturnal emissions, and petting. The fact remains that the principal outlet for maximum satisfaction in our culture is orgasm reached through intercourse.)

What does this amazing difference in sexual behavior connote? It suggests that the poorer and less educated classes in the community have a philosophy of life fundamentally different from that of the more highly educated groups. For nothing short of fundamental differences in basic values could explain such gross differences in sexual behavior.

The values we live by are the values which have been inculcated into us, above all by the training and indoctrination which we received at home. Within broad limits these values are the regulators of our behavior. It need hardly be stressed in this post-Freudian era that the contention that we regulate our lives in terms of our values in no way denies the strength of unconscious forces which so relentlessly hold us prisoner and which so effectively limit our scope for rational action. Our unconscious is largely our cumulative reactions to the behavior and values of our parents to which we were exposed, without opportunity of escape, throughout our childhood.

The manner in which the individual regulates his sex behavior, then, is conditioned by the values, including those in his unconscious, which grew out of the training he received at home. At least this is true for all who are not in major rebellion against their parents.

In general, people who come from the same background, who work in the same types of trades, who live in neighboring houses, who participate in the same forms of recreation—in short, people who were born into and who remain in the same environment—are likely to adhere to the same set of values. It is small wonder that their children also have much in common.

Although there are many forces at work in every society that exercise a common influence on all classes, these forces have never been strong enough to obliterate significant variations which grow out of differing environmental conditions. In the Western world, all classes adhere, at least formally, to the Judeo-Christian tradition. Now Christianity has a very definite attitude towards sexual behavior; it disapproves of sexual relations except within the bonds of marriage. Yet all groups flout its tradition—the poor to a much higher degree than the middle class, at least with respect to premarital intercourse.

The significant differences between the poor and the upper classes which Kinsey found with regard to premarital intercourse could conceivably be explained by the stronger hold which formal religion has on the more affluent and better educated. But this explanation is highly questionable.

A more likely explanation recognizes that classes differ with respect to their "evaluations of the future." We have learned from Freud of the inexorable hold of the past over the present; we should learn from the economists of the significant role that expectations for the future play in the determination of present behavior.

There are good reasons for the poor to "discount the future" more heavily than the better situated classes. With only a smattering of education, without capital, with a wage that is scarcely sufficient to provide their families with essentials, without powerful friends who can smooth their way, with no resources available to meet the scourges of illness and unemployment; in short, without basic security—and with little prospect of obtaining security by their own efforts—what reasons have the poor to discount the future other than very heavily?

How different from members of the middle class! They frequently have had the opportunity to acquire a considerable amount of education; they have usually inherited a little capital which facilitates their acquiring some additional; their earnings are sufficient not only to provide their families with all necessities but also with a considerable number of luxuries; they can usually cope successfully with the drains of illness; and they may even be able to withstand moderate spells of unemployment; in most instances they can secure help when they need it from relatives and friends.

No effort has been made to detail, no less exhaust, the significant differences in the "reality conditions" of the poor and the middle class. But the factors which have been made explicit should strengthen the presumption that the poor have every reason to have a different view of the future from that of the middle class.

The poor have no reasonable grounds for withstanding the temptations of the present. Even in the United States where opportunity has been greater than in any other Western country, the ability of the poor to change their circumstances materially through their own efforts has been much smaller in fact than in theory. From the log cabin to the White House was rare in Lincoln's day and it has become still rarer in recent decades.

If it is true that the poor have little hope of materially enhancing their security, it is also true that they have little ground to fear that their circumstances will worsen substantially. In case of illness requiring hospitalization, they will be better cared for, in an urban community, than at any other time in their lives. Nor will unemployment be fraught with great deprivations; they will continue to live in the same houses, eat the same food, and wear approximately the same type of clothes to which they have been accustomed. The real costs of unemployment are emotional—the loss of status and all which that implies for the man, his wife, and his children.

Differences between the poor and the middle class can be highlighted by considering the way in which the two prepare for life. The poor boy leaves high school usually at the end of his second year and frequently he has lost interest in his studies before then. He then becomes a full-time wage earner, a step of major emancipation from family restraint. How different with the middle-class boy, who stays with his books not only through high school but usually through college and frequently even longer, during which time he is supported in whole or at least in part by his parents. His entire life is geared to the future; he may experience great difficulty in "finding himself" but he knows that this is his primary task.

The essential difference between the two classes revolves around the fact that the entire constellation of the poor boy's environment operates to place a premium on current gratification, for the future is not propitious, at least no more so than the present. There is little or no rational basis for his "delaying gratification." As far as the college boy is concerned, his entire existence is in the nature of a postponement. He is using up parental capital rather than adding to it; he is studying today in order to profit tomorrow. His training is a necessary prelude to the accomplishment of his goal. He may engage in regular sexual intercourse while in college (about one in six do just that), but the environment places difficulties in his path. More important than the objective difficulties are the forces working to deflect him. He has been trained to accept postponement in gratification and he has also been encouraged to seek gratification from other experiences—his studies, his sports, his extracurricular activities. By recourse to masturbation and petting, he manages to reach a tolerable, if not a desirable, equilibrium. He can wait: for him the future is propitious.

The differences in the premarital behavior of the two classes must be explained largely in terms of differences in discounting the future —or put the other way, in willingness and ability to accept some postponement in current gratification. That this explanation is substantially valid is reinforced by still another finding of Kinsey's, one of the most interesting and challenging in the entire work and one for which Kinsey himself had no ready explanation.

The preceding analysis was made in terms of two sharply defined classes without reference to any movement of individuals from one to the other—a reasonable procedure if one deals with rather widely separate groups in the social and economic hierarchy. The fact must not be overlooked, however, that there is constant movement of people both upward and downward, especially between adjacent groups. Kinsey found that persons who managed to climb out of a working-class group into a proprietary or professional class followed the sexual pattern of the group which they eventually joined, not the pattern of the group into which they had been born. Kinsey noted with some amazement that these "successful" people followed the pattern of the new group long before they had joined it.

The explanation of this admittedly startling phenomenon must also be sought in the "training-postponability" complex. Either the parents of these successful individuals inculcated into them a scale of values at variance with that of their class; or else these individuals, out of inner emotional needs, planned their entire life around an escape from their parental class. Such a charging of their goals made it possible for them to inflict on themselves a high degree of postponability of current gratification.

The deprivations of the poor who climb into a higher class are not so great as might first be assumed, because they derive considerable satisfaction from the progress which they are making towards accomplishing their objective. Here is a striking example of the close relation which exists between the way an individual manages his sex life and the way he manages the rest of his life. Here—in the balancing of the current versus the postponable gratifications—is the bridge between sex and economics.

To juxtapose sex and economics may at first appear startling, but there are sound historical grounds for doing so. The two have been intimately linked from the very beginning of economic thought. Adam Smith, the founder of economics, was dead but a few years when there appeared in England (1798) an anonymous book entitled *An Essay on Population,* whose author was later identified as Robert Malthus. With great persuasiveness Malthus contended that the key to economic analysis was to be found in a study of sexual behavior. Of course, Malthus did not use the word "sex," but his analysis centered on sex.

Malthus argued that the optimism of the radical philosophers who looked forward to the perpetual betterment of mankind was unwarranted unless they could demonstrate how the tendency of the population to increase could be brought under effective control. Malthus himself had serious doubts about the possibility of successful control. He did not agree with those reformers who believed that increased education would enable men to deflect their sexual energies into intellectual pursuits—in modern language, to sublimate them. He held that "passion" was good; that "virtuous love" was the best of life; that men were always tempted by a good meal, good liquor, and a desire to possess a beautiful woman.

Although Malthus recognized the great satisfaction that men derive from the exercise of passion, he was oppressed by the serious consequences resulting both to themselves and to society. The more people indulged in sexual intercourse, the more children there would be. In the decades before the widespread use of contraceptive devices, sexual union very frequently resulted in conception. Since the food supply could not be increased at the same rate as the population increased, general impoverishment was a certain consequence of overindulgence. The balance between the population and the food supply could then be re-established only through famine, pestilence, and war. The sole alternative was to employ the "preventive check," which to Malthus meant a delay in marriage and continence during marriage.

Francis Place, a contemporary of Malthus, took the position that acceptance of the principle of population did not force one to choose between the positive checks (famine, pestilence, and war) and the preventive check (delayed marriage and continence in marriage). He claimed that "it was not disreputable for married persons to use precautionary means. . . ." However, it was not until many decades later —after a long and hard struggle against tradition and ignorance—that birth-control techniques became widely adopted by members of the laboring classes.

Malthus used his principle of population not only to puncture the foolhardy optimism of the French reformers and their English allies but also to advocate the need for a radical reform in the English Poor Laws. During the last decade of the eighteenth century, England was in great turmoil, externally because of her conflict with Napoleon, and internally because of convulsions incident to her rapid industrialization. During this period of storm and stress, Parliament had liberalized the conditions under which relief was granted to the indigent. The poor were guaranteed a basic allowance, adjusted to the size of the family. The British worker had security—at least security against starving to death—not only for himself but for all the children whom he might father.

David Ricardo, who shared with Malthus the leadership of what later became known as the classical school of economics, argued with the rigorous logic that was his that "if every human wanting support could be sure to obtain it, and obtain it in such a degree as to make life tolerably comfortable . . . the tendency of such laws would be to change wealth and power into misery and weakness; to call away the exertions of labor from every object, except that of providing mere subsistence; to confound all intellectual distinction; to busy the mind continually in supplying the body's wants; until at last all classes should be infected with universal poverty."

Ricardo was greatly impressed with the hardheadedness of Malthus, who had pointed out that the laboring poor "seem only to live from hand to mouth. Their present wants employ their whole attention and they seldom think of the future . . . even when they have the opportunity to save . . . their money goes to the ale house . . . they enjoy themselves while they can."

Ricardo shared Malthus's pessimism about the future of the laboring class and saw no hope for general betterment unless one could impress on the poor the value of independence "by teaching them that they must look not to systematic or casual charity, but to their own exertion for support."

Several decades later (1848) John Stuart Mill, the heir to Malthus and Ricardo, saw no reason to question the principle of population. The Malthusian analysis was sound: unless the tendency to population growth is checked, the poor are doomed to perpetual poverty, if not to outright starvation and death. (In years of high food prices, the death rate increased materially!)

However, despite Mill's acceptance of the Malthusian doctrine, he differed from his teachers in the morals that he drew. He himself believed in the optimistic doctrine of Adam Smith that "a plentiful subsistence increases the bodily strength of the laborer, and the comfortable hope of bettering his condition and of ending his days perhaps in ease and plenty animates him to exert that strength to the utmost." Using this doctrine as a basis, Mill concentrated on positive incentives rather than on negative compulsions.

Ricardo had placed his principal emphasis on the abolition of the Poor Laws, for he saw no hope of the poor becoming responsible and self-reliant citizens as long as their keep was guaranteed them by the state. Mill believed that the basic objective of a responsible citizenry could be secured, but more successfully and at a lesser social cost, if instead of employing the threat of starvation society resorted to the incentives of higher wages and better working conditions.

Mill knew that as long as the laboring masses had little opportunity to cultivate their minds and as long as they suffered the oppression of poverty, they would have "neither the fear of worse nor the smallest hope of better . . . which would make them careless of the consequences of their actions and without thought for the future."

When Alfred Marshall brought the classical theory of economics to the highest point of systematic formulation in his *Principles of Economics* (1890), he found it desirable to tread carefully through the population controversy. Almost a century separated Marshall from Malthus and a century was long enough to provide facts and figures which could either substantiate or deny the principle of population.

Marshall was confronted with incontrovertible facts—vast increases in the total population of Great Britain, in fact of the entire Western world, and parallel increases in the standards of living of the average man. Was Malthus wrong? By no means. Marshall said that it would be unfair to hold Malthus responsible for not foreseeing the strength of new forces—forces which greatly cheapened the cost of producing the food supply (development of new lands and cheaper transportation); the direct and indirect effects of industrialization and urbanization on the birth rate; the tremendous advances in productivity through the greatly expanded use of technology. Marshall held that the combined force of these developments had "suspended" but not invalidated Malthus's analysis.

With technological changes and urbanization facilitating the suspension of the principle of population, Marshall was able to follow the more optimistic Mill rather than the more somber Ricardo and look to positive incentives rather than to heightened insecurity as a way of insuring that the world's work be done. He found the vigor and energy of men to be primarily "in the hope the freedom and the changefulness of their lives . . . a given exertion conserves less of the store of nervous energy if done under the stimulus of pleasure than of pain and without hope there is no enterprise." Mill had taken the position that "no remedy for low wages has the smallest chance of being efficacious which does not operate on and through the minds and habits of the people."

So great were the changes in the minds and habits of people during the second half of the nineteenth century that Marshall questioned whether the highest ideals of human aims were not absent in the case of many people who artificially limited the size of their families. The low fertility of the more favored classes and the political dangers of a stationary or declining population were just coming into view. Time proved that Marshall's caution was not out of place.

Reduced to essentials the Malthusian doctrine was very simple. There was little or no prospect of social and economic improvement for the mass of mankind unless the lower classes exercised "preventive checks" on passion. Men of liberal education, the upper classes, do not follow their nature; but others of "stronger passion and weaker judgment break through the restraints." Only if the mass of mankind would learn to "look before and after" is there much ground for hope.

Malthus postulated that a significant difference existed in the sexual behavior of the upper and lower classes and that the sole prospect of social amelioration resided in the adoption by lower classes of the restraints practiced by those of higher station.

Malthus had only a few facts at his disposal at the time when he wrote his *Essay on Population*. After its publication he went to work assiduously to study not only British but also foreign sources for the light which they might throw on the key determinants of population. The later editions of his work are a testimonial to his skill as an empirical investigator. Despite long years of conscientious labor, he was never able to secure reliable data about the sexual behavior of different classes. He had to content himself with more generalized information about birth and death rates for the population as a whole.

We now have the most striking empirical verification for the Malthusian assumption that differences in sexual behavior between the lower and the upper classes must be found in the varying capacity of the two to accept "delayed gratification." Admittedly, the population problem, as Malthus saw it, is not our population problem. Reference need only be made to the widespread adoption of birth-control techniques in the twentieth century to emphasize the magnitude of the change. Yet we still have serious "population problems" that we dare no longer neglect. Even if we have succeeded in checking overpopulation in the Western world, no traveler to China, India, or the Middle East can doubt the continuing validity of Malthus's insight. There may be others of serious, if not comparable, magnitude.

From one point of view, the classical economists were too successful. They persuaded the dominant groups in Britain and America that salvation could be achieved if every man assumed full responsibility for his own actions and strived his utmost to gain his own ends. But they failed to perceive that this doctrine would result in an extreme atomization of society. This is exactly what has happened, especially in urban communities, which have been unable for some time to reproduce even their own number.

But the existence of overpopulation in the East and the imbalance in birth rates among ethnic groups and lower economic classes in many parts of the West are not the only problems. There was doubtless much wisdom in the economists' contention that a prosperous citizenry would be assured only if each individual assumed a high degree of responsibility for himself and his family. There is still much wisdom in this position, for the history of recent times underlines all too clearly the incompatibility of excessive paternalism and virile democracy.

But enterprise without hope is impossible. We have noted that large numbers of citizens have reached such a negative conclusion about bettering their prospects through their own efforts that they have concentrated on maximizing the pleasures of the moment. We have also noted that those in our society for whom the future holds out reasonable hope have found it possible to withstand the temptations of the present in favor of the delayed gratifications of the future.

The difference between the two is not one of moral fiber but rather of realistic opportunities. John Stuart Mill saw the issue clearly—over a century ago, and expressed it in these words: "If the bulk of the human race are always to remain *as at present*, slaves to toil in which they *have no interest*, and therefore *feel no interest*—drudging from early morning till late at night for bare necessaries, and with all the intellectual and moral deficiencies which that implies—without resources either in mind or feelings—untaught, for they cannot be better taught than fed; selfish, for all their thoughts are acquired for themselves; without interests or sentiments as citizens and members of society, and with a sense of injustice rankling in their minds, equally for what they have not, and for what others have; I know not what there is which should make a person with any capacity of reason, concern himself about the destinies of the human race."

The greatest advance in biological theory—Darwin's *Origin of Species* —was stimulated by Malthus's *Essay on Population*. It is fitting that economics should seek to profit by the contribution that Kinsey has made to increasing our knowledge of sexual behavior.

Every society must find a balance between sex and food, between the desire of people to obtain current gratifications and their need to forgo them so that their future can be made more secure. Without some control over sex, economic well-being cannot be insured. To some degree, probably to a very high degree, the present must be sacrificed to the future. But such sacrifices will be possible only if people can secure important compensations for renouncing the gratifications of immediate sexual enjoyment.

Meaningful work can make this possible, for work can yield great current satisfactions. Only a society that succeeds in solving its work problem can solve its sex problem—in short, can solve this problem of society itself.

8.

THE NEW PSYCHOLOGY

Of all the intellectual developments in the twentieth century none has had a more direct and widespread influence on the theories and practices of child-rearing than what can be subsumed under the heading of the new psychology. Because the term "the new psychology" does not have accepted usage, let us first say very briefly what it covers. It includes a series of approaches to the study of thought, emotions, and behavior that stand in sharp contrast to theories of an earlier day when psychology was just beginning to emancipate itself from philosophy, on the one hand, and a preoccupation with vision, the study of traits, and the functioning of sense organs, on the other.

Encompassed under the term "the new psychology" are the important contributions starting around the turn of this century of developmental psychology, psychiatry, and psychoanalysis to the widened understanding of emotional growth and development, learning, and intellectual functioning. These major areas can be distinguished from each other, from such related fields as intelligence testing and child psychiatry, and from specific schools of psychoanalytic thought. But for the purpose at hand, which is to trace the impact of the new psychological ideas on social thought and behavior, it is preferable to deal with the several currents as a single stream.

The first question that suggests itself is how did it happen that the American environment in particular proved so receptive to the new ideas, or at least to many of them?

A partial answer lies in the weakening of the traditional belief in revealed religion, which left the moral underpinnings of Western society greatly in need of shoring up. For more than fifteen hundred years,

Europeans had found in religious teaching their basic guideposts to conduct. However much individuals had deviated from the teachings of the church, neither the leaders nor the masses had any serious questions about the basic principles of human conduct.

However, in the second half of the nineteenth century, a major assault on the truth of revelation destroyed this foundation of ethical conduct. And many who had lost their traditional faith were in search of a new one. At a minimum they wanted something to replace what the critical approach to biblical scholarship and the evolutionary doctrines of Darwin had shaken.

The fact that the new psychology was a "scientific" discipline based on rationality and buttressed by experimentation helped greatly to heighten its prestige and to facilitate its acceptance. For the decline in religious belief was paralleled by a deepened respect for science. Many developments in psychology required the use of laboratory techniques and procedures so that it was not long before the prestige of the natural sciences began to rub off on the new discipline.

While this ideological shift was probably the main factor in the receptiveness to the new psychology, other factors also played an important role, particularly in the United States where rapid changes in the social fabric left many unresolved tensions between past and present.

As has been pointed out earlier, the United States was to a marked degree a child-centered culture even before the rise of the new psychology, and as such it had long been restive toward orthodox Calvinist doctrine with its emphasis on predestination and evil. Many Americans did not find it congenial to look upon the behavior of children as something inherently evil. The new psychology with its emphasis on the "naturalness" of child behavior provided a welcome alternative to dour theological doctrines stressing the intrinsic evil in child and man.

Freudian psychology with its focus on the role of sexuality in human life also became part of the struggle, then under way, to win full rights—both social and political—for women. For Freud's contention that lack of normal sexuality would lead to egregious difficulties in human adjustment provided intellectual ammunition for those seeking acceptance of woman as a whole person with a wide range of feelings, desires, and needs of her own.

Finally, as an increasingly productive economic system provided the public with more and more resources to invest in schooling, the question of whether these resources were being used most advantageously arose. With the passage of every year, it became increasingly clear that conventional theories of learning were a weak base on which to erect a much enlarged and hopefully also a much improved educational structure. The strict authoritarian approach, with the teacher putting new knowledge before the child and drilling it into him, frequently with the aid of a hickory stick, began to impress many Americans as a somewhat doubtful and inefficient method. Hence, they were on the lookout for theories of child development and learning which might provide a more satisfactory basis for restructuring the school. And the new psychology seemed to meet this need. For it threw important light on learning at the same time that it established a connection between the development of the child's personality and motivations and on his acquisition of knowledge and skills. Dewey's stress on interests was strongly reinforced by Freud's emphasis on emotions.

The thrust of the new psychology was in four major directions. First, it focused attention on the overriding importance of the family situation in the development of the child's personality. The key to emotional development, the new psychology pointed out, was the individual's experiences during infancy and early childhood—above all else his relationship with his mother, father, and siblings. Emotional disturbance in later life was almost always rooted in a trauma experienced during childhood. Second, the new psychology took a more favorable view toward human potential. In contrast to the early geneticists who had placed major emphasis on heredity, the new psychology said that the processes of development, particularly emotional development, determined whether individuals would be encouraged to make the most of their aptitudes. While the new psychology stopped short of saying that the level of human accomplishment was solely a matter of early conditioning—a position developed by Watson and other behaviorists—it nonetheless held that the quality of the environment was a major determinant of later performance.

Probably the most revolutionary effect of the new psychology was to force a radical shift in the attitude towards child behavior. Since so much of what children did was at variance with adult standards, it had long been dealt with by repressive methods. By stressing the extent to which child behavior was dictated by natural drives, the new psychology shifted the focus from a moralistic to a naturalistic basis. This shift was part of a much broader social movement whereby religious and moralistic interpretations were increasingly superseded by scientific and naturalistic explanations.

Finally, the new psychology provided an understanding of the ways in which emotional disturbance in later life was linked to defects in the developmental process. The inability of a child to concentrate in school, the excessive shyness of an adolescent, the alcoholic proclivities of an adult could, for the first time in the history of human thought, be understood by tracing them to the emotionally disturbing and distressing experiences in the earliest years of a person's life. If the child was deprived of a mother's love, if he was treated as a baby beyond infanthood, if he grew up in terror of a domineering and harsh father, if he was the continued butt of an older sibling's hostility —if he experienced any such trauma, he would likely manifest serious emotional disturbance that would interfere with his ability to function effectively or gain satisfaction from life. Here were important new vistas. But first the new theories had to be adopted and applied.

With the realization that most child behavior was the expression of instinctual drives, parents and educators began to adopt an attitude of permissiveness rather than of restriction and frustration. Instead of trying to prevent children from expressing themselves—which had long been the accepted practice—the experts now argued strongly in favor of avoiding frustration by permitting each child the maximum degree of freedom to express himself. The turn-around was complete: parents hesitated to establish any limits, even when they recognized physical dangers in not doing so, for they stood in fear of stunting the child's sound emotional development.

The new psychology played a major role in freeing American society from its prudish attitudes towards sex, an inheritance from its religious and, more particularly, its Calvinist tradition. The theory that sex was normal and natural, that children had sexual interests and desires, and that nothing could be gained but much might be lost by harsh repression of these instinctual proclivities helped bring about a more tolerant attitude toward relations between the sexes. Coeducational schools had long been accepted, if only for economic reasons. It was simply not practical, outside of large population centers, to provide separate schools for boys and girls. But the new attitudes towards sex went much further. No longer did it appear necessary or even desirable that parents should keep girls and boys apart. Just the reverse was true. Boys and girls were given increasing opportunities to meet and get to know each other. In place of the long-established tradition of denying sex, or at least fearing it because of its connection with the doctrine of original sin, the new psychology produced what can only be called a positive attitude toward the long-forbidden subject.

Since the new psychology traced emotional development through a series of stages, each with a potential for crisis, parents, teachers, and others in authority became much more understanding of aberrant behavior. When a child of three suddenly developed what seemed to be excessive stubbornness, when eight-year olds would have nothing to do with members of the opposite sex except perhaps to torment them, when adolescents became excessively moody so that a parent could not ask a simple question without receiving an uncivil reply—when these and similar types of "bad behavior" were encountered, adults were no longer deeply disturbed. They had come to recognize, from the teachings of the new psychology, that these crises were more or less part of normal emotional development, that the more extreme forms of behavior would recede almost as quickly and as unexpectedly as they had originally emerged.

Understanding led to changes in action. Sanctions formerly applied to unruly children were now withheld. Parents became less insistent on the child's conforming to their own standard of behavior. They recognized that even with the best will in the world, a child going through a difficult stage in his emotional development needed toleration and possibly even special support.

The new psychology had further impact. It led to an increased demand for psychotherapists and others skilled in the diagnosis and treatment of emotional disorders. Many children with emotional difficulties, it was realized, could be helped by these experts, particularly when they were in a period of special tension. As time went on, this type of assistance was even provided by others besides the psychotherapists, for the new psychology became part of the training of other specialists—physicians, teachers, social workers, and ministers. With their broadened and deepened insights, many of these specialists were able to see more clearly and to act more wisely than laymen in dealing with young people experiencing emotional difficulty. In the case of pediatricians and nursery school teachers, the new psychology, in particular, revolutionized their approaches and techniques.

The new insights also led to radical changes in child rearing within the home and in pedagogy within the school. Previously, parents and educators had relied on their authority as adults to impress upon the young the right way of doing things. Whenever this failed, they resorted to punishment, physical and otherwise. That infants and very young children might not yet possess the minimum degree of understanding required to comply with the demands made of them had, of course, been appreciated. But once the age of understanding had been reached, children were likely to be held strictly to account. If they failed to do what they were told, the pain of punishment, it was felt, would sharpen their memories and lead to correct behavior in the future.

The new psychology, however, showed that establishing an environment of love and security was more important and crucial to healthy emotional development, especially for the infant and the young child. It also shed light on the important role that certain adults play in the emotional development of children by serving as their models. Drawing on these new ideas, parents, teachers and others involved in child development came to appreciate that fear of punishment was one of the least desirable methods of controlling behavior. Many young people, for example, could be encouraged to do something difficult or disagreeable if asked to do so by somebody who loved them. For, to retain the love of those whom they love in turn, children can, if put to the test, call on hidden resources to surmount difficult situations. Similarly, young people, in the process of growing up, need to model themselves after adults whom they love. They, too, can be encouraged to do much that they might otherwise avoid because it is difficult, disagreeable, or takes them away from something that is fun, if they come to appreciate that the behavior required of them is an essential step in their efforts to grow up in accordance with the model set up for them.

The new psychology led to the awareness that there were important instinctual energies that could be harnessed to get children to study and to learn. Children had interests of their own, the new psychology pointed out. If given an opportunity to gratify these interests, at least in part, within the school, they could more easily be taught. Clearly, it was better for young people to learn because of interest than out of fear.

Other types of motivation, it was discovered, could also be used to encourage learning, such as the thrill of competition, the desire for group acceptance, and the drive for self-expression. These and many more motivations were slowly harnessed for use in various facets of child-rearing, particularly in education.

One important aspect of the new psychology was to bring the study of man within the orbit of scientific inquiry. This was a radical change from earlier generations. As long as man was viewed as the unique creation of a Divine Being, a powerful barrier stood against treating him as a natural phenomenon subject to systematic study like the stars, rocks, or animals. Once Darwin established the link between other members of the animal kingdom and man, scientists no longer hesitated to apply the tools of science to the study of human behavior. The new psychology appeared on the scene at a particularly propitious moment, when the barriers against the scientific study of man were just in the process of being overcome. This undoubtedly contributed to the advance of the new discipline.

In no field did the theories and techniques of systematic scientific inquiry have more impact than in the study of intelligence. In France, England, and the United States the first decade of this century saw a rapid advance in the design and standardization of intelligence tests, thanks to men such as Binet and Thorndike.

These studies of intelligence laid the foundation for a wide range of programs aimed at strengthening the education of youth. They helped to establish the existence in a great many cases of a gap, sometimes large and sometimes small, between the intellectual potential of a child and his actual school performance. On the basis of these and other, more refined analyses of children's intellectual strengths and weaknesses, educational psychologists could help school authorities to place children in learning environments that were more conducive to their intellectual development. Now, for instance, there was a way to determine a child's intellectual potential and assign him to a class where the instruction was geared to his capacity to profit from it. The new testing instruments, moreover, made it possible to spot children whose school achievement was below their tested potential. They could then be given special attention.

The new psychology left a mark upon many crucial aspects of child-rearing and education. The atmosphere in the home was considerably altered. Parents loosened their reins; they became increasingly permissive. The atmosphere in the school was likewise altered. No longer did the teacher rely primarily on his authority as a teacher to force knowledge upon the recalcitrant child. Instead he tried to elicit and hold the interest of the child in the subjects under discussion and in the complete learning process. The atmosphere also changed in the society as a whole. It came to understand more fully the role of instinctual forces, including the sexual ones, in the development of behavior. It also came to understand more fully the nature of emotional disturbances and the steps that could be taken to alleviate or otherwise deal with them.

But not all influences of the new psychology were positive. An infatuation with the new led to extravagances and excesses. Many who had to aply the new knowledge had only a limited understanding of what the scientists and scholars were uncovering. They frequently failed to appreciate all the difficulties of adapting the new knowledge to the problems of every day life, with its complex institutions and multiple objectives. The intervening decades have witnessed an increased acceptance of the new psychology. But the problems that have developed as a result of misunderstanding and misapplication of the new doctrines have not yet been eliminated.

Reducing the extent to which children were dealt with harshly, were forced to conform to adult standards, and were subject to considerable frustration undoubtedly represented a social gain. But some misguided devotees of the new psychology went too far in holding that children should not be frustrated at all. When a young child is given everything he wants, his emotional development is certain to be seriously damaged. Sound growth and development requires that a child do things new and difficult, so that he can build up his capacities and self-confidence. Such learning will inevitably involve many unsuccessful trials. These, in turn, will inevitably lead to frustration. If parents seek to protect him from this frustration, they will deprive him of an important aspect of personality development. For the child who is protected from frustration will grow up not only deficient in skill but also deficient in the emotional resilience he will need to tolerate the inevitable frustrations that are part and parcel of every adult's life, no matter how well-endowed he may be in the gifts of nature or of property.

The frank recognition of the important role played by the instinctual forces, including the sexual ones, also helped to reverse what was often a most unhealthy situation. It helped free the child from fears about feelings that he could not repress. But the liberation that took place often went too far. Men are not animals and the sex drive must be controlled. Many parents, misunderstanding the necessity for limits, failed to set any. They exposed their children to more sexual stimuli than they could successfully cope with; they failed to indicate their disapproval of certain types of sex play; and some even gave young adolescents tacit and overt approval to engage in sexual activity before these youngsters were mature enough to guide their own behavior effectively. In these and in other respects, the new freedom went too far.

The new psychology, furthermore, contributed significantly by alerting parents and teachers to the potential emotional difficulties of certain children. It also helped by pointing out the possibility of successfully treating these children. But the new doctrines also led many adults to believe that it was possible for children to grow up without any significant tensions and problems. Some parents became so enamored with the potentialities of psychotherapy that they were on the phone every day—and in the office almost as frequently—seeking expert advice on how to deal with their children's emotional problems. And there were teachers, social workers, and others in a position to counsel parents who also saw in psychotherapy the only solution for almost any type of problem. Such attitudes were falsely based, on two accounts. First, they frequently saw serious problems where none existed. Some tension and difficulty is inherent in the growing up process. Every child, as he passes through certain stages, must loosen his emotional dependence on those to whom he has been very attached and must learn to cope with new challenges in the world outside his home. While support and reassurance may help if the child begins to experience difficulty, excessive concern can only lead to a heightening of the child's anxieties, making the ultimate resolution of the problem even more difficult. Whether a person successfully copes with his difficulties may often depend on whether he believes that he is supposed to cope with them on his own rather than seek someone else's help.

In broadening our understanding of the maturation process, the new psychology made another important advance. But once again, it was misused. Many parents and teachers feared to use punishment as an instrument, not recognizing that without punishment, effective education is frequently impossible. Why, for example, should a lazy child attend to his homework if he is promoted to the next class regardless of his performance? How can a child engaged in socially disapproved activities recognize that they are disapproved of unless he is punished for his actions? Delinquent behavior must be reprimanded before it can be treated.

Even in the case of intelligence testing, where the applications of the new psychology were relatively less complex, difficulties and errors arose. For one thing, measuring intellectual potential proved much more complex than the early investigators had suspected. Eliminating the effects of a testee's unfavorable environment, it has come to be realized, is not a simple matter. Furthermore, many users of tests, not appreciating the complex nature of intelligence itself, failed to realize that a single measure might not reveal a person's great variety of differing strengths and weaknesses. Then too, some experts for a long time failed to appreciate that intelligence scores, though supposedly reflecting potential, and thus immutable, were actually subject to significant change over time. Finally, judgments based on a test score were not always borne out by later observation. In predicting a person's success in school or at work, counselors frequently gave too little weight to the important role played by interest and motivation.

While these various aspects of the new psychology led to much-needed reforms in child-rearing and education, they were also over-generalized and sometimes misapplied. As a result, many faulty practices were introduced into the home, the school, and the community at large.

Since the ideas were revolutionary, error was probably inevitable. But today, a half century after they first saw the light of day, confusion is still widespread. In sum, continuing difficulties arise out of three basic failures. The first is the failure to differentiate between understanding behavior and controlling it. The life history of an adolescent may provide good reasons why he committed a crime. But society is still faced with the problem not only of understanding why it was committed but also of what action to take.

The second basic confusion equates education with therapy. Education, by its very nature, involves demands made upon the child, including the acquisition of knowledge, skills, and controls. In the judgment of his elders, these acquisitions are essential to the survival of society. Therapy, on the other hand, to be effective must in large measure be permissive and must elicit the voluntary cooperation of the individual. Unless the child in trouble wants to be helped, nothing can be accomplished. Hence the psychotherapist must often be supportive and noncritical, at least until the individual is somewhat advanced in his treatment.

Finally, widespread misconception results from equating the psychological facets with the whole of life. It is true that emotional considerations are likely to touch every aspect of human life, for humans when they act and react are inevitably subject to psychological forces. But this is not the same as saying that human behavior is determined exclusively by psychological factors. Much of what goes on in the world also reflects the compelling forces of social institutions—how men make a living, when they marry, how many children they have, whether they are called to arms, how their time is divided between work and leisure, when they retire, and even when they die. And what is true of adults is also true of children. Their development, while certainly influenced by psychological forces, is also a reflection of those dominant social forces whose role must never be ignored or minimized.

9. LEADERS AND LEADERSHIP

Leaders

For centuries, the writing of history was limited to the exploits of military leaders: Alexander the Great, Caesar, Charlemagne, Cromwell, Napoleon. Sometime during the nineteenth century, this type of history-writing fell out of fashion and its place was taken by more sophisticated approaches. Consideration was given to the ideas that motivated the warriors. The new history concentrated upon the great architects of thought: Plato, Aquinas, Leonardo, Galileo—these were the true leaders. Then the fashions changed again. Students began to consider great men the products of their times, and they shifted their attention to analyses of the social and economic environment.

Ordinary folk, however, continued to be vitally interested in the dramatic and to learn what they could about the African explorer, the business magnate, the successful revolutionist, the founder of a new religion. Although most professional historians failed to cater to the public, there has been a never-ceasing stream of books these many years dealing with the exploits of leaders.

Yet we know next to nothing about leadership. We have the detailed records of some great men, but about others we have only scanty information. When this material is put together we have some knowledge but little understanding. We have a surfeit of names, dates, and banal facts, but concerning the whys and wherefores of these leaders we are still very much in the dark. We possess some knowledge, many impressions, and a few good hunches. A beginning should be made to assort this jumble of truths and half-truths.

Starting with elementals, leaders are not predominantly one physical type, although statistics may yet prove that they tend to be taller and stronger than the average. In Western culture, strength is commonly identified with the tall and broad. Police regulations make it difficult, of course, for the physically well endowed to take direct advantage of their superior strength. However, we probably overlook the many areas of our civilization—the boxing ring, the pulpit, the screen, even mercantile and industrial employments—where the tall and the strong have the advantage.

They are twice blessed. First, they stand the pace better, and in the competition that prevails for leadership, the ability to stand the pace is no small asset. The late President Franklin D. Roosevelt, despite his disability, was uniquely endowed. He stood the strain of office perhaps better than any predecessor. It is worth pointing out that the United States has only two living ex-presidents. No one who has seen a union president in action during a prolonged convention can doubt that physical stamina is a prerequisite for successful leadership. To preside all day, to speak at length whenever the occasion demands, and to negotiate all night, is not for the frail.

A second advantage of the tall and strong is the admiration which comes to them. Women are not alone in trusting their emotions. Men also have idols. It does not follow that the undersized and the nondescript have no chance to rise to power. Clearly they do. Napoleon, with his paunch, the midget Dollfuss, and clubfooted Goebbels are only a few examples. They were able to overcome prevailing prejudices. Modern psychology would have us believe that all undersized men undergo a constant struggle to compensate for their shortness, a handicap they cannot hide. In our culture, short men are seldom able to win women taller than they. What is worse, their sexual potency is under suspicion. Hence many short men feel a great need to prove that they are not only normal but superior.

What is true of height and strength is probably true of all significant characteristics. Men who most closely approach the social ideal have the advantage, and deviants are hard put to overcome their handicaps. It need hardly be emphasized that ideals change with time, and in a fluid culture like ours several ideals may be enthroned at the same time. Some were enamored of the uncultivated speech of Alfred E. Smith, while others trembled when they thought of his occupying the White House. There was a time, not so long ago, when a man born to wealth, a graduate of Groton and Harvard, would have been severely handicapped in campaigning against a farm boy who had been educated in a little red schoolhouse. We are still in the grip of the past; we fear the trappings of wealth and exaggerate the virtues of poverty.

Deviants can, however, in the absence of absolute prohibitions, succeed to power. Potential leaders must surmount not only legal and administrative barriers, but also the prejudices of the dominant group. The Constitution of the United States has no stipulation regarding the religion of the President, but only one Catholic, not to mention a Jew, has yet been elected.

Some men have the physical and social prerequisites for leadership; others have great determination and capacity. They too belong to the leadership group. But if there be a leadership group, then there must also be followers. A shipwrecked man on an uninhabited island cannot be a leader. The distinction between those who lead and those who are led is important. Some people want to lead, must lead, devote their every ounce of energy to obtaining positions in which they can lead. Others are content to follow, find security in their dependence on a leader, in fact would never permit themselves to be catapulted into a position of leadership. This contrast in the personality structures of leaders and followers does not imply that every leader fulfills an inner need to command and control. Circumstances bordering on the accidental might place a man at the top, in a position he never sought, but one he will occupy as long as the demands upon him are reasonable. Had it not been for the sudden death of President Harding, Calvin Coolidge would probably never have become President of the United States. Nor does it follow that all who are led are content. Many have the desire, but not the ability or the opportunity, to rise out of the ranks and assume a position of leadership.

There is much that is obscure about leadership, such as the source of the demonic energy that enabled a poor Corsican lad to conquer Europe or that which enabled an Austrian paper hanger to repeat the story one hundred years later. Less spectacular, but equally impressive, are the achievements of many other lowly born who, against great odds, succeed in fighting their way to the top. If we really understood what made Napoleon and Hitler tick, we would have come close to unraveling the major tangle of the leadership problem. However, we would still be faced with the question of whether Napoleon accomplished what he did because the time was ripe or because he was Napoleon.

We have a clue or two, but no more, to this problem of energy. No one who has observed newborns can fail to be impressed with their physical differences. Some babies sleep peacefully from one feeding to the next, while others howl in anticipation of their bottle. Some are content to amuse themselves, while others demand constant attention. To prove that people are born with differing energy potentials is not easy, but one should think twice before denying this assumption. The source of adult differences may well be present at birth.

Psychoanalysts have an alternative explanation, one which seeks to understand adult aggressions in terms of childhood frustrations. They cite innumerable cases to prove that premature weaning, harsh discipline, parental preference, and a thousand and one other circumstances lead to frustrations out of which are generated the aggressive drives that only later come to the surface. But this must be remembered: many frustrated children never develop evidence of overt aggression in later life. It has never been proved that the quantity of adult aggression stands in any fixed relation to the quantity of childhood frustrations. Nor do we really understand the multiple opportunities for the discharge of these aggressive drives in socially acceptable in contrast to socially reprehensible activities. It is surely not a matter of indifference, at least to society, whether a person frustrated in childhood eventually kills a man or becomes a judge; and it is surely an imperfect psychology that cannot prognosticate the probable outcome of infantile frustration.

Whatever be the explanation for the marked differences that we find in the energy drives of adults, the fact cannot be gainsaid that differences do exist. Some people have an inordinate need for power, and it is no accidental matter that they achieve it, for they devote their every waking hour to getting ahead. They are driven as if by the furies, and they can no more retire from the race than retire from life itself.

A study of the great captains of American industry—the same findings would probably be revealed by a study of any other group of leaders—disclosed a pattern of dominant characteristics. Most men possess some of these traits, but only the leader has all of them. First, these leaders had an inordinate capacity for work. In the middle of the nineteenth century the average workday was twelve hours or more, but these leaders usually worked much longer.

A second characteristic was their constant planning and scheming. They could not rest with the completion of their daily task, for if they did they ran the risk of finding themselves in the same position the next day. This they could not contemplate. When the next day came they had to be one or two rungs up the ladder. In order to push ahead they had to gain an advantage over their competitors. They burned the midnight oil to find ways and means of getting ahead.

This group had energy, lots of it. They also had talent; a few even had genius. Their strong points differed. Some had a flair for trading, others for mechanics, still others for social relations. The important point is that, once they decided upon action, they were able to carry through.

In almost every instance the future captain of industry ran into a "do or die" situation early in his career. He was face to face with a unique opportunity, but one which usually presented serious difficulties. The opportunity may have demanded only a minimum investment, but it was beyond his immediate resources. Faced with a major challenge, the future leader reacted with boundless confidence. Needing capital beyond his own resources, he threw all his savings into the venture and then browbeat relatives and friends into lending him the additional funds, for which he could offer no security other than his own confidence. Those who gave up their jobs manifested the same self-assurance. They threw over the work they had been doing and set out on new and risky ventures, firmly convinced of eventual success. When opportunity offered they backed up their confidence in their own judgment with a willingness to stake their all.

These men were ruthless. To achieve their ends they used every weapon at their command, not hesitating to transgress law or custom to avoid defeat. Their actions were frequently in the twilight zone of criminality. It is noteworthy that their ruthlessness was directed not only towards opponents, but also towards close associates and friends. The primacy of their aggressive needs was reflected in the doggedness with which they sought to enhance their power. Their need for power was so overwhelming that they made short shrift with all other emotional and social values. Difficult to appreciate is the coldbloodedness with which they would unhesitatingly ruin a friend if he stood in their way.

The fact that these men worked very hard, were amazingly self-assured, and were frequently ruthless explains why so few were successful in their personal lives. They were unable to make essential marital adjustments, and they had neither the time nor the temperament for successful parenthood. Marital discord runs through their biographies.

In contrast to the stockbrokers who dealt in pieces of paper, the industry builders—the railroad kings, the steel masters, the oil tycoons—identified themselves intimately with their undertakings. They had good reason for doing so. Not only was their work their life, but the industrial empires that they came to own were, much more than carping critics think, their handiwork. This intense identification helps to explain their uncompromising, pugnacious attitude whenever their establishments were under attack by competitors, labor, or the government. The attack on their empires was an attack on them, on their very vitals.

A further characteristic of the group was their insatiable drive for power. Most leaders found it difficult to stop even when further accumulation had lost all meaning. They frequently kept on, even at a risk to their health. Late in life a few were finally deflected and found other outlets for their all-consuming energies, but the majority died with their boots on.

Such were the lives of these leaders. How different from ordinary men! Most people find it difficult to get through their working day, be it twelve, ten, or eight hours, and once through, they are glad to let the matter rest until morning, when they must again sweat in order to eat. Although now and again they are willing to gamble a few dollars on a horse or cards, they do so for relaxation. Their behavior has nothing in common with the desperate "risk-all" plunges taken by leaders.

Ordinary folk plan, but not in the same way as leaders. They put a few dollars aside for a rainy day. They are polite to superiors, frequently from necessity. They will read a book or attend a lecture because it may prove useful to them. However, their work does not mean enough to them to scheme, plot, and plan all with an eye on the main chance. There is no doubt that many people do not possess the qualities that would make their planning a success, but there are many others who have the ability but fail to exploit it.

Ordinary folk are under no compulsion to be ruthless. True, they are not as vulnerable as leaders, for, having less to lose, they are seldom under attack. But this is not the entire difference. The average person is not under the same inner necessity to sacrifice every value that stands in the way of his self-aggrandizement. He seeks his satisfaction from many areas: home, job, club, and church. If he has friends, and most people do, he will protect his relationships, and if necessary he will pay a price, sometimes a high price, to cement them.

Unlike the highly aggressive who has neither the time nor the interest to spend on familial relationships, the average person finds his principal interests in his home. He is much more concerned about his wife and children than about his business associates and competitors. Although most people find pleasure in their work, their satisfactions do not derive primarily from their job. Reflecting the many hours he spends at work, the average man tends to identify himself with his job, but he seldom becomes deeply involved in the problems of his employer, for they are not his problems. Living from day to day and year to year, and seeing the future largely in terms of his children, he does not possess the incessant drives of leaders, whose whole beings are bent under the yoke of their power needs.

The striking contrasts between the behavior of leaders and the living patterns of the masses are not derived solely from innate physical and emotional differences. In our society important values attach to leadership posts, a fact that helps to explain the intense desire of many to achieve these positions.

Top positions carry top rewards, in income and prestige. It is a widespread misconception that aggressive people are always money-mad. True, the future leader must keep an eye out for reasonable income, especially in our society, where so many opportunities are open only to men of means. However, except for the pathological individual who keeps accumulating because he cannot stop even to spend his gains, wealth has little attraction for most leaders. Goering, not Hitler, is the exception. Power over men and the prestige that came to him as the leader of all Germans sufficed for Hitler. He had little need either for bank balances or hunting preserves. There is an obvious reason why money can be of only secondary importance to the real leader, why it can be useful to him only as a means, never an end in itself. One needs time to enjoy luxuries, and time is the one thing a leader does not have.

Men must satisfy their basic instincts of hunger and sex, but most of their activities are socially determined. We seek to achieve what society holds desirable. The top positions carry rewards of money, titles, privileges—above all they carry the esteem of the group. For those who succeed in arriving at the top, victory has deep meaning. The approval and acclaim of the group reassures them.

The insatiability of their power drives is so great that leaders can derive satisfaction only by capturing the most important positions. They view their accomplishments, not in relation to the road they have traveled, but rather to the one they see stretching ahead. Since the number of top positions is always limited, the struggle is never over.

It is a long way from office boy to vice-president, from $55 to $1,500 weekly. But objective facts are brushed aside by those set for the kill. Many a vice-president continues to strive and strain as before, for the bigger the prize the harder the struggle.

The incessant fighting, the ever-present risks, the constant need to be on guard—these are a few of the liabilities of leadership. No wonder many able people refuse to compete.

The leader is lonely. He has many followers, some associates, but no intimates with whom he can share his work and worries. In the last analysis he can trust no one, for his goals are always personal. The power that he wields and the power that he seeks are eyed greedily by others. He knows that his competitors, like himself, would not hesitate to use every advantage.

Fear of responsibility, which excludes many from the competition for leadership, may have its roots in this fear of loneliness. For the top executive, sharing of responsibility is impossible. He must make his decisions, change them if necessary, but he must live with them. If his calculations go awry he cannot place the blame on others. Nor has he anything to gain by passing the buck, for failure leaves him vulnerable. If a general loses a campaign, or a high command loses a war, they have lost it and must suffer the consequences no matter who else has failed. Even the master propagandist, Hitler, was unable to shift the blame for Germany's defeat in World War I from Ludendorff and the high command to labor and the bourgeoisie.

We are face to face with the basic paradox of leadership. Inordinate power drives and all that they connote frequently have their roots in man's need for reassurance. This is a hostile world, and many individuals feel their insecurity acutely. They are oppressed by what fate has in store for them and seek to protect themselves by striving ceaselessly to gain power to ward off the hostile forces. Yet their every move conjures up new opponents.

Not every leader is trapped. Many find a resting place along the way; they are satisfied by modest achievements. Others stop not from choice but from necessity. They realize that personal limitations or social barriers block further progress. A man can never fool himself all the time.

There are men, however, who drive on to find rest only in the grave. They are a small group, but their influence is tremendous. Sometimes they master history. Paul's influence on the peoples of the Mediterranean cannot be viewed as just another step in their historical development.

Not good nor evil but change is the handiwork of leaders. Sometimes their work is good and sometimes evil, but always the world is different because a man was born who lived to lead. Ominous it is, but true, that we cannot foretell the end to which leaders will devote their power. Most leaders tear down much that was, as well as create much that was not. Even after the passage of many years it is usually difficult to reach a balanced judgment. Napoleon slaughtered thousands, but he also carried the French Revolution into the hinterland. He destroyed the last vestiges of representative government in France, but he greatly improved her legal and administrative structures. Our business tycoons bribed legislators, blackmailed innocent business-men, tricked investors, and cheated the public, but they also laid the foundations for the industrial strength of this country.

Leaders act as they do because they cannot act otherwise. All con-tend that they seek to improve the world. Actually they use the world for their laboratory. Whatever they contribute, either good or bad, is incidental. This probably explains what Byron meant when he wrote: "When we think we lead we most are led."

Leadership

A study of leadership must distinguish between the great leader who founds a new religion, creates a dynasty, or leads a successful revo-lution, and the rulers who follow in his footsteps. With the tools at our disposal we are in no position to analyze Mohammed, but we can learn considerable about the Caliphate, about the leaders who ruled the Prophet's followers in matters spiritual and temporal.

To take a more contemporary illustration: It would be exceedingly difficult, in fact impossible, to analyze the wellsprings of Lenin's genius and strength. The fact that he was a genius is no longer doubted even by the most rabid anti-communist. But even admitting the tremendous role played by Lenin, and more recently by Stalin, in directing the policies of the Soviet Union, it should be obvious that no one man can rule a nation of one hundred and fifty million. No matter how intensively power is concentrated, it requires a sizable leadership to rule one-sixth of the earth.

The study of leadership in the Soviet Union would involve several distinct approaches. A first step would be to identify the significant positions, governmental and other. A second would be to specify the occupants of these posts as leaders. This second step would not be entirely valid, since certain incumbents probably are little more than figureheads while others, without recognized position, are probably wielding great power.

Admitting this limitation, the next step would be to submit these leaders to detailed analysis. Since the Russian Revolution professed to broaden the opportunities for the hitherto disenfranchised, a study of the social origin of the leadership class would prove relevant. Are the leaders sons and daughters of the bourgeoisie or did they come from workers' and farmers' homes? Their educational and occupational experiences would also be illuminating. Such data would indicate the extent to which opportunities for leadership in the Soviet Union are dependent upon formal educational achievements and specific job experiences. If the answers to these questions were secured, our understanding of the Russian leadership pattern would be greatly enhanced.

But this would be a beginning, not the end, of a study of Soviet leadership. In addition to data concerning the social origins and education of the leaders of the Army, the Communist Party, important national groups such as the Ukrainians, it would be necessary to study Soviet leaders in terms of the organizations they lead and to see how they solve the problems that present themselves. To contend, as many do, that Soviet Russia will prefer to move in this or that direction completely disregards the fact that even a dictatorship is bound by its own history. Every leader, even the most powerful, is limited in his scope of action by the structure and functioning of the organization he leads. Stalin was no exception. The policy of Soviet Russia is the resolution of the wills of its many leaders whose roots are deep in Russian institutions.

Only a beginning has been made to study the patterns of leadership in different organizations. A graduate student in search of a subject for a dissertation might find it rewarding to collect and review the available studies. In the absence of such a review, a start can be made by pointing up the similarities and differences in the leadership patterns of the Church, army, business, politics, and trade unions.

Among the oldest of institutions, the Church illuminates many interesting facets of the leadership problem. The recruitment of the clergy depends upon the place of religion in the culture of the times. In colonial days, Harvard College concentrated on training ministers. The sons of leading families chose the ministry for a career. How different today! Almost never does a boy, born to wealth or position, enter a Protestant, Catholic, or Jewish theological seminary. Today the clergy is recruited almost exclusively from low and at best middle income groups. The rich no longer hear the call.

It is well known that for many generations the younger sons of the landed gentry entered the Church of England. The law of primogeniture and the entailing of estates prevented younger sons from enjoying a life of respectable indolence. Nor was it considered proper for them to enter business to seek the fortune they could not inherit. Their one choice was army or Church. As the industrialization of England progressed, the power of the Church declined. The prejudices of the aristocracy against money-making likewise declined, and its sons no longer had to enter the Church for a livelihood. As time went on, the middle and even the lower classes filled the gap. A poor boy with scholastic ability had a good chance of securing an ecclesiastical sinecure.

Certain parallels and contrasts are found in the recruitment of the Catholic clergy. During the centuries when the Church ruled in matters temporal as well as spiritual, the offspring of prominent families took orders. The Church rules today in the United States only in spiritual matters, and the wealthy no longer give her their sons.

Throughout the many centuries when feudal barons ruled Europe and the door of opportunity was kept shut to the lowly born, the Church alone offered them a chance to advance. Although a Borgia or

Medici might secure a red hat with relative ease, the gifted son of a cowherd or artisan had at least an outside chance of becoming a Prince of the Church. The Jewish communities, with their deeply ingrained respect for learning, also facilitated the advancement of poor but brilliant lads. Able students were subsidized, and the wealthy sought them for sons-in-law.

As far as Catholics and Jews are concerned, and the same is true of most Protestant sects, admission to and graduation from an authorized seminary is prerequisite to ordination. The basic conservatism of organized religion is maintained largely through its control over the curricula of theological schools.

If one seeks to identify the important characteristics that contribute to outstanding leadership in the Church, first and foremost is that elusive quality which, for lack of a better word, is called "spirituality." It does not follow of course that the average clergyman, or even one who rises high in the ecclesiastical hierarchy, always possesses deep religious emotion. But one cannot be a great religious leader without this inner resource.

Spirituality is not enough. Congregants must be inspired and colleagues impressed. Hence, the importance of the spoken and the written word. Learning is important. A knowledge of the past and an intimate acquaintance with contemporary forces are essential for the leader. The fact that Leo XIII had such a deep understanding of the political crosscurrents of his day goes far to explain his masterful steering of the Church through troubled waters. The renaissance of the Church of England that loomed on the horizon largely reflected the broad vision of the late William Temple, Archbishop of Canterbury.

What of the army, which shares with the Church the distinction of being among the oldest forms of social organization? The attitude toward the military has differed from century to century, from country to country, and recruitment has always been directly affected by prevailing opinion. The impression is widespread, and it is probably well founded, that the regular officers of the United States Army have been drawn to a disproportionate degree from southern families, rich in tradition but small in purse. With limited opportunities in agriculture and industry, it is not surprising that many southerners chose the Army for a career. In the more prosperous northern and western states, few youngsters gave the Army a second thought. The fact that northerners shied clear from a military career has led some to advocate that, if we are forced to mobilize again, specific efforts should be made to recruit officer material from the ranks of northern business where executive talent abounds. These critics believe with General Wavell that, as far as strategy is concerned, "the main principles . . . are simple and easy to grasp." The real test is tactics—the handling of troops and munitions on the battlefield. The leaders of American business have been tried and tested in the most competitive of environments, and they should be able to distinguish themselves in solving problems of military logistics.

The selection of officers for the German Army had long been under the strictest controls. Limitations were placed even on their marital choices. Marriage to a woman without social standing meant the end of promotion, if not dismissal from the service. Organizational discipline was so great that the military machine was able to survive the disastrous defeat of 1918, and it may yet recover from the overwhelming defeat of 1945.

Like the Church, modern military organizations rigorously control the education of officers. Great importance is placed on training. Even in war, when many officers are chosen from the ranks and when promotions are accelerated, final control is kept by professionals who are graduates of the military academies. The army, like the Church, has a hierarchal structure, and the future leader does not advance solely on the basis of technical capacity. He must get on well with subordinates and superiors, and when he reaches the top he must inspire the confidence of his own and allied governments, for, to quote Wavell again, if he fails to do so he "may forfeit both fame and victory."

Business leadership stands in sharp contrast to leadership in the Church or army. The scale of commercial and industrial activity, especially in the Western world, is so large that the number of business leaders far exceeds the number of ecclesiastical and military leaders. The significance of this fact is heightened when one realizes that the road to business success until recently has not been cut through the campus. There are more corporation presidents in the United States who never saw the inside of a college than those who hold a degree from the Harvard School of Business Administration. Even in England and Germany, men with minimal formal education have been able to amass fortunes. But these facts should not obscure the obvious—that a man's chance for success is greatly enhanced if he has wealthy parents and has enjoyed the educational and other advantages of property. Although many men are self-made, many others owe their positions to relatives. The sons of the wealthy are not once but thrice blessed.

In recent decades educational prerequisites have assumed greater importance in the struggle for business leadership. With modern industry increasingly dependent upon scientific processes, many executive posts are reserved for the technically trained. The obverse is also true: the uneducated are precluded from competing for many jobs.

It is not easy to isolate and describe the specific talents that contribute to business success. Money-making is an art, and artists have different talents. One man may have a flair for correct timing—when to buy cheap and sell dear. The money-making capacity of another may be grounded in a mechanical genius seasoned with enough practicality to prevent others from appropriating his inventions. In certain instances success may depend on personality. The successful salesman needs no introduction.

The analysis of political success hinges on a prior analysis of political power. Today the successful politician must be able to capture and hold the populace. But this is recent. Only yesterday small cliques ruled without regard to the wishes of the masses. In this country the direct election of senators is of recent date; and in England a small leadership group has long been in control. The narrow leadership base in Great Britain probably explains the many tragic errors committed by Baldwin and Chamberlain. These older men went unchallenged because of the manpower losses of World War I. Those who should have been on the front bench and in the important ministries during the twenties and thirties were only names on the memorial tablets of Cambridge and Oxford.

In the United States political leaders come from many classes. The children of the poor have a real chance to get ahead in politics. As is true of business, political success depends only slightly on formal education. Although many politicians have studied law, there are no educational requirements for election to Congress.

The ability to speak well, especially on the air, is a major asset, much more so than a knowledge of science or history. The phenomenal success of the late Franklin D. Roosevelt was dependent to a large degree on his forensic abilities. Nor should one overlook the fact that in the First World War as in the Second, the leaders of the United States and Great Britain were distinguished orators: Wilson, Lloyd George, Roosevelt, and Churchill. A great orator has more than a flair for words and a resonant tone. To give expression to the latent emotions of the masses so as to nourish and strengthen their hopes and aspirations—that is the genius of the orator.

The political leader must also have a knack for negotiations. He must know how to win friends and influence people, and he must avoid unnecessarily making enemies. The statesman needs more. He must have vision to find his way through the mass of detail and emotion and use today's challenges to create a better tomorrow.

Labor leadership has much in common with political leadership. One distinction must, however, be recognized: In a democracy politics is the concern of all classes, while trade-unionism has a more limited appeal. Although competition for labor leadership is technically open to all, prejudice militates against the success of one who does not belong to the working class. Education is of relatively minor importance, especially formal education. Few serious attempts have been made to establish schools for training labor leaders.

In England the Labor Party has long been seriously handicapped by the limited education of its leaders. Many trade-union bureaucrats were pensioned off with seats in Parliament, where they proved no match for the Eton or Harrow graduate. Nor was it possible to solve this problem by relying on intellectuals who for the most part had no real appreciation of the structure and functioning of the trade unions, the backbone of the Labor Party. In the late thirties Bevin experimented with subsidizing the education of a few young people preparatory to launching them on parliamentary careers. He had grown dissatisfied with the innate limitations of the typical trade-unionists as well as with the impractical intellectual.

In trade unions, as in politics, oratory plays an important role in the leadership pattern. An appeal to the group is frequently necessary—before calling a strike, when settling a contract, when fighting insurgents. The silver-tongued orator has the edge. But the successful leader cannot rely on words alone. Once again the parallel to politics is striking. He must negotiate—inside his organization, with employers, with the government. Moreover, he must know how to administer: he has the responsibility for keeping the organization on an even keel, solvent, and free from discord. A great leader must also have vision. He must use his power not only to control the present but to mold the future.

This brief sketch of the leadership pattern in Church, army, business, politics, and trade unions has disclosed interesting parallels and differences. In general, the poor are at a disadvantage in competing for power, although they have the field more or less to themselves in the modern church and in trade unions. Formal training is of much greater importance to churchman and soldier than to politician and labor leader.

Certain qualities stand all leaders in good stead, while others have more restricted value. Ease in social relations is an asset to cardinal, general, or trade-union president. Oratorical gifts, essential for politicians and labor leaders, are relatively unimportant for business magnates. The organization sets the challenge which the successful leader must meet.

Studies of leadership will always prove difficult, for the principals see little gain and considerable danger in revealing what they know about the process. But there are more facts and figures available about patterns of leadership than have as yet been collected and analyzed. Considering the important role that leaders play, this neglect should be remedied.

10. THE DETERMINANTS OF PERFORMANCE

We have used the term *personality* throughout our analysis to encompass the totality of an individual's qualities, that is, his strengths
and weaknesses which have a bearing on his ability to perform. We
have used the term *performance* to refer to the individual's response
to the demands that are made on him by his family, his employer, and
the community of which he is a part. While the level of demands tends
to be geared to the level of responsibility that individuals are able to
discharge we have concentrated on exploring the reasons why large
numbers of people cannot meet the minimum demands that are made
on them. We know that great individual and social wastes result when
talented people perform at a level far below their optimum. But a
democracy, which is dedicated to the concept that the individual has
primary responsibility for himself, must be even more concerned with
the wastes that result when many of its members are unable to perform effectively even at a minimum level. For when this happens the
community must step in and assume responsibilities that should
normally be carried by the individual.

Performance Potential

There is no doubt that an individual's personal characteristics have a
bearing on his performance. This is borne out in every-day experience
and is generally in accord with the many observations that we were
able to make on the basis of the analysis of our materials. Yet no one
characteristic can adequately explain performance except in an extreme case, such as a mentally deficient man who cannot take care of

himself. When we seek to account for the successful or unsuccessful performance of a group of people, any attempt to rely solely on an analysis of their personal characteristics will generally fail. Repeatedly, we found that our expectations about how people would perform based on our interpretation of their qualities were at variance with their actual performance record.

We see, then, that there is no simple one-to-one relationship between an individual's qualities or traits and his performance except in extreme cases such as the one mentioned above. How well an individual performs depends rather on an interplay between his qualities and traits and the factors in the external environment which present him with opportunities and limitations. Therefore, instead of considering personal qualities as if they were isolated or independent factors, it would be better to recognize that the performance potential of an individual involves more than their sum. We pointed out in *The Lost Divisions* how inadequate the prediction of performance is even for groups that had been carefully studied, and certainly it is more so when based on such evaluations as were made in connection with the large-scale screening of selectees during World War II.

We did not choose the concept of performance potential because of its predictive value, but rather to stress that the individual's qualities can be properly appraised only as they are revealed in given situations, under given circumstances. In spite of this indeterminate nature of the performance potential, it is possible to single out some of the constituent factors even though they can be subjected only to a broad analysis.

Personal Characteristics

Whether an individual can perform effectively depends in no small measure on his endowment and on his life experiences, especially those during the formative years of childhood and adolescence. At one extreme are those who are so seriously handicapped that they can never acquire the minimum knowledge and skills necessary to perform at even a minimum level. Fortunately, the number in the population who are truly mentally deficient has been estimated at not more than 1 to 2 percent. In terms of the manpower of World War II this would point to a mentally deficient group of between about 200,000 and 350,000 in the age group eighteen to thirty-seven who were screened for military service. But the difference between this significant but fortunately relatively small number of truly mentally deficient persons and the ten times larger group who were rejected for service or prematurely separated from the Armed Services during World War II for mental or emotional defects points to the need of considering a much wider range of personal determinants.

Intelligence is an important determinant, but the evaluation of a man's intelligence is frequently difficult because even specially designed tests do not enable one to distinguish adequately between the individual's innate capacity and the opportunities that he has had to learn. Nevertheless, the evidence in our three volumes clearly indicates that intelligence is among the most important determinants of performance. Those with low intelligence scores and with limited schooling—the two tend to go together, although it is not always so—had a poorer performance record in both civilian and military life than men with more intellectual capacity and a greater amount of schooling. But we must be quick to add that high-school graduation or even college attendance was no guarantee that a man would perform effectively, although the odds were very much in favor of his doing so.

Effective performance implies that the individual is able to establish and maintain relationships with others, both superiors and associates, on the job and with relatives and friends off the job. Seriously disturbed individuals who do not have control over their emotions, who may not be able to differentiate between reality and fantasy, will be unable to perform effectively no matter how intelligent they may be. One must have a minimum emotional stability to be a satisfactory member of a complex society that requires every person in it to adjust his needs and desires, at least in some degree, to those of others.

But even men of intelligence and emotional stability will not always perform in an effective manner since without adequate motivation individuals do not mobilize their strengths. While most men will, by virtue of their upbringing and the pressures exerted on them by their environment, put forth the effort required to become and remain self-supporting and upright citizens, some few will not be motivated to meet society's standards and ideals.

In addition there are physical characteristics which, though they fell outside of the main concern of the study of *The Ineffective Soldier*, should not be overlooked or underestimated in their bearing on performance. What a man is able to make of his strengths, intellectual and emotional, and how well he can surmount his weaknesses depends in considerable measure on his physical condition and in particular on his stamina. This is as true in many civilian occupations as in military service. Illness is debilitating and the individual must draw upon his reserves to cope with it. The more a man is ill, the more he must use his reserves just to keep going. In contrast, the man with a strong constitution who is free of organic complaints has a distinct advantage, other things being equal. He is much more likely to be able to perform effectively because his body is his ally. If he must labor long and hard, if he is exposed to inclement weather, if he misses meals or sleep, he can take these and similar deprivations in his stride and they do not scar him easily. Moreover, he can recover very quickly. The physical condition of a person is often the crucial factor which determines whether he will be able to perform effectively or not. This is true particularly of those whose other strengths and disabilities are in precarious balance.

Organizational Policy

Years ago when most men were self-employed in farming, business, or the professions, a consideration of the factors determining their performance could be reasonably limited to their own strengths and weaknesses. Whether a man made good or failed appeared to depend primarily on whether he was intelligent, stable, well-motivated, and healthy. But the pattern of contemporary life is quite different. Most men do not work for themselves. Many are members of large organizations. This fact has a significant impact on their performance, for all men react—some more, some less—to the organizational policies to which they are exposed.

No man is indifferent to the policies which determine his specific assignment, his wages, his opportunities for promotion, the type of supervision and discipline to which he is subject, and other essential aspects of his job. Individually and in combination, these facets of his job shape his attitude towards and his performance at work. The policies pursued by the organization may result in his working more effectively or less effectively. But they cannot be without effect, even though some policies may operate in one and others in the opposite direction.

Most men must work, but how much they apply themselves and how conscientiously largely depends on the way in which they are treated by their supervisors and employers—or how they think they are being treated. Students of human behavior have long recognized that the underlying weakness of a slave society was the hidden costs involved in forcing people to work. The major challenge to management is to develop policies which encourage rather than discourage men from applying themselves to their work. Effective work must be elicited; it cannot be commandeered.

Organizational policies also affect performance by the obstacles that they place in the way or by the opportunities which they provide for people to make use of their skills and potentialities. As we have suggested, a major challenge that an army at war faces is to find the time and personnel to screen the millions of recruits in order to assign them more nearly according to their capacities and potentialities. Similar difficulties, although of a lesser order, confront every large organization. There is no way of finding out what a man can really do except by the slow and costly process of trying him out. And while measurement instruments are constantly being improved, they cannot foretell the capacity for executive leadership which a recent college graduate will eventually develop.

It is no easier to design policies which will enable men to add to their skills. Those concerned with industrial training have come to recognize that while some men are eager for the opportunity to study and grow, others will ignore the opportunities which are made available to them. But the difficulties of differentiating between those who really want to and would make effective use of learning opportunities and those who would only go through the forms should not discourage management from facing up to the important challenge to provide adequate opportunities for the continued growth of its work force.

Men resent being employed at work which does not make use of the skills which they have acquired, often arduously. They may tolerate such a situation in war or in a depression when they recognize the pressure of overriding considerations, but in peacetime such a working environment can lead only to their frustration and lessened productivity.

One important way in which organizational policy can enhance performance is through special measures designed to facilitate the indoctrination and orientation of new members. This is true for every type of organization—a college, an army, an industrial concern. The newcomer is likely to feel ill at ease as he enters a situation where he has only a hazy notion of what is expected of him and how he can meet the new demands. Even men who have performed quite well in other environments may be unsettled by a new situation. The bright high-school graduate who has never been away from home may find his first months at college very upsetting. This happens to many young men who are drafted into the Army, especially in wartime when there is a premium on their speedy conversion to soldiers. During their early weeks of active duty they are likely to be subjected to truly harassing circumstances which force them to change their habits. Although a new job in civilian life seldom represents quite such an extreme challenge, since most men continue to live in accustomed surroundings with their relatives and friends, it does imply a large number of new and frequently difficult situations. Under pressure to do well, a young man in a new job is likely to be anxious.

Since uncertainty, stress, and strain are likely to be present whenever men confront new situations, it is wise for an organization to provide orientation and indoctrination to help the newcomer better understand his new environment. Every superior has known men who showed great promise but who resigned or had to be discharged early in their employment. There is much that an organization can do to prevent such needless waste—although no program can help everybody.

Organizational policy can also contribute to the reduction, and possibly the elimination, of ineffective performance by preventing the build-up of high orders of stress. Under accumulated tension, some men who until then had performed with real effectiveness may break down, reducing their level of performance temporarily or even permanently. Although most individuals usually protect themselves if they feel that they are nearing the point of physical or emotional exhaustion, there are some situations, especially in periods of national emergency, in which men may be driven to breakdown. In the Armed Services in war this is most likely to occur when, because of lack of planning or inadequate reserves, commanders have no option but to push their troops to their maximum—and beyond—and take whatever casualties they must. But it is always preferable when possible to plan ahead for the use of manpower so as to avoid undue stresses and strains by removing men for rest and rehabilitation or reassignment before they break. Analogous situations can also be found in industry, particularly among an executive group that is confronted with a major emergency that cannot be quickly resolved.

Organizational policy that provides appropriate supports for those who suddenly encounter difficulties can help to reduce ineffectiveness. Some men who break down may become so disturbed that it is better for the organization to discharge them since there is little likelihood that they will soon again function effectively. Many others, however, may require only modest help before they can again become effective.

Some of these men may have run into conflict with their superiors or fellow workers. Others may be in emotional turmoil because of difficulties at home. Still others may be overwhelmed by an inability to cope with new responsibility. They are disturbed and therefore the quality of their performance is likely to deteriorate, perhaps at first imperceptibly, but later more noticeably. They feel tense and anxious. Frequently their fears are grounded in fact; more often they exaggerate the real situation which confronts them. Often they need only a sympathetic listener. In many cases an opportunity to talk out their problems might be all that they require. As they verbalize their problems, their difficulties may start to shrink or disappear completely. Others may not be so fortunate. They may be face to face with a realistic problem which only reassignment, additional training, or financial assistance can relieve. But if they receive such support, many of them straighten around and quickly. The wise organization will provide it.

A leadership must insure that all who are in a supervisory position clearly understand the basic principles and procedures on which the organization's operations are based. For only if the several echelons have a clear understanding of the aims and objectives of policy will they be able to use it constructively. This also indicates why the leadership of an organization must avoid instituting frequent and radical shifts in policy. For policy can realize its constructive potentialities only to the extent that it is stable. In fact, policy that is subject to frequent and large-scale changes is a contradiction in terms, for shifting principles cannot be communicated and absorbed sufficiently rapidly to serve as effective guides to action.

The burden of these considerations is that organizational policies can either strengthen or weaken the motivation of men to perform effectively; to the extent that policies facilitate a man's using his skills and adding to them, his performance is likely to be improved; policies which smooth the adjustment of new members, that prevent the accumulation of extreme stress and strain, and that provide supports for members of the organization who need them can help men to attain and maintain a satisfactory level of performance.

Environmental Factors

In addition to the part played by an individual's strengths and weaknesses and his experiences in the organization of which he is a part, his performance will be significantly affected by conditions in the broader environment and by the pressures with which he must deal. These can affect him both directly and indirectly.

To begin with, ours is a society with certain pervasive values which help to mold the attitudes and behavior of the great majority. A man, if physically and mentally able, is supposed to work. In fact our society does not look kindly on even a wealthy man who does not work. This fundamental responsibility that is inherent in our culture provides a very strong propulsion on men to meet it.

This is reinforced by the parallel responsibility that a man has to support not only himself but his family. We had occasion to note particularly in *Breakdown and Recovery* that many men were heartened during the war by their close ties with their loved ones at home and that many others finally were able to throw off the lethargy and depression resulting from their war experience and to return to gainful employment when they saw again the need to provide for their wives and children. This is a second powerful spur to effective performance, and it is the more powerful because it goes beyond the simple question of responsibility. Many men are able to keep working at their jobs only because of the substantial emotional support that they receive from their wives or other members of their family.

It would be hard to exaggerate the importance of still another facet in the effective performance of so many men under the major stresses of war—ordinary men who had nothing of the hero in their makeup. Many kept going because they "could not let their buddies down." Unlike in some societies where the individual's responsibility does not extend beyond the confines of his family, the American soldier's behavior was greatly conditioned by his feelings of comradeship with the others in his unit.

Important as the cultural values are which spur men to assume the obligation of work or military service and to perform effectively, they cannot by themselves assure the result. It is also necessary that the environment provide an opportunity for the discharge of these obligations. The depression of the 1930s put an end to the widespread belief that a man who was willing to work would always be able to find work. In passing the Employment Act of 1946 which charged the Federal Government with taking all necessary action to establish and maintain a high level of employment, Congress underscored the new understanding which the American people had gained through adversity that a man in a modern industrial society can meet his obligations only if there are jobs available that he can fill. Whether a larger or smaller number are able to perform effectively depends on the range of opportunities available.

In a labor market in which the numbers seeking employment are far greater than the jobs available, employers will pick the potentially abler and reject those who have major and possibly even minor defects. No matter how strong their motivation for work may be, the physically handicapped, the emotionally unstable, the intellectually retarded, the former criminal, the reformed alcoholic often will be passed over not once but repeatedly. They will be barred from demonstrating that despite their handicap or record they are capable of performing effectively. Many of them will simply not have a chance.

But when jobs are plentiful it is much easier for the handicapped group to succeed, not only because employers are less critical, but because the marginal group realizes that others like them, and some possibly more handicapped, have succeeded in getting a job and performing satisfactorily. The knowledge of this fact is a substantial reinforcement of their own drive to try, and helps to still the uncertainties and doubts which might otherwise immobilize them, especially if they have been repeatedly rebuffed.

The challenge that the more seriously handicapped face is to build up and exploit their strengths to compensate for their defects. There is, however, little incentive for a man to put forth the effort if he knows from the outset that his chances of succeeding are very slim indeed. Rather than to try and fail, he prefers to let his strengths lie idle. At least he need not compound his difficulties by being rebuffed. But if he sees all about him men whom he considers no better, or perhaps even less able, than he getting and holding jobs, then the spur is great indeed. And the chances are greater that if he makes the effort, he too will succeed.

A full employment economy makes still another contribution to marginal persons. When employers recognize that the only way they can add to their labor force is by employing people who have shortcomings, they will be encouraged to restudy their jobs to see whether some of the more difficult ones might be simplified and thereby brought within the competence range of the potential working group. To the extent that this is done, the handicapped will be in a better position to find work within their competence, and if they do, they will be much more likely to perform effectively.

This comment about the matching of jobs to men points to another facet of the problem. In a country as large as the United States with such a highly diversified economy, it is exceedingly difficult for men to know the range of work which is available and for which they might qualify. Men cannot make the most of themselves and their assets unless they know about the opportunities that are available. The handicapped person who has not been regularly employed is likely to be poorly informed about the jobs that are available or are likely to become available. Yet his need for this information is the greater since he can qualify for a smaller number than a worker without disabilities.

While improved guidance and counseling services and more active employer participation in providing opportunities are required if larger numbers of marginal people are to perform effectively, they need further help. They frequently cannot meet the demands of a job without some prior medical or other rehabilitative assistance. While voluntary and governmental efforts along these lines have been expanded considerably over the past years in many parts of the country, they are still inadequate. But it must be emphasized that rehabilitation can only help a handicapped person get a job; it cannot insure that he will do so. Whether he does or not will continue to depend primarily on the total availability of jobs.

The availability of jobs and widespread information about them and how they can be secured can contribute more than any other factor to helping people become and remain effective. The more jobs there are, the easier it is for a person with a handicap to find one with which he can cope. And as more handicapped people succeed in getting jobs, others who have defects will be encouraged to make a special effort to do likewise.

The foregoing summary of the more important individual, organizational, and environmental factors that influence performance should indicate its complex nature when it is viewed as a social phenomenon. Because of this complexity we will order some of our more generalized findings around three basic concepts of performance—those of level, range, and time, the last conceived in terms of continuity. Each will be considered briefly in turn.

Level of Performance

One of the striking characteristics of every technologically advanced society is the very wide differences in the occupational levels at which individuals perform. Contrast the man who holds down a simple laboring job which makes the most modest demands, intellectually and emotionally, with the work of Einstein who transformed for all time the world of ideas and action.

These differences in levels of performance, while reflecting in the first instance marked variations in the individuals' qualities at birth, may also mirror the external environment and the opportunities and stresses it presents. As we have noted, in the depression of the 1930s many millions of capable persons were unable to perform effectively for the simple reason that jobs were not available. And many hundreds of thousands of men who had been able to cope, by and large, with the demands of a civilian environment were unable to meet the special challenges involved in serving in an army at war.

Our industrial society with its exceedingly fine division of labor contributes greatly to enabling the maximum number of people to perform at a satisfactory, if not optimal, level by presenting such a grading of opportunities that men of vastly differing capacities, interests, and motivation can find appropriate jobs. The fact that many Americans have been willing, if not eager, to move from one region to another and from one job to another in the hope of bettering themselves has insured that they avail themselves of the advantages inherent in our increasingly differentiated labor market.

The major factor which determines the level at which an individual performs is his education and training. Every year more and more jobs in the economy are open only to men who have graduated from high school, college, or professional school. Increasingly, employers are less concerned about what a man has already learned than about his potential for further learning on the job. This is also true of the Armed Services, which have repeatedly sought relief from the Congress so that they would not have to accept for military service poorly educated men with little potential for learning the new skills required.

While education, skill, and the potential for acquiring further skills are the most important factors determining the level of a man's performance, they are not the only ones. One of the outstanding characteristics of present-day America is the high proportion of young people who graduate from high school—almost 7 out of every 10—and the strikingly high proportion of male high-school graduates who go on to college—approximately 1 out of every 2. We will not consider here the crucial question of the relationships between the years of formal schooling and the quantity and quality of knowledge acquired; it is sufficient to note that if a high-school or college graduate is emotionally unstable or poorly motivated, his education and training will not of themselves insure that he performs effectively, surely not at a level commensurate with his preparation. Since performance makes a demand on the whole person, not only on his skills, many fail because of emotional or behavioral defects.

The fact that our society offers a great variety of jobs and patterns of life with tremendous variations in demand, however, markedly reduces the number of individuals who cannot find a level of work at which they can meet at least minimum performance requirements. Relatively few jobs make a demand on all of an individual's competences. This means that men with some kind of defect, even a serious one, may be able to perform effectively in a vast number of even demanding jobs. A minor impairment in eyesight or hearing may prevent a young man from gaining admission to West Point, but severe paralysis did not prevent Franklin Delano Roosevelt from being elected President and serving as Commander-in-Chief of the Army and Navy during the most important war in the nation's history.

Individuals will usually seek out work which will enable them to make the most of their strengths and where their deficiencies and defects will handicap them as little as possible. The freer the economy and the society and the more rapidly it is expanding, the greater opportunity individuals will have to find a niche where they will be able to perform effectively. One of the serious handicaps which encumbers an army during a period of mobilization is the pressure of time, which precludes giving soldiers an opportunity to explore where they can best fit in.

Sometimes it is not lack of time but lack of flexibility that interferes with people finding the most suitable level at which to perform. For centuries it was taken for granted that the younger sons of the British nobility had a choice only between a military career and the Church. If they had an inclination towards neither, they were likely to encounter serious difficulties in finding a career since the mores of the culture presented few, if any, alternatives.

College advisors in the United States are often confronted with a contemporary manifestation of this problem. The sons of professors often have no special intellectual aptitude or interest. Yet many of these youngsters feel that their parents and friends expect them to do well at school and enter a profession. For many years they are prevented by their family and class ties from acting to circumvent their weaknesses and building on their strengths. Some never succeed in facing up to the fact that they are not suited to an academic or professional career, but the world of business has begun to have sufficient prestige in the United States to offer most of them a suitable alternative.

While American business is constantly raising its educational and training requirements for employment, it is incorrect to assume that most jobs require a high order of mental and emotional effort. Some do, but the majority do not. No competent observer of the American scene would question the generalization that the vast majority of the population are working below, some considerably below, the level of which they are capable of performing.

Moreover, there are many millions of jobs in the economy which are sufficiently routinized that individuals with quite modest intellectual or emotional equipment can handle them. In fact, the low order of demands built into many of these jobs makes it possible for individuals even with severe handicaps to handle them.

Historically, farming and other types of family business presented an ideal environment within which marginal persons could work. The demands of the job could be adjusted so that individuals with special disabilities could meet them. The contemporary counterpart for this historically protective environment is employment in simple service or clerical jobs. The fact that there is such a great diversity of jobs available, many of which make only the most modest demands, doubtless contributes to increasing the numbers who are able to perform at least at a satisfactory minimum level.

This diversity has another important advantage. It implies that there are many opportunities and significant rewards available for the man who wants to apply himself to his work. And while outstanding success may require talent as well as motivation, diligent application will enable many to advance.

A job helps to give structure and meaning to one's life and a person of limited strength is likely to gain considerable reassurance from the fact that others are willing to employ and pay him. As long as such a person is able to keep his place in the productive economy his self-doubts are less haunting. And the longer he succeeds in performing effectively, the less worried he will generally be about his deficiencies.

Range of Performance

A second major facet of performance is that of range: there are marked differences in the performance of individuals in similar jobs. Every supervisor knows that when he must get extra work out, there are some men on whom he can rely and others who will probably hamper the effort. In many organizations, men with the same title and the same salaries differ greatly in their actual performance. These differences often reflect varying orders of personal strengths or weaknesses. One man may be much more intelligent and well-trained than the next; and if he is also more stable emotionally, more strongly motivated, and has more physical stamina, his performance is certain to be superior.

But often differences in the range, i.e., quality, of performance reflect not individual differences so much as variation in leadership and organizational policy. Senior executives of large organizations frequently see that similar work teams have quite different production records. One is conspicuously better than the other. Inquiry usually discloses that part, and sometimes all, of the difference in the range of performance can be traced back to differences in the quality of the leadership in the two units. In one the supervisory group knows how to elicit the best that is within their work force; in the other the supervisors and the men are in conflict with the result clearly reflected in output. An outstanding example of this from World War II was when Headquarters in the European Theater had to relieve four commanders in turn before it found one who was able to get a particular division, whose men had been well-selected and trained, to perform effectively.

Sometimes differences in the range of performance can be traced more to variations in policy than to the leadership per se. For example, some hospitals in the United States have been reluctant to permit nurses and medical technicians to assume responsibilities commensurate with their training and competence. Others have been eager to delegate as much responsibility as the law will permit. Employees of the latter group are much more likely to perform at the upper range of their capacities.

The way in which an organization assigns men may also affect the range of their performance. When during World War II a Southern farmer was put into a company of tough boys from a Northern city, he felt lost. Had he been with men whom he knew and liked and from whom he could have drawn support, he would have been much more likely to have performed successfully.

Differences in the range of performance may also arise because of conditions existing in the environment which directly or indirectly influence the attitudes and behavior of men. Sometimes the environment has a positive effect, as when men are fighting on their own land to protect their homes and loved ones. It is generally recognized that the heroic defensive fighting of the Russian people during World War II against the invading Nazi armies arose out of such a situation. In sharp contrast was the depression which afflicted many American prisoners of war in the Pacific who had been captured by the Japanese early in the war and who were cut off for years from any contact whatever with the outside world. Many died because they could not make the effort required even to continue living in the face of great deprivations. The situation was so terrible that they lost the will to live.

Although the evidence is not easy to come by, many employers are convinced that in periods of prosperity when the demand for labor is very strong, many individuals slacken their efforts and their performance begins to slip. In contrast, when a recession gets under way and particularly if the numbers of unemployed should increase significantly, most members of the work force put forth additional effort and pay more attention to their work, with a corresponding gain in their output.

Another example of how the environment may affect the range of performance was the substantial testimony from the field commanders in Korea that after Negroes were integrated into combat units, most of them made a special effort to do well for they realized that they were being watched by all—white and Negro alike. Those who were prejudiced against them were sure that they would not stand up in combat. And their friends were anxiously awaiting proof that they would do as well as the next man, if not better. It soon became clear that the performance of Negro troops improved markedly when the Army began to treat them without regard to their color.

Under certain conditions the environment can encourage men to draw on their reserves and perform better than previously; in other instances it can be so depressive or overwhelming that men lose hope and their spirits flag to a point where their performance deteriorates badly. We have seen, then, that the environment, like an individual's characteristics or an organization's policy, can operate either positively or negatively to alter the range within which men perform.

Continuity in Performance

The third important facet, that of continuity and therefore also of discontinuity, can help to clarify the relative importance of the basic determinants of performance. We have seen that if minor fluctuations are disregarded, some men tend to perform at the same level or in the same range—be it high or low—throughout most or all of their lives, while others show marked variations in their patterns of performance which follow changes within themselves or within the external environment.

While no man goes through life performing always at his highest possible level, a considerable proportion of the total population succeed in maintaining a basic continuity in their performance pattern.

When crisis or illness strikes, they have sufficient resources so that they are not overwhelmed, and although their performance may deteriorate, they keep going until the difficult situation is behind them and they can again build up the resources which will enable them once more to perform effectively.

Another pattern of continuity is reflected by people who are born with or early develop such severe handicaps—physical, emotional, or mental—that they never even acquire the basic education and skills which in our society are prerequisite for effective performance. And there are others who, while they succeed in going through school and sometimes even college, develop major emotional disorders in late adolescence or young adulthood which may hold them prisoner for the rest of their lives.

Still other groups have a more or less consistently poor record of performance. They are the men with serious behavior problems who seem to be in constant conflict with the rules of society; some become alcoholics, others use drugs, and still others engage in overt criminal behavior. While some of these men do succeed in bringing their aberrant behavior under control, a high proportion are unable to do so and their record is one long story of ineffective performance.

Many individuals perform well, even with outstanding success, in certain environments but fail in others. We are not considering in this connection those whose failure is caused by a lack of knowledge and experience required to cope with the specific problems in the new environment. Our interest here lies with the individual who does not have the emotional elasticity required to meet altered circumstances. It has been noted by many historians that the man who successfully engineers a revolution seldom if ever is able to consolidate and stabilize the gains. To take another example: the British public questioned Churchill's skill for peacetime leadership, but they had correctly estimated his potentialities for taking the helm in war. Much less spectacular examples were the many members of the Regular Army and National Guard who had excellent and sometimes even superior ratings in peacetime, but who failed when confronted with the exigencies of war. Apparently they could perform well in the stabilized environment of peace, but were overwhelmed by the speed and flux which characterized the emergency.

Individuals perform differently in different circumstances but the change in their performance is often a reflection of internal factors. Acute observers have noted that certain individuals appear to do better under the severe stresses of modern war when their life is endangered than in the normal pursuits of peacetime. This happens, but it is the exception. We also called attention to the more typical situation where individuals who perform effectively in the normal pursuits of life may fail to do so if they are forced to confront a new and strange set of circumstances. Both of these instances involve individuals who sometimes perform effectively, and at other times do not.

The more supportive and rehabilitative services which a society provides, the larger will be the proportion of those who have failed who can later succeed. We noted earlier that large organizations are likely to be able to provide various kinds of support which will reduce the toll of ineffectiveness and which will speed the recovery of those who break down. But voluntary and governmental agencies also have a major responsibility. Many types of assistance go far beyond the resources of even the largest employer. For instance, since many become ineffective because of the onset of a serious emotional disorder which requires hospitalization, the nature and speed of their recovery will depend in the first instance on the quality of the mental hospitals in the community and their follow-up services. There is increasing agreement among experts in the fields of medicine and rehabilitation that the crucial time for helping people who become emotionally disturbed is at an early stage of their illness before their ties with the world of work become severed. After a man has tried several times to return to a self-supporting status and failed, he is likely to develop an adjustment to his disability that will prove very difficult to reverse. Society has a major stake in providing sufficient services to help all those who begin to fail so as to prevent a permanent adjustment to failure.

Fortunately, the factors responsible for the onset of ineffective behavior in many individuals prove to be self-limiting and these people are usually able to reknit their lives with little or no assistance from the outside. This may be the case when ineffectiveness is precipitated by a major personal crisis, such as the death of a spouse or the recurrence of emotional depression. In such cases time may bring relief and provide the basis for recovery. As his depression lifts, the individual again feels capable of coping with the demands of reality and can again perform effectively.

These findings about continuity in performance point to four major life patterns of performance. Some people tend to perform effectively almost all of the time. Others tend to do well most of their lives but experience a period of ineffective performance when in a new environment or because of an emotional disturbance. If they can escape from the difficult environment, their difficulties may largely disappear. And, if their ineffectiveness results from an emotional disturbance that is not too deep, time is also likely to bring a change for the better. Still other men perform satisfactorily for some period of their lives but then encounter a situation which appears to "break them." They are unable to recover from this experience or rather from what was touched off by it. Finally, there are some who never perform effectively.

**THE WASTE OF
HUMAN RESOURCES**

Many years ago Dean Swift commented on the fact that there were more holidays than workdays in Ireland. Even today, most agricultural countries are characterized by heavy underemployment, even unemployment. But it was not until men left the farm for the city and had to buy their bread with their wages that the problem of jobs assumed a new significance.

It was a long time before economists realized that unemployed men represent a great waste, since the labor that they could have performed was lost forever. Since they did know how to control the business cycle, the economists—together with the bankers and industrialists—waited for conditions to right themselves, which they usually did.

However, the problems that England faced in its coal-mining regions after World War I and the blistering depression that began in the United States in 1929 took an unparalleled toll affecting not only adults but children, not only the unemployed but the entire society. This story is told in Chapters 11 and 12.

The wastes of manpower stemming from unemployment are important, but they are not the only ones. The more our economy becomes dependent on skill, the more we need to invest in people. The illiterate and the uneducated have no position in an advanced technological society. We see this in Chapter 13.

There are other sources of waste in addition to the wastes which result from unemployment and underinvestment in people. When the market acts to discriminate against certain groups or when management is inept, manpower will be misallocated or underutilized. Chapters 14 and 15 are focused on these important sources of waste and on the ways in which the waste can be reduced, if not eliminated.

Since the end of World War II we have come increasingly to appreciate that human resources are the key to economic development, that the rate of economic progress depends in large measure on the level of skill of the population, and that therefore the reduction and elimination of the waste of human resources must be a principal objective of a progressive economy and society.

11. UNEMPLOYED COAL MINERS

During a motor trip from North Wales on a road that traversed beautiful woods and rich agricultural lands, the visitor to South Wales was repeatedly warned by his companions about the intolerable conditions that he would find in the coal mining villages. When the map showed South Wales to be just over the hills the visitor was certain that his companions had been exaggerating, for the landscape continued warm and friendly. Soon the car was in Bwlch Pass on the road from Brecon to Abergavenny. Tradition has it that once through Bwlch Pass, a Welshman never returns. Crickhowell came into view and in the background was the Sugar Loaf, scarcely discernible through the rain. South Wales was wetter than North or Central Wales, but this was the only difference. Because of the torrent the charming village of Gilwern and the heavy woods of Clydach were difficult to appreciate, but that South Wales was charming was easy to establish. Established it was, but not for long, for there soon came into view the industrial ruins and human tombs of the Northern Outcrop, the oldest and most depressed region in South Wales: Nanty-Glo, Blaina, Brynmawr. It was clear that the mines had long been inactive. But not so clear was the fact that men, women, and children were living in the foreshortened houses that lined the streets and the terraced hills. These houses looked like stone blocks, chipped and dirtied by an active child who had put them together in a pattern all his own. These were the homes of His Majesty's subjects at a time when Great Britain was enjoying great industrial prosperity.

At Tredegar the visitor left the car to await the bus for Merthyr Tydfil. The square in Tredegar could boast of the office of the Tredegar

Workmen's Medical Aid Society, the society for which Cronin's hero had labored and lost. Although it was five-thirty in the afternoon, a time when streets are usually thronged with men and women on their way home from work, the square in Tredegar was deserted. Nor was there a single customer in the sweets shop where the visitor took refuge from the rain. And while his cup of tea was brewing he concluded that the proprietor had made few sales that day or on previous days, for the merchandise on the ancient fixtures was heavy with dust.

The bus to Merthyr finally came! The proprietor of the shop had been uncertain from what corner it would leave or at what time. It was a new and spacious bus in striking contrast to the houses and shops that lined the square. After a short distance, people going to Merthyr had to push their way through the crowded bus and out into the rain in order to transfer to another that would take them to their destination. There were few people abroad when the bus reached the outskirts of Merthyr, for the rain was ever heavier and even a record sprinter would have been soaked to the skin in running the block between the bus depot and the hotel.

It was a hotel with neither office nor clerks, and one was fortunate indeed to stumble across a chamber maid who knew which rooms were vacant. If four walls, a ceiling, and a floor make a room there were many rooms; and if a bed, chairs, and a bureau furnish a room then there were many furnished rooms. The bed posts sloped, each in a different direction; the mattress, in harmony with the contours of the land, had deep valleys and high hills. The mirror was so badly shattered that it reflected only its own cracks, and if one sat on the chair one came into contact with exposed nail heads. There were a dining-room and a parlor also in a state of great disrepair, and the waiter who served supper wore garments from another age.

Through the sheets of rain one could dimly discern, on the farther side of the street, shops without merchandise in their windows and others with boards nailed against their panes. Neither man nor beast was abroad that night, because the rain was now torrential and the only thing out of doors that moved was the occasional trolley, whose parts must have been wrought of the best Merthyr iron, for its design permitted of no doubt that it had been in operation since the days of Queen Victoria. There were only two men in the hotel that night—one a refugee manufacturer from Czechoslovakia, who told of the tragedies that had befallen his country when Hitler brought culture from Berlin to Prague; the other a Scottish engineer who was supervising the installation of machinery in a new factory that the British government was erecting nearby, out of reach of Hitler's legions if ever they should turn their attention to the West. Sometime after midnight the heavy rain let up, and shortly after dawn there was a noise that sounded like hail. But soon all was quiet, and the calm remained unbroken, for in Merthyr people did not go to work in the morning except for a few miners whose nailed boots sounded on the pavement shortly after dawn. These men left their homes at 4:30 A.M., for they had to travel as much as twenty miles to the mine and the morning shift began at 6:00 A.M.

So long have unemployment and destitution been part of the life of South Wales that only visitors are struck by the patterns of living; the people of the valleys are no longer aware of the transformations that have taken place. Work and wages are only dim recollections and to the young they are not even recollections. The visitor to South Wales soon loses the strength of his first reactions to a country in which work is the exception, and comes to accept as normal the life he sees about him. A sensitive observer once remarked that the towns of the Northern Outcrop appeared to be asleep.

Sleep and unemployment are closely associated. When the mines first closed down men enjoyed the luxury of sleep; but after several years rising late was no longer a novel pleasure, yet the unemployed miners continued in their new ways and remained in bed until late in the morning. They discovered that it was easier to idle time away in darkness than in daylight and therefore preferred to turn day into night and night into day. Moreover remaining in bed had the advantage of offering protection from damp and cold, especially when garments became thin and fuel had to be hauled a long distance. Most important, it was easier if one remained in bed to do with less food. Late rising permitted one to telescope two meals, breakfast and lunch, as many Americans do on Sunday.

Twice a week the unemployed would rise somewhat earlier, for during the course of the morning they would sign on at the employment exchange. This was not an unpleasant chore, for it gave them something to do, and if the weather was good a man could hang around the exchange for a few hours talking with his buddies. The week had several other breaks, especially for the able-bodied who supplied their households with coal of their own picking. The journey to the coal level and the journey back usually took the better part of a day.

Many men spent several mornings or several afternoons a week working on their allotment; some became expert in getting their small strips to yield large quantities of potatoes and greens. It was indeed unfortunate that were were too few allotments, for not only did the potatoes and greens help to check malnutrition but cultivating a plot was a great boon to the unemployed since it gave them something useful to do. Occasionally an ex-miner became so attached to his strip of land that he adamantly refused to consider migration or training. Allotments, however, contributed more to slowing the demoralization of the unemployed than to hindering their successful transference.

There remained many hours in the week when the unemployed were not busy signing on at the exchange, collecting fuel, or tilling their allotments. Time hangs heavily on the wealthy who can buy what they desire and travel where they please, but for the poor idleness is really painful. Walking up and down the main street in the company of their buddies and taking careful note of the position and price of every article in the windows offered the unemployed companionship and activity. And it cost nothing. This walking to and fro continued for hours on end, especially after dark. The more observant window-shoppers knew when an article disappeared, was shifted to another place, or was reduced in price, and many merchants related that the unemployed were better acquainted with their stock than were their own employees.

But there were many days in the year when walking was difficult, for the poor could not indulge in the luxury of walking in the rain—at least not without serious consequence. Their clothing was poor protection against the elements and the food that awaited them upon their return was insufficient to replenish their energies. On wet days —and there were many such—and even on dry days the men passed many hours sitting at home. They just sat. Occasionally they would read a book or magazine, but frequently they would be preoccupied only with their phantasies.

Once or twice a week there was greyhound racing and for threepence one could gain admission and watch the sleek hounds chasing the electric rabbit. One could watch a favorite win or lose, a favorite because it belonged to a friend and one had had a hand in training it. At the races one could give advice to the betters, who seldom knew much about the finer points, and on rare occasions one could even place a shilling bet.

In season the monotony was also considerably reduced by football, for whether one bet or not—and most people did place small bets— one had favorites whose playing one followed in great detail. Rare indeed was the man who was as concerned about Hitler as he was about his favorite team.

Of course there were movies, with glamour girls and cowboys, and the unemployed could gain admission in the afternoon for as little as threepence. But few among the older men enjoyed the movies. When they took a few pence from their unemployment allowance they preferred to spend them in the pub, not on whisky or even beer, for these were too expensive, but on draught cider. This was not a real drink, but at least it was served in a pub, and real drinks might not have been good for men who neither ate properly nor worked regularly.

There was the perennial question of cigarettes. The Unemployment Assistance Board did not include cigarettes in its budget and many worthy citizens were outraged when they saw the unemployed enjoying a few puffs. The men of South Wales took puffs, they did not smoke. A cigarette would be lighted and after two or three draws it would be extinguished, to be relit later. Frequently a cigarette was divided into three or four parts so that one could share a smoke with one's buddies.

Such was the daily existence of tens of thousands of men in the valleys of South Wales, who in a better day had swung their picks for eight long hours, had drunk many quarts of beer on the way home, and after eating a ravenous meal had fallen exhausted into bed only to start the round again next morning. But this was hearsay, for now one saw emaciated, toothless figures aged much beyond their years, with threadbare garments hanging loosely from their stooped shoulders. These were men in a trance.

While the unemployed man succumbs to idleness, his wife deteriorates from overwork. In the days of prosperity the lot of the miner's wife had been far from easy. With a husband and perhaps a son or two in the mines, and with younger children at school or at her apron strings, managing a household was a formidable undertaking. Cooking and scrubbing alternated with scrubbing and cooking; coal dust could easily be washed from the bodies of the men, but it was difficult to keep the floors free of it. In South Wales the women had always been the managers and except in emergencies had been able to run their households without difficulty. The postwar years, however, were one long emergency, and as the spell of their husbands' unemployment lengthened management became increasingly difficult. Since the relief allowances were woefully insufficient, the housewife was constantly perplexed in meeting the most insistent needs of her family. In most homes children took precedence, and every effort was made that they should not go hungry. Next came the men, for despite everything most wives continued to have real affection for their husbands and realized that the family's plight was not due to personal failings of their menfolk. The women also realized that their husbands, deprived of the pleasures and companionship of work, were suffering grievously, and they strained to check the despondency of their men. But it was not easy to find money for the glass of cider or the package of cigarettes that they knew would help, and many were the deprivations that the women inflicted on themselves so that their husbands might not become utterly miserable.

Well-informed observers in the valleys, physicians and laymen alike, testified to the fact that the women carried the major burden of hard times. That the incidence of illness and death among them did not mount by leaps and bounds can only be explained by the fact that the women had a struggle from which they could not retire. So long as the struggle did not appear hopeless, just so long could a wife find satisfaction in keeping the gloom from settling completely on her husband and in helping her children prepare for adulthood.

Of course poverty took its toll; even the best-natured wife and the most devoted mother—and many were neither good-natured nor devoted—would sometimes snap under the strain. Conflict could not be avoided when her husband wanted a shilling to have a blow with, while she wanted it for the clothing fund so that one of the youngsters might have a pair of shoes when school opened. And it was not always easy to avoid quarreling, especially during spells of bad weather when the men were continually under foot.

Harassed with duties and bereft of clothes, at least without the clothes that would not shame her in public, the wife of the unemployed man had little relaxation. She neither went visiting nor encouraged visitors. Gossip with the neighbors next door alone remained. Naturally there were movies and fiction magazines, good escapes but occasionally a little too good, for they dealt primarily with people who restrained themselves from eating because of their figures and who wore few clothes for reasons of style.

The women suffered most, however, from being precipitated into the position of head of the household, and, although the more sensitive tried hard to protect the morale of their men by usurping as few male responsibilities as possible, more and more women came to treat their husbands as their eldest children, a relationship demoralizing not only to their husbands and themselves, but especially to their children.

From one point of view the young were the most fortunate, for misery was part of their world from the day of their birth, and they were therefore spared the hurt that came from memories of older and better days. But the failure to have known family life when father worked all day, when there was ample food on the table, when the cost of amusements did not have to be calculated to the last penny—the failure to have known all this was sadly crippling, though the injury was not painful. There was much damage done to a child who grew up in a home in which the mother was straining herself constantly; in which the father was frequently the head of the household in name only; where the pay packet was unknown and disciplined routine something encountered only in school; where mealtimes were so far apart and food so scanty that discomfort was frequent; where one was forced to wear the already much worn garments of other children. A child forced to do and suffer these many things from the first days of consciousness might take them for granted, especially if the same conditions prevailed in other homes; but ignorance of better things was no protection against evil, for, as the statistics of infant deaths and children's diseases so clearly showed, poverty insisted upon claiming its victims.

South Wales had an infant mortality approximately 20 per cent greater than that of England, and the virulent childhood diseases, especially diphtheria and scarlet fever, struck with greater intensity in the impoverished coal-mining villages of South Wales. Nutritional examinations of school children further confirmed the physical deterioration that followed in the wake of poverty. In Merthyr Tydfil statistics showed that 25 to 35 per cent of the children in grade school were suffering from either bad or subnormal nutrition, and one can be sure that the examining physician in establishing a norm erred on the side of optimism. With a community largely dependent upon public assistance it would have been risky for him to do otherwise. In his Second Report, the Commissioner for the Special Areas of England and Wales called attention to the low medical standard of boys and young men in the areas, and confirmation of the Commissioner's statement can be found in the examinations made by a physician attached to an important Birmingham firm. Out of a group of 64 boys he found only 17 to be in adequate health.

Although successive Ministers of Health reiterated that the nation's health was satisfactory, other experts were less sanguine. The latter were not always able to support their contentions with statistics, but they knew that the children of the poor were not receiving an adequate diet. In 1936 the School Medical Officer of Merthyr Tydfil remarked in his report that "it is an extraordinary thing to me, knowing intimately the distressed economic conditions under which the great majority of the people of this borough are living, that there are not a greater number of malnourished or subnormal children." A child may not present a clinical picture of malnutrition and yet be suffering from insufficient and poor feeding.

The Report of the Committee of Inquiry into the Anti-Tuberculosis Service in Wales and Monmouthshire presented considerable evidence of excessive mortality in respiratory tuberculosis in young adults between the ages of fifteen and twenty-five. Although the mortality rate in England for this group showed a steady decline in the period 1921–25 to 1931–35, the male death rate in Wales fell only slightly and the female death rate actually rose. The female death rate from respiratory tuberculosis in South Wales during the years 1931–35 was almost 70 per cent higher than the corresponding rate for England. In Merthyr Tydfil the mortality rate for females between the ages of fifteen and thirty-five was about two and one-half times the expectance standard for England and Wales. The Report suggests that poor nutrition had probably played an important part in heightening the susceptibility of females to this disease. Several well-informed medical men in the valleys suggested that the excessively high rates for young women must in part be explained by the fact that after a childhood of deprivation they left for posts in the Midlands and London, where their work taxed their strength and endurance, and their already weakened constitutions were not up to the strain. They suffered breakdowns and then returned to South Wales to linger or die.

For the entire country 9 per cent of the male and 18 per cent of the female applicants in receipt of Unemployment Assistance Allowances in October 1938 commenced their current spell of unemployment after a period of illness. Only 7 per cent of the men were below thirty-five but as many as 17 per cent of the women were less than twenty-five. Clearly the health of young adults left much to be desired, especially the health of young women. Nor were many young men in good health, as can be seen by the large number of applicants who were refused admission to the army for reasons of health.

Offspring of the poor were more likely to die in infancy than were the offspring of the rich; if they did not die, they were more likely to contract infectious diseases in childhood; if they survived, they were more likely to become tubercular in adulthood. Children of the unemployed ran all the risks of children of the poor and some additional ones. Not only their bodies were likely to be crippled, but also their souls. School teachers complained bitterly about the inability of their charges to arrive on time. But, what was worse, once the youngsters were in their seats instruction proceeded slowly, for most pupils were apathetic. The more sensitive teachers realized that this dullness, which resembled paralysis, was not hereditary. Accuse the Welsh of anything else, but not of slow-wittedness. The lethargy of the pupils was clearly the result of conditions at home, where prolonged unemployment had broken the morale of their fathers and had added substantially to the burdens of their mothers. Where life tomorrow could only be more difficult than life today, no child could be reared normally, not even if parents strained to hide their true feelings. The fact that father was under foot all day with nothing to do, and the further fact that mother was constantly harassed and therefore had little free time—these simple and persistent facts which could not be brushed aside wrought most of the havoc.

Unemployment has persisted for so long in certain parts of South Wales that children have come to working age without ever having seen their fathers in employment. This is true not only for one family but for many. Not knowing the meaning of work, these adolescents are adjusted to unemployment without ever having been in employment. The Commissioners for the Special Areas repeatedly warned that many young men were content to live in idleness as state pensioners and unwilling to make any effort to find work. Although the Commissioners realized that the demoralization of these youths derived from circumstances beyond their own control, for they had grown up in an atmosphere of idleness and had never had a chance to experience the inspiration of work or the pride of earning a living for themselves and their families, they felt that despite these extenuating circumstances these youths represented a most unhealthy element in the body politic.

Toward the end of 1937 the Unemployment Assistance Board made a study of its younger applicants, i.e., those under thirty years of age, and discovered that a large number, though a minority, showed a tendency to settle down on the allowance and to accept as inevitable a life of idleness. Of course if jobs were offered them in their own locality at wages substantially higher than their allowances, and if the conditions of work were pleasant, only a few would refuse employment. The most thorough study of unemployed young men in South Wales suggested that the "work-shy" did not exceed 10 per cent; but this figure does not allow for all the conditions that would have to be fulfilled before many would accept work, and since these conditions could seldom be met insistence upon their fulfillment was the equivalent of refusal to work.

Although a small number of young men were disinclined to accept any sort of employment because they found the allowances of the Unemployment Assistance Board sufficient for their needs, and although others were inclined to trade their allowance only for desirable jobs, the majority sought private employment because they were thoroughly dissatisfied with a life of leisure. The unemployed young man could usually scrape together enough to attend the cinema once or at most twice a week. Occasionally he could afford to go to a dance, but even though the admission price was low dancing was more difficult; one could wear patched garments in the dark recesses of a modern theater, but not at a dance. Unless the weather was very bad one could walk about, usually with one's buddy. Once a week one might take a girl for a stroll, though it was difficult to keep company with a young lady unless one had money to spend, at least a little money. But just this little was hard to get. Nor were sports an easy outlet. There were few playing fields in the valleys, for the land was uneven and there was the further problem of equipment and clothing. It was difficult enough from the meager allowances of the Board to provide shoes for ordinary use let alone sneakers or other specialized clothing.

The young women who remained in the valleys usually assisted their mothers or, if their mothers were ailing or dead, carried the entire burden of running the household. Although they did not earn wages, they were not unemployed and leisure was no problem. Like the boys they spent their evenings walking the streets in the company of their friends and once or twice a week tried to lose themselves by watching the lives and loves of their favorite actors and actresses. The prettier among them attended a dance now and again, or at least had male companionship for an evening.

Unemployment and poverty forced the older folk, men and women alike, to sacrifice one after another the activities which in the days of prosperity had given meaning to their lives, whereas unemployment and poverty made it almost impossible for their children even to become acquainted with these activities. In former decades chapel and trade-union gave meaning and direction to life in South Wales. At the time of Wales's greatest trial, however, chapel and trade-union were unable to help. In fact, the strength that had been theirs had ebbed away and what remained was a shrunken framework from which the spirit had departed. True, street cars did not run in Merthyr on Sunday mornings and no pub could be open on the Lord's day, but the survival of these prohibitions reflected the lethargy and poverty of the populace rather than the strength of the chapel.

Church buildings were in great disrepair, and church finances were even worse. In the later thirties the total debt of the churches situated in the more depressed regions of South Wales was over 400,000 pounds, a debt that swallowed all current income. Although the towns and villages in the Special Areas of South Wales could boast of more than 1,100 churches, less than half were able to support ministers. Attendance was poor and the congregations were composed largely of people too old to change or of juveniles too young to revolt; these few were drawn primarily from the thin ranks of the employed. In part this decline in chapel life reflected the mediocre quality of the ministry, which possessed neither the spiritual nor the intellectual stamina of the ministry of an earlier day. Ministers in South Wales, like ministers elsewhere, sought to distinguish between the material and spiritual, an especially dangerous dichotomy for South Wales, where men's beliefs and actions had long been of one piece. When unemployment struck the valleys the chapels could have held their own only by a heightened concern for man's relation to man.

In its heyday the chapel in addition to being a house of worship was school, political forum, and social club. The young received instruction in the Holy Scriptures and in Welsh. In his sermons the minister emphasized rather than eschewed contemporary problems. Most important of all, the chapel was the center of social activity. It was in the chapel that choirs practiced and sang, and boys met the girls who were later to become their wives. All this and more the chapel contributed to the culture of South Wales, and from all this the unemployed were cut off. Poverty was largely responsible, for attendance at services meant dressing in one's best clothes and offering a contribution. As unemployment came and stayed, best clothes became ordinary clothes and eventually patched garments. In these circumstances attendance at chapel became exceedingly difficult. Moreover without money for food it was not easy to contribute to the upkeep of the chapel. Poverty explains much of the decline, but not all, for a ministry sensitive and virile could have salvaged much. But such a ministry did not exist.

Second only to the chapel in molding South Wales was the trade-union. In struggling to escape the serfdom of an exploitative mining industry the men of South Wales contributed bone and blood to form a union, and their sacrifices were not in vain, for at the outbreak of the first World War the miners had an organization second to none in the British trade-union movement. In 1921 organized labor in South Wales suffered a minor defeat, for the strike ended with a reduction in wage rates and a worsening in working conditions. During the next few years the South Wales Miners' Federation was further weakened by the closing of pits and the migration of miners. Despite these reverses organized labor in the several coal fields of Great Britain was sufficiently strong in 1925 to obtain for the coal industry a substantial subsidy from the government. Then came the General Strike of 1926. The General Strike was over in a few days, but South Wales fought on for many months. It was a fight that could never have been won, and when it was finally lost the Federation was broken, its treasury depleted, and its membership distraught. So badly did ranks break in retreat that one expert estimated that the panic cost the coal miners of South Wales millions of pounds in privileges.

With an empty treasury and a disheartened membership, the South Wales Miners' Federation was forced to fight for its very life during the succeeding years, for there sprang up in the valleys of South Wales a dual union. For twelve long years the struggle continued, and it was not until 1938 that the dual union, the South Wales Miners' Industrial Union finally ceased functioning. During its life it precipitated many deplorable incidents, contributed to accelerating the decline in wages, and even led to the imprisonment of members of the South Wales Miners' Federation and their womenfolk.

The Federation was up against it during the years when unemployment was rampant in South Wales; and rampant it was, for in November 1932 more than 40 per cent of all coal miners were out of work and the unemployment rate remained for a long time around 33 per cent. In the more stricken areas many lodges were forced to close because of insufficiency of dues from working members, and many others were forced to merge. In the active lodges considerable friction arose between employed and unemployed members over such questions as the right of the unemployed to vote on strike issues and the use of facilities by the unemployed. With the passage of time a deeper cleavage developed, for the unemployed felt that the Federation was neglecting them, while the employed began to chafe at being forced to carry almost the entire financial burden.

In 1935 the South Wales Miners' Federation included 85,000 employed members and approximately 25,000 unemployed members, and by 1938 it had more than 103,000 employed members and less than 18,000 unemployed. In 1938 the members contributed 86,000 pounds to the union and in addition contributed 9,000 pounds in the form of a political levy for the Labor party. A special Spanish levy netted more than 2,300 pounds, and refunds in compensation cases amounted to another 2,000 pounds. Additional income brought the year's total to more than 100,000 pounds. The union also had, on the 31st of December 1937, reserve funds of approximately 100,000 pounds.

With an income of 100,000 pounds a year, and with a membership of 121,000 out of a possible maximum of 133,000, the South Wales Miners' Federation in 1938 surely presents a picture of strength that substantiates the claim of the executive council, which stated in its Fifth Annual Report that the "organization is healthy and still retains the confidence of the great mass of the workingmen and, we believe, of the general community in the mining area. There is probably no other organization in the world that plays such a vital part in the daily lives of its members and their families and in the community in which it operates as does the South Wales Miners' Federation."

It must, however, be recalled that the Federation revived in the later thirties, partly because of the revival in the coal trade coincidental with the armaments boom, partly because of the exceptional leadership of Arthur Horner. Although Horner's affiliation with the Communists stood in his way while he struggled to become president of the Federation, his commitments to the Party did not prevent him— once he had secured office—from being a very able president. World revolution was forced into the background while Horner used his talents to further organizational drives and to win important negotiations. Despite Horner's phenomenal success in obtaining for the Federation for the second time in its history almost complete control over the coal fields of South Wales, he was unable to win victories for his unemployed members, a failure that reflected inherent difficulties rather than lack of sympathy.

In the decade following the General Strike of 1926, especially in the period after 1929 when the miners of South Wales were in dire need of guidance and assistance, the Federation was unable to help. Organized around the struggles of employed workers, the Federation showed little flexibility in grappling with the problems of derelict communities, but actually even greater flexibility would have been of little use so long as the Federation's financial stringency was not relieved. In the days of its strength the trade-union movement in South Wales had nurtured the growth of Workmen's Institutes, many of which could boast of excellent libraries and fine recreation rooms. The books would have graced the shelves of any college library, and the billiard tables would not have been out of place in exclusive clubs; but that was in the old days. After 1926 many libraries were unable to purchase a single book, and billiard tables were not repaired. Because of fast dwindling resources the Institutes had fewer facilities available, and the unemployed suffered inhibitions and prohibitions about using these facilities that were supported by the employed. Like its sister institution, the chapel, the trade-union suffered from lack of leaders and lack of money at a time when South Wales needed both. But, unlike the chapel, the trade-union toward the end of the thirties made a remarkable recovery, although it was a recovery that contributed little to lightening the burden of the unemployed.

During the General Strike of 1926, especially during the later months of the strike, there could be found in the valleys of South Wales a vanguard of social workers distributing food and essential clothing to the needy. In this advanced guard were members of the Society of Friends who because of training and experience realized that the havoc which they saw was not likely to disappear when the strike was ended. They believed that the basic institutions of South Wales were in collapse, and were convinced that the destruction, unless checked, would feed on itself. Hence they turned part of their energies to the salvage of South Wales, and as early as 1927 in Maes-yr-Haf in the Rhondda Valley opened the first settlement house. Although patterned after settlement houses in English slums, where major emphasis was on educational and social activities, Maes-yr-Haf paid more attention to the direct relieving of distress. In the following year the Society established a community house in Brynmawr in the hope of contributing to the economic reconstruction of this stricken town. Emphasis was placed on retraining coal miners for new industrial activities and on establishing new industries that could use these retrained workers. Some time later the Society established a furniture factory and a shoe factory; but these two undertakings, despite liberal contributions from private sources for developmental and managerial expenses, offered employment to only a few men. The years that followed saw the establishment of additional settlements at Risca, Merthyr, Bargoed, Aberdare, Pontypool, and Pontypridd.

As the late twenties turned into the early thirties the foresight of the Quakers was proved correct, for the economic, social, and cultural deterioration of South Wales accelerated. As conditions deteriorated the need for counterattack became more pressing, but a successful counterattack meant more than settlement houses.

Aware of the horrible ravages that unemployment was causing, not only in South Wales but throughout the whole of Great Britain, the National Council of Social Service organized an important meeting in Albert Hall, London, in January 1932, on which occasion the Prince of Wales broadcast a national appeal to the citizenry to cope with the consequences, if not with the causes, of unemployment and reminded the public that unemployment need not be accepted fatalistically. He viewed it as the work of the devil, which could be exorcised by men of faith and courage. Largely as a result of his appeal the government put funds at the disposal of the National Council of Social Service to enable the Council to extend its work among the unemployed. Specifically the subvention aimed at increasing the number and resources of clubs for unemployed men which had been springing up in the more stricken parts of the country. So rapid was the growth of these clubs after 1932 that the First Annual Report of the South Wales and Monmouthshire Council of Social Service (1934–1935) stated that within the Council's area there were nearly 200 clubs and centers with a total membership in excess of 20,000. Of these clubs 78 were more or less closely linked with settlement and community houses.

The most pressing need of the clubs was adequate premises, and even before government funds were made available the unemployed in many parts of the country—especially in South Wales—had shown great ingenuity and persistence in transforming unused garages, warehouses, and other buildings in noticeable disrepair into quarters that were usable if not entirely suitable for their purposes. The work gave the unemployed something useful to do, and many men were pleased to discover that they had talents previously unknown to them. Boards had to be planed, wires connected, plumbing fixtures installed, and many ex-miners were genuinely surprised at their ability to do such work.

The clubs were largely recreational centers. Billiard tables were their most prized equipment; chess, checkers, and darts were usually provided. The men were also encouraged to work on various materials—leather, wood, pewter—not with the aim of becoming skilled workers nor even with the aim of earning money, but rather with the idea of developing hobbies. It was believed that the unemployed, like the mentally ill, while cut off from normal living would thus find satisfaction. Nor must it be overlooked that when conditions favored—and this meant when able leadership was available—the clubs frequently devoted considerable attention to cultural activities, especially to music, drama, and lectures.

Once government funds were made available for its use, the National Council of Social Service offered the clubs the services of visiting instructors, for the purpose of guiding and supervising their recreational, occupational, and educational activities. The instructor who was able to win the confidence and respect of the club members frequently assumed a dominant position in the community. Dependent largely upon the Council for grants with which to pursue their activities, the clubs nevertheless offered opportunity for the emergence of leaders from the ranks. The fact that men of talent and energy had some opportunity for constructive activity was a major contribution of the clubs toward neutralizing the ravages of persistent unemployment. Moreover, although the South Wales and Monmouthshire Council of Social Service contributed during 1934–35 approximately 8,000 pounds to the clubs, an equal amount was contributed by the members, whose weekly dues of a penny or twopence helped to cover the regular maintenance charges of the club—heating, cleaning, and lighting, the purchase of newspapers, wireless licenses, and sometimes even the payment of rent and rates. The grants from the Council were usually spent for the purchase of equipment, furniture, heating apparatus, tools, gymnastic kits, and other items. The average membership in the clubs varied from 50 to 200; the average for South Wales was 135 members. At first the clubs were limited almost exclusively to unemployed men, but the revival of business throughout the greater part of Great Britain after 1933 changed many unemployed into employed workers. Despite this important shift in status many employed members refused to sever their connections with the clubs, and there is evidence to suggest that they remained among the most active members.

On the basis of a survey completed toward the end of 1937 it appears that about 70 per cent of the membership in South Wales was unemployed. This represents an average for all the valleys, but it must not be overlooked that in the more severely stricken regions, such as the Northern Outcrop, the membership was predominantly unemployed. The survey revealed that over 82 per cent of the unemployed members in South Wales had been out of work for more than one year. The clubs made their greatest appeal to older men, for approximately 70 per cent of the unemployed members of South Wales were above thirty-five years of age.

Although the clubs failed to attract men between the ages of eighteen and thirty-five, a failure sufficiently marked for the Council to comment upon it in its Annual Report of 1937–38, they were nevertheless able to interest the womenfolk—not only the wives of the unemployed, but also the wives of the employed. In 1939 there were 260 women's clubs in South Wales with a membership of approximately 18,000. This was a noticeable achievement, for women in South Wales had always been tied to the home, and it was not easy to break this tie even for a few hours weekly. Even when this was accomplished real difficulties remained, for most women's clubs were forced to depend for their premises upon the good will of the men. Usually the men set aside the entire club at stated periods in the week, or else set aside one or two rooms permanently. The programs of the women's clubs expanded despite these handicaps, for during the first quarter of 1939 attendance during instructional visits of the Council's officers totaled about 50,000 in the handicraft classes, 53,000 in the home classes, and 85,000 in the keep-fit classes.

Transplantation of the English settlement house to the valleys of South Wales was a mistake. The only bridge between the settlement house and Welsh life was the strong tradition of adult education, and an able warden could use this bridge to advantage; but classes in psychology, history, French, and German were not attractive to men and women beset by worries and plagued by hunger, and only a skillful warden who knew his community intimately could overcome its lethargy. Competent wardens and staff members were rare, however, and the failure of the settlements to become integrated with the culture of South Wales must be ascribed primarily to inadequate personnel. The clubs were more nearly indigenous; their growth was therefore more rapid, and their position more secure. But it must not be forgotten that the clubs never served more than one-quarter of the unemployed of South Wales, and the majority of men and women remained cut off from social life. Great poverty and poor leadership explain much of this failure, but mendacious propaganda also contributed, for settlement house and club were constantly under attack.

Some critics ridiculed the teaching of foreign tongues and esoteric subjects to the unemployed. Other critics disparaged the keep-fit classes for women which emphasized "rhythmic exercises to music calculated to give balance to the whole personality; dancing of various types, designed to produce lightness and grace of movement." To these sophisticated objections were added the direct attack of the Communists, who feared the expansion of the Social Service movement, since any alleviation of the plight of the unemployed would reduce their political radicalism. The Communists had a nickname for the settlement house—they called it "the dope house," where injections were administered to the unemployed so that they might more willingly bear their lot. If the salvation of South Wales depended, as the Communists were certain it did, upon political action, their objections were not without point.

But the clubs suffered most from the indifference of the chapel and the antagonism of the trade-unions. Instead of contributing facilities and leadership, the chapel and the trade-union viewed the growth of the clubs with suspicion. Each, intensely jealous of its preserve, looked with disfavor on the growth of a new competitor. Not until the end of 1938, when the competitor could no longer be ignored, did representatives of the Workmen's Institutes and the Social Service Clubs agree upon a *modus vivendi*, and not until war loomed on the horizon was it possible to hold a joint conference of Welsh voluntary organizations.

Exaggerated statements that referred to settlement houses as "power houses of friendship and service" and remarks to the effect that "Mr. Peter Scott had taken this little town (Brynmawr) under his wing" could not fail to outrage the local populace and prejudice it against the Social Service movement. Moreover, distrusting the government, the populace distrusted the Society of Friends and the Council of Social Service, for it believed that these organizations were under government control; and when the populace learned that the government was actually giving financial support to the Council its distrust turned into hostility. Yet despite widespread suspicion, criticism, and antagonism the clubs were able during the nineteen-thirties to gain and hold sizable membership. These members found that the clubs made life a little more tolerable. Not that making toy boats, playing cards, and attending lectures were to be compared to hewing coal, drinking beer, and going to chapel. At best the Social Service movement fought a rear-guard action that aimed to reduce the destruction wrought by unemployment.

So devastating was this destruction that the efforts of the clubs were well-nigh nugatory. Natives of South Wales who had left the valleys in the heyday of their prosperity and who returned for a visit in the late thirties were choked with feelings of sorrow and anger because of the wreckage they saw about them. Their eyes told them that the mines had long been shut and the furnaces had long been dismantled, that the trade-unions no longer celebrated victories, and that chapel services were sparsely attended. The visitors became even more disturbed when they realized that the strength had gone out of the men, the beauty out of the women, and the joy out of the children. All these changes were clear, all too clear. More difficult to probe were the feelings and the thoughts of the people who had suffered these changes. Idleness could not take the place of work nor unemployment allowances be substituted for wages, trade-unions could not flounder nor chapels be boarded up, without radically influencing the hearts and minds of the people of South Wales.

Substantially unimpaired was the family. Men were thankful that they did not have to go the road alone, and women still found pleasure in their husbands. The joy and happiness of shared experience of earlier days cushioned the fretful anxiety that came in the wake of idleness and poverty, and most men did not seek escape by chasing other men's wives. Family life gave way very slowly. As had his father before him, so now a young man when reaching maturity took a girl to wife and established a home; unlike his father, however, he could not support his wife by his own labor but only by his unemployment allowance.

Nevertheless it was in religious behavior and beliefs rather than in the institution of the family that radical changes were to be found. The handful of worshipers on a Sunday morning, the dwindling membership in Bible classes and singing groups, the sinking roofs on the chapels, the shabby clothes of the ministers, all pointed in the same direction—the estrangement of the populace from the chapel. And it was more than a physical separation. With it came a real questioning of the nature of the Divine, for His ways appeared more questionable than inscrutable. Men who asked no more than an opportunity to eat their bread in the sweat of their brow were denied their petition. And there was more evidence of Divine harshness than of love, for babies died from lack of milk and young girls developed pneumonia from lack of clothes. One verse from the Bible appeared relevant—"to him who hath shall be given and from him who hath not, even that which he hath shall be taken away."

The Welsh had loved their Bible so dearly that they probably would have continued to find much joy in it even if forced to shiver during services. That chapels were able to hold only the stolid bourgeoisie and a handful of old women who had attended services for so long that they could not break themselves of the habit, must in large part be ascribed to the incompetence of the ministers. By their acts and by their words the ministers proved that religion was for the well clothed and for the well fed, not for families on relief. And they alienated not one generation, but two, for parents who broke with the chapel not only absented themselves but no longer sent their children to Sunday School. And so one finds today, in the valleys of South Wales, an older generation that has lost its faith and a younger generation that knows not what faith is.

Before the first World War the national government played a role in Wales only slightly different from that which it played elsewhere. Now and again it interfered in the bloody labor struggles that flared up, and it passed rules and regulations about the Welsh language—only the King's English could be used in the courts. For all this, the government interfered little. When colliers were no longer permitted to go down into the mines and steel hands were unable to tend the furnaces, representatives of the Crown came to the valleys to give the people money so that they could live even though they were no longer able to earn wages. But the Welsh were not grateful to these government officials—not grateful at all—for they preferred to work as they had of old, to live on the pounds that they earned rather than on the shillings that were doled out to them. They resented the smallness of their allowances, but what they resented most was the fact that the government was largely responsible for their plight.

The General Strike of 1926 might never have come to pass, and its outcome would doubtless have been different, had the government remained neutral. In short, having been precipitated into their misery by the government, they had little reason to think well of it even when its servants came to offer them allowances for the taking. Their resentment mounted noticeably when Parliament tightened the regulations which made it more difficult for them to obtain even their paltry allowances. They found particularly obnoxious the new regulations which forced them to present evidence that they had tramped to neighboring towns in search of work, that forced them to allow inspectors into their homes, that forced them to report all work which they had the good luck to secure. Despite their feelings of hostility toward the government their behavior was noticeably restrained, because like children in a rage against their parents they dared not strike for fear of the consequence. Only the most brutal of the new regulations aroused them to action. When the Unemployment Assistance Board suddenly applied a new scale of allowances rioting actually broke out.

The Communists preached that nothing would be altered for the better until the government, Conservative and Labor, alike, was chased from office and honest representatives of the working people were entrusted with power. Many believed that there was some truth in the Communist contention; for, although Baldwin and his henchmen ruled in London, representatives of Labor filled most of the posts in the towns and boroughs of South Wales, and these Laborites were as inefficient, as incompetent, and as petty as were the Conservatives in London. They were interested in their jobs and in securing jobs for their relatives and friends, but they were little concerned about the plight of the populace. The knowledge that their own leaders had let them down disgusted the people of the valleys with politics and politicians while it reduced their relative hostility toward the national government, for it made all governments appear evil. In the Rhondda large numbers threw in their lot with the Communists, whose leaders at least appeared honest and courageous—which was more than could be said of the other parties. But when one got to know the Communists better one discovered that they were usually more interested in fighting for China or for Spain than for South Wales, and that they fought more among themselves than against Conservatives, Liberals, and Laborites. When this became general knowledge most people in South Wales became convinced that all governments were engines of oppression. The majority continued to vote, as they had in former years, for representatives of the Labor party; but they did so without enthusiasm, as was proved by the light vote on election day.

A study of the divorce rates would have suggested that the family had not changed; a study of the election returns would have suggested a stability in political life. But nothing could be further from the truth, for South Wales in the nineteen-thirties was not the South Wales of old. Idleness and poverty had done their work. Men were in a trance; the community was asleep.

12. THE GREAT DEPRESSION: LIVING ON RELIEF

We learn from contrast. We learn from unemployment the true significance of work. Only when a man is thrown out of employment does he perceive how much of his life is under the dictatorship of the job.

Work establishes the basic routine of modern living. Men must get out of bed, whether they like to or not, to get to work at a stipulated hour. This they must do day after day. Even when they work only a 40-hour week, men see relatively little of their wives and children, for they are away from home at least 10 hours daily. This explains why Mr. Israel "always helped his wife with the dishes, not because he liked housework, but he wanted to have her free in the evenings so they could talk or listen to the radio. While she is preparing supper, he will come out and set the table for her, just to be near her so that they can talk."

What is pleasure to the employed man—to be at home with his family—is a burden to the unemployed. With no job to report to, and no place in particular to go, the man who had previously been at home only evenings and weekends was now constantly underfoot. He could not always be looking for work, for among other things carfare and lunches cost money. Nor could he listen to more than a limited number of refusals per week. Every "no" was a stab.

The fact that the men hung around the house led to friction. Mrs. Silverman said: "There is constant bickering and quarreling in the household. Her husband is nervous. He yells at the children and at her and she nags at him because she can't stand this poverty. Maybe it is not his fault that he's unemployed, but it's a man's business to support his family. Sometimes she feels sorry for him, but her children's needs are more important." Mrs. Berkowitz exploded: " 'He hangs around most of the day and drives me crazy.' She cannot stand it when he is at home because they quarrel and it seems to her that usually they do not even know the reason for the quarrel. They are both nervous and pick on each other. She is glad when he goes out and leaves her alone. But he has less and less to do in the repair shop, and therefore finds it more comfortable, especially when it is cold, to sit at home. He does not help her with the housework because she does not want him to. She has always managed her own affairs in the home and prefers to continue to do so."

Mr. Berman, who is forced to stay at home a large part of the time because of his hernia, reacts badly to his confinement. "He cannot listen to the radio during the day because it makes him too aware of the fact that he is not working. It is unnatural for him to have time to listen. Evenings, he enjoys it." The tension in the Wolf household is so great "that Mr. Wolf clears out of the house every morning. He feels that he is going 'nuts.' He just keeps walking around town all day long. Mrs. Wolf described the situation as one in which 'nerves are worn thin.' She yells at him and he yells back, 'Do you think I don't try?' She is sorry after she has yelled at him, but sometimes, when she is sufficiently miserable, she isn't even sorry. Then she feels malicious enough to want to hurt him, for this is the only outlet she has for her pent-up emotions."

One might think men would welcome the opportunity of getting out of the house, if only to visit museums, attend lectures, or read in the library. Such was not the case. Mr. Levin related that he went to libraries "from time to time but has little patience to read the books or papers that he finds there." Some men felt that they were not making the best use of their time, but they doubted whether they could really profit from lectures since "one could not learn from words, one only learned from trouble."

These men were not used to reading for relaxation and they did not acquire the habit during their unemployment. Some tried to acquire a taste for books but found that their diffuse restlessness and nervousness made it difficult for them to concentrate on anything other than their own plight. Apparently, they could not shake free of their unemployment; cosmic problems—such as wars, revolutions, presidential elections—had little meaning for them.

The loss of a job also deprived a man of friends and acquaintances, who play such a large role in the life of the average citizen. Men travel together; they work together; they play together. Most unemployed men were deprived of companionship.

Depressed by his failure to provide for his family, the unemployed man suffers additional frustration. He cannot spend his energies in work. He is deprived of the pleasure that a farmer has when he sees the wheat which he has sowed blowing in the wind. And the butcher, the baker, and the candlestick maker also experience satisfaction at the end of a day's work. Even the man on the assembly line or the clerk behind a counter feels that he has contributed something useful. The unemployed man goes to sleep with his strength unspent, or worse still, dissipated in frustration. He has seen the clock go round but he has nothing to show for the hours that have passed.

This is not altogether true, for many unemployed, in a desperate effort to do something, lend a hand at home. They take care of the shopping, the heavy cleaning, the laundering, and even act as nurse-maid. If his wife is in poor health, the man can be extremely helpful. Mr. Levin said that he "keeps fairly busy helping his wife, who is frequently incapacitated by arthritic pains. He does her shopping, helps her with the washing, and even with the cooking. All in all, this takes considerable time each day." Even Mr. Shea, who drinks and beats his wife when she nags him, helps a little around the house when he feels well enough. He does most of the shopping because Mrs. Shea is unable to climb stairs.

In the McCarthy household, Mrs. McCarthy "goes for surplus commodities and their daughter, Nora, does most of the shopping. Mr. McCarthy is at home most of the time and does all the cooking. Mr. McCarthy stated that he is very proud of his ability to cook and bake, that the men in his family have always been interested in cooking. His father liked to cook and taught his children, just as he is teaching his son. His wife laughed and said that, while it was to her advantage to say that he is a good cook, even if he were not, in order to encourage him to continue, she has to admit that he cooks and bakes a lot better than she."

The Kennedys always work together. "Mr. Kennedy does the washing, cleaning, and anything else that needs doing. 'It's my home as well as my wife's, so why shouldn't I help?' " Mr. Eisner felt differently, however, for he refused to help with the housework and especially with the washing. " 'Washing is women's work' and under no circumstances would he do such a thing."

Sometimes, even men on WPA helped out. Mrs. McCabe said that her husband "does her work for her at night after working all day on the job. Despite her illness, she tries very hard to get some of her work done in order not to put too much pressure on him." In the Wharton family, one finds much the same situation. "The woman is not at all well and is unable to do her housework most of the time, which places a great burden on her husband."

The work which men do around the house helps their morale and also eases their wives' burden. Some women, able to handle their own work, deliberately encouraged their husbands to help them, because they thought the men would be better off for having something to do. But working around the house was not all profit to the unemployed man. By taking on feminine duties he widened the breach between his old life and the new. His failure was underlined by this transgression of sex boundaries. Some men took so easily to their new work that one must suspect that it fulfilled an inner need. The better adjusted the unemployed man became, the more difficulties he had fighting his way back into private employment.

Many women were distressed by their husbands' failure to provide for the family. They had taken it for granted even prior to marriage that a husband would provide for his wife and children. When a man failed to carry out his obligations, his wife frequently lost her balance.

The most telling evidence is found in the changed attitude of many women toward intercourse. Mrs. Berkowitz said "that she had always hated 'it' but never felt that she could do anything about it. But now, 'thank God,' it was possible for her to sleep apart from her husband." Mrs. Wolf, a much younger woman, was even more outspoken. "She said that she had always been a cold person, little interested in sexual matters. When her husband was working and supporting her, she supposed it was his right to have sexual relations and she therefore acquiesced. Now she avoids it. She has limited sexual relations to once a week, and even tries to get out of this. She has not gone to the birth control clinic because she saw no reason for going through an examination and using contraceptives just to give her husband pleasure."

The excessive demands of Mr. Cohen had long been cause for friction, but Mrs. Cohen said that "as long as he made a living, they went along from day to day. Now it was impossible." In his office interview, Mr. Cohen plaintively remarked "that his wife is now 'wearing the pants' and this makes for disturbance in the family. He said that not even in Italy or Germany, where all sorts of queer things are happening, did the man fail to remain the head of the household. He realized that his wife had reason for complaint, now that he was no longer earning money. She keeps repeating 'F.D.R. is the head of the household since he gives me the money.' "

Even in families free of marital tension, the failure of the man to continue as breadwinner led to a shifting in authority, usually to his wife, occasionally to an older child. Mr. Jacobowitz knows "that his wife has lost all respect for him. She keeps nagging and annoying him for not being able to do better, but makes no helpful suggestions." Mrs. Jacobowitz is aware that when she is very much discouraged she scolds and nags him, but she tries to make up for it afterward. However, she feels sure that "the mother must be the backbone of the family." Conditions have changed in the Jaffe family. "Mr. Jaffe is no longer the man he once was. He was proud, confident, and admired. His wife looked up to him and was happy with him. She did her job in the home, and he out of it. They had many friends. Now they seem to be crawling around in a hole which seems to be closing over them. She is cross, scolds, and nags. She tries to stop, but cannot."

No family on Relief escaped without some heightening in tension, but most men and women tried hard to keep the tension within bounds. The Davidowitzes said "that they know how each suffers, and they do all that is possible to understand and help each other." Mrs. Finkelstein believes that not only "have family ties not suffered during unemployment, but, if anything, they have been strengthened 'since they all recognized that there was a need to work together and make a go of a very difficult situation.' "

When women understood that the men were not personally responsible for the family's plight, but were victims of circumstance, they had little reason to nag and scold. But they did not always understand, at least not at first. Mrs. Finnan remarked that "she had not realized that her husband had been caught in a widespread economic disaster, and at first had believed that he failed to put forth the effort necessary to support the family. She had even gone so far as to leave him temporarily. She quickly realized, however, that she had been very unjust and came back, and spent the remainder of the time trying to encourage him and helping him to keep up his spirits." Few wives went so far as Mrs. Finnan, but many went through the same cycle of accusation and understanding.

Despite the genuine efforts of many wives to support their husbands emotionally, the man's status deteriorated, especially in households with adolescent children. The fact that their fathers were not working, the fact that they were around the house all day, the fact that their mothers had to budget every penny—all these things proved their fathers were failures.

Many men were particularly sensitive about their failure to provide adequately for their children. Mrs. Atkinson said that her husband is most concerned about his inability to give his young daughter the things she really needs and wants. Her daughter, however, is very understanding and has never alluded to her deprivations. The Brills have a less understanding daughter. She wants things that other girls have and does not understand why she cannot have them. She does not see why her father cannot get a job like other men, and she tells him so. Mr. Brown related "that it makes him feel badly that his children have so little. It hurts him particularly because his daughter lets him know how little she has in comparison with other children." In the Gallagher family, things have reached an even worse impasse. "According to both parents, the older children are unhappy because they want things they cannot have, and refuse to listen to reason when their father tries to explain why they cannot have certain things. They point to other fathers. This leads to much quarreling, for Mr. Gallagher has no patience with them because they are so unreasonable. When they make noise or annoy him, he flies off the handle."

Younger children were frequently unaware of being deprived, and many older children, sympathizing with their father's plight, spared him. Occasionally, as in the Solomon family, the father was able to give the children something other than money. "He has always taken an interest in the children and allowed them to monopolize as much of his time as they wished. Although he has had no schooling in this country, he is able to help them with their homework, and they are particularly proud of his mathematical ability."

Although few children went to the extreme of Mr. O'Brien's daughter, who said "that she does not believe her father is the person to criticize her because he doesn't have a real job himself," they observed that unemployment had deposed their father as head of the household and turned him into just another member of the family.

While the unemployed man was hard-pressed to find something to do for the sixteen hours that he had to wait until he could again escape into sleep, his wife was under pressure for the opposite reason. Although used to hard work, most women found running a household more difficult as they grew older. When family income was cut in half or even one-third, the pressure became great. Yet many continued to keep their homes in good condition. Mrs. O'Connell related "that the landlord tells her that if he paints he will have to raise the rent and this, of course, would be impossible." Although her rooms are small and dark, her home was spotlessly clean and attractive. "While the furniture is obviously old and somewhat shabby, it has been extremely well taken care of. Mrs. O'Connell showed the worker a crocheted bed-spread which she now uses as a cover for the dining room table. She said that it was at least thirty-five years old and yet is as good as new. She washes it very carefully, as she does all the other crocheted pieces on the bureaus, tables, chairs."

Despite the many hardships under which they labored, few women gave up the struggle. Only 12 per cent could be called "poor" house-keepers; 20 per cent were "passable"; and almost 70 per cent were "good." The key to this good housekeeping record is found in Mrs. Horowitz's statement. "She had always taken a good deal of pleasure in her home, and now it was almost her only pleasure. Her furnish-ings were lovely and looked like new, although Mrs. Horowitz said that she had had them for nineteen years."

To keep a home looking nice with no money available for replace-ments meant extra hours of labor. Many women did all their laundry and spent their few free minutes repairing and otherwise lengthening the life of their aging possessions.

The women were constantly harassed—they walked long distances to save a penny or two on purchases; they washed and ironed every-thing, even the heavy sheets; they tried to cheer up their husbands; they helped their children to get along on very little. However, they found time to worry. Mrs. Shannahan said "that she worries and wor-ries about her troubles and does not see any way out. She worries a great deal about the children because she wants them to have what they need, but it is very hard to manage. It is extremely important for her to keep her home scrupulously clean and to follow a prescribed routine for her children as to their food and exercise. In her attempt to do all this, she sometimes has trouble keeping her courage up. Al-though she is not yet 31, she sometimes feels that she has been work-ing for centuries and cannot remember when she last had a rest."

Although most women, especially those who had been on Relief for a considerable time, had a minimum wardrobe, we heard few com-plaints. Only when they had nothing warm to wear did they call attention to the inadequate clothing allowances. Style was no problem. Apparently these women were so overburdened with household duties that they did not need clothing for social purposes. Except for an occasional movie in the afternoon—and one could slip into the local movie house in a work dress—these women seldom went out.

The most serious strain was their gnawing fear that they would never escape from their present predicament. Many women cried during the interviews. They excused themselves by saying that they were depressed, not only by what they had been through, but what they feared they would still have to go through. Mrs. Ryan is an extreme example. She was so rundown that one of the social agencies sent her to a nursing home to recuperate. "They were very good to her at the home and she tried to do as they told her in order to show her appreciation, but it was almost impossible for her to pull herself together. She said that when other patients would talk about their husbands' jobs, she would feel so sick 'inside' that she almost fainted. She felt sure that if her husband were working and she had enough money to run her home adequately, her health would be all right and she would be a real person again."

The influence of unemployment on the children is of the utmost importance. There were few childless families in the Home Relief and WPA group—9 in all, of which 8 were in the WPA group. However, at the time of the interview, 26 families, or more than 20 per cent, had no child living at home. There was evidence to suggest that in 66 of the 94 families with children living at home unemployment of the father had adversely affected the physical, emotional, or occupational condition of the children. In larger families, sometimes only one child showed ill effects, sometimes all had been harmed.

However, there were only a few cases in which unemployment and its associated stresses appeared to have aggravated a medical condition. The Corcorans believe that they lost their little girl because she contracted pneumonia while they were on Relief. Mrs. Corcoran said "she had been unable to afford medical care and had not known they could get a doctor through Relief. Her children had been sick before, and her investigator had not suggested medical care. For this reason, she failed to realize that it was available." The Brennans feel certain that their daughter suffered an aggravation in her condition because they were on Relief. "After two attacks of scarlet fever within one year, the child developed a serious cardiac condition. The parents know that if they could have given her better care, she would not have become so ill, and this has been one of their bitterest associations with unemployment." Mrs. McCarthy had the misfortune to lose her twins, John and Joseph, from pneumonia. "The mother wept as she talked about the cruelty of Lincoln Hospital which refused to admit John until a few hours before his death. She firmly believes that had they not been on Home Relief and had they been able to afford a private physician, John would be alive today."

Even if the Corcorans, Brennans, and McCarthys were correct in their appraisal, the fact remains that in only 5 of the 66 families did children suffer a marked physical deterioration because of the Relief status of their parents.

One reservation is in order. This low percentage relates only to marked deterioration, not to minor handicaps. For instance, malnutrition was widespread, although in the absence of a physical examination no definite proof can be adduced. The records and interviews are replete, however, with indirect evidence: "Judy was a slight, fragile child; Jean also was a slight child with poor coloring, yet looked stronger than Judy; Frances had better coloring, yet looked small for her age and is undernourished; Catherine seemed small and undernourished; John, the exception, was a sturdy, healthy-looking boy." This is the social worker's impression of the McCann children. In the Gallagher family, James and Daniel were not at home when the social worker called, but she met Catherine, "a tall, thin, pretty child with good coloring, and Leroy, who is a thin child with deep circles under his eyes." Mrs. Gallagher says she does not know why Leroy looks so sickly. She thinks he gets adequate food, although he does not get enough milk and she cannot afford cod-liver oil. The Callahans have two children, John "who is big for his age but seems slow in developing. He is not very strong, has poor coloring, and talks very little." His younger brother, Hughie, is "a thin, bright, very active baby, but his color also seems very poor. His mother has not taken him to the baby clinic for some time, since she is afraid that they will put him on whole milk and she does not see how she will be able to provide it for him." Home Relief provided extra allowances for undernourished children, but not all families knew their rights.

Tooth decay, like malnutrition, took a steady if silent toll. Home Relief provided dental service, but only extraction work. Many youngsters, especially girls, refused to avail themselves of this service, for they saw no reason to mar their looks by needless extractions. One boy, recently returned from a CCC camp, complained about inadequate dental care at the camp. He related that "he had suffered a great deal from toothache but refused to allow his teeth to be removed." No matter how low dentists kept their fees, the unemployed could not afford to pay them, even on the installment plan.

Children probably suffered from other conditions associated in whole or in part with the fact that their families were on Relief. Poverty, however, stood in the way of periodic medical examinations and thereby conspired to keep such conditions from being recognized and treated. Examinations in school helped a little, especially in picking up youngsters with defective eyesight.

If the effects of malnutrition or dental neglect can remain hidden for a score of years, emotional disturbances can escape detection for even longer periods. Great care must be taken, however, not to ascribe to unemployment emotional difficulties predating the family's acceptance on Relief. This is well illustrated by the case of Miriam Cohen, who was nine at the time when the family first came to Relief. According to her mother, "she had been a 'problem child' since birth. In infancy, she had colic, slept poorly, and was a feeding problem. Even now, at the age of nine, she asks her mother to feed her. Her mother answers 'that even if she were to look at her food until she was old and gray, she would not lift a spoon.' Since infancy, Miriam has had nocturnal enuresis. She does very poorly in school and has been tardy almost daily. She is in the slow class, but fails to do satisfactory work. Her I.Q. is normal, hence her failure in schools points to emotional difficulties. Miriam verbalizes intense jealousy toward her younger brother, whom she says she hates and with whom she fights whenever they are together. She tells her mother that she knows her mother hates her and prefers her brother. Miriam also expresses self-hatred. She says that she does not know why she is living and that if she is careless and allows a car to run her down, everyone would be satisfied since there is no point in her going on."

Clearly, Miriam was disturbed long before the family came to Relief, but her father's unemployment probably intensified her difficulties. One illustration will suffice. Following Mr. Cohen's unemployment, Mrs. Cohen, seeking to limit intercourse, had Miriam sleep with her and banished Mr. Cohen to a couch in the living room. Frequently, Mr. Cohen is unable to control himself long enough to get Miriam out of her mother's bed, and the parents have intercourse with the child present.

Mrs. Solomon does not believe that her two younger children are affected by the Relief situation, but she knows that Robert "worries about the family and about the future. He is nervous and bites his nails continuously." During the office interview, Robert stuttered badly.

"Because his carfare and necessary shoe repairs used up the money which he might otherwise have had for spending purposes," John Duffy dropped out of high school before completing his course. He did not feel that additional education was sufficient job insurance to warrant the sacrifice. He has been unable to find anything to do and just hangs around all day. Only nineteen, he is already disgusted with life. John does not like the people in the neighborhood and when he can afford it he goes back to University Avenue to visit his friends. But when he sees that they have good clothing and other nice things he gets embarrassed and is cross. He quarrels with his parents all the time.

The Browns have three children, Evelyn, Charles, and Wallace. "Both parents say that Charles is backward. From his appearance, the social worker would judge that he is borderline. He is a quiet child, gives no trouble, and apparently the parents ignore him. Evelyn gets her own way quietly but surely. Her father complained that she has little respect for him. When she is listening to a radio program and he wants to tune in on another station, he cannot do so because she always has her own way. Wallace also manages to get his own way all the time. He gave evidence during the interview of having the upper hand and flaunting his parents' authority. Mrs. Brown said that she did not mean to have Wallace—he was an accident—and she certainly will not have any more children."

If relatively few children deteriorated physically because of the unemployment of their fathers, the opposite was true of their emotional state. In 80 per cent of the families, one or more children showed evidence that their psyches had been damaged. True, the damage frequently predated the family's acceptance on Relief, but Relief usually intensified it.

Most children were too young to be faced with occupational problems or even with educational decisions related to occupational choices. However, several older children showed occupational frustration. Mrs. Gallagher said that her daughter, Alice, "left high school six months before she was to graduate because the family could not afford the carfare and clothing that she needed. The only thing that Alice was fit for was domestic work, but she considered this beneath her. However, to get better jobs, children needed a college degree. Mrs. Gallagher is certain that Alice married very young because she was jobless and feeling unhappy."

Mrs. Horowitz's boy, Daniel, had always been a good student but had never been fond of school, for he was taller than most boys of his age and strangers thought him retarded. "When he became aware of the financial problem the family was up against, he decided to leave school. He completed the sixth term and then found work as an errand boy." The Brills' eldest son dropped out of college at the end of his second year because he was assigned by the National Youth Administration to a laboring job. "He thought it silly for a laborer to be going to college." Robert Solomon was confronted by a real dilemma: "He does exceptionally well in his studies and is now completing the first year of high school. His principal believes that if he continues to do good work, he will obtain free tuition at the College of the City of New York, and therefore advises him against taking the commercial course. He and his mother are both confused because if he takes the commercial course, he will have a better chance of getting a job when he finishes high school; but such a course would spoil his chance of going to college."

The economic pressure under which these Relief families lived was responsible for much waste of personal and communal resources. As was true of most poor children, talents remained undeveloped and skills could not be acquired, for immediate rather than prospective earning power was a prime consideration. These unemployed families were very poor and their children were therefore under extreme pressure. The $5 or $6 a month that a student needed for carfare, lunches, and incidentals presented such a huge sum that many left school prematurely. The $5 bill which the employment agency demanded for a registration fee also was hard to find.

Adolescent children had almost as difficult a time out of school as in. Finding a job was no easy matter, and deriving any benefit from one was even more difficult. Children living at home could retain only a part of their earnings; the remainder was deducted from the family's Relief allowance. The rough formula was 60-40: 60 per cent was considered available for the family, 40 per cent could be retained by the worker. At first glance, this might appear liberal, but if one makes allowance for carfare, extra cost of meals, additional clothing, expenses for tools and other accessories, a person could frequently be working for nothing.

Many young adults resented what they believed to be the excessive harshness of the partial-earnings formula. Ruth Levin found a Christmas job which paid her $11 a week. Home Relief budgeted $6.50 and the girl was allowed $4.50 for herself. "She resented this very much, constantly scolded and nagged at her mother because she thought a sacrifice was being demanded of her. She felt that other girls were permitted to keep their earnings, and saw no reason why she should contribute to the household budget. Both parents felt that, although Ruth's attitude was affected by their Relief status, it was only one further manifestation of her usual lack of consideration."

Daniel was different. When he found work, he looked forward to paying his parents for room and board, and thus help the family to become independent. "He was very much upset when he found that his earnings were so closely budgeted that there would be almost nothing for himself. His discontent grew, and finally he threatened to move out of the house. His mother, seeking to have the investigator reduce the amount that was budgeted, mentioned Daniel's threat. The investigator pointed out that the family could be removed from Relief, and Daniel sent to jail, if the threat were carried out. This threw Daniel's mother into a panic, for she remembered that Daniel had recently said that it might be better to be in jail, since one could be as free there as on Relief."

The strict budgeting of minors' earnings not only created familial conflicts but also helped keep many young people out of the labor market. The following notation in the Hollingsworth record illustrates this: "Although the investigator has been urging her to look for employment, Bertha, the eighteen-year-old daughter, said that she was not interested in work outside the home. Her earnings would be deducted from the Home Relief allowance, and neither she nor her family would be better off. Her energy could better be spent in her own home, where her mother can use her assistance in taking care of the three youngest children." Ralph Brill is another case in point. He was called into the office for failing to report to the occupational division. "He said that he saw little point in reporting, since his father was already on WPA and he knew that two members of the family could not be employed at one time. He did not go to the New York State Employment Service because he was too discouraged." Later in the record, Mrs. Brill reported that Ralph was making between $10 and $11 a week. Since this covered the deficit supplemented by Home Relief, the case was closed over the protests of Mrs. Brill, who pointed out "that her son needs this money for clothes and expenses."

Some boys, like Charles Adams and Harry Epstein, were willing to turn over all their wages to their parents. Mrs. Adams said that Charles had "recently been placed on an NYA job that paid him $22 monthly, all of which he turned over to her without any question. He occasionally asked for a few cents for cigarettes or a show, but he did not think that he had any more claim to the money than any of the other children." The Epsteins' poverty made it impossible for Harry to go to college. For a while he set his heart on attending the Delehanty Institute with the intention of studying to become a policeman or fireman, but he found even this beyond him. His mother said "that he took the application for Relief harder than any other member of the family. He threatened to kill himself if anyone found out that they were on Relief. His parents did not consider this an idle threat and they were terrified that they could not keep the secret. Harry is a little happier now but still is very restless. He gives every cent that he makes to the family and is constantly asking whether it is enough to get them off Relief."

Home Relief insisted on the 60-40 formula because the administration believed that employed children should contribute an amount equal to the cost of room and board. As long as children lived in their parents' homes they were unable to have the psychological gratification which comes from true independence. The fact that the deductions were compulsory deprived them of any pleasure which they might have had in making voluntary contributions. In the Israel and O'Brien families, both on WPA, the older children were glad to contribute a share of their earnings because they could see how their action helped the other members. Thomas O'Brien gives his younger brothers and sisters "their spending money and, from time to time, buys things for them." James Knight was lucky. Although his family was on Home Relief, the investigator shut his eyes to his earnings. "From his $15 weekly wages, James buys his clothing, takes care of his lunches and carfare, and gives his younger brothers and sisters their spending money."

Children growing up in homes where their fathers were unemployed missed the subtle discipline that work and wages bring. It was shortsighted policy, therefore, to reduce whatever incentives these adolescents might have to find employment in private industry.

When unemployment struck, life became much more difficult for the man, his wife, his children. The fact that tension seldom reached the boiling point should not obscure the finding that almost every member of an unemployed family, young, middle-aged, and old, had increasing difficulties in adjusting to each other.

Unemployment also left its mark on the external relations of these families. In an effort to reduce expenses, many families "doubled up." They usually achieved their primary objective of reducing living expenses, but frequently at high emotional cost. Mrs. Klein had her parents living with her. "The present situation is rapidly becoming unbearable. She hopes for the day when she can again have her own home as had been the case when she was first married. Her mother is not so difficult, but her father, who has had two strokes, causes considerable disturbance. His nose runs because he has no control over it, and he is unaware that it runs. When eating, he makes a sighing, gasping noise which proves very disturbing. The children become upset when they see him at the table. If the children are noisy, their grandfather yells at them. The old folks, simply by sitting around and looking so sad, make Mr. Klein uncomfortable."

Mrs. Jaffe's father was such an irritant that the Jewish Social Service Association agreed to move him out of the home and supplement the Home Relief allowance by $10 or $12 monthly. They thought this a necessary step to safeguard the family. Shortly after he became unemployed, Mr. Silverman moved his entire family back to his mother's home, which she shared with two unmarried sons. Mr. Silverman's brothers were so resentful that there was nothing left for the Silverman family to do but move out again. Occasionally, "doubling up" did not lead to emotional friction but the anticipated gains seldom materialized because of Home Relief's strict regulations which forced a pooling of all available resources.

About 80 per cent of the families incurred debts prior to coming to Relief. Much of their borrowing was from relatives and friends. Once on Relief, such borrowings declined but they did not cease completely. The Mittlemans "had always been helped and protected by Mrs. Mittleman's sister. When the Relief investigator visited this sister, she said that 'she cannot continue to help any longer because her husband quarrels with her for giving the Mittlemans money.' " The same thing was true of the Finkelstein family, which had received considerable assistance from Mrs. Finkelstein's brother. "A conflict was started when Mrs. Finkelstein's sister-in-law wanted her husband to help her family rather than his." The Silvermans had some well-to-do relatives, but they refused to help because of an earlier experience with unemployed relatives.

Many relatives were in no position to extend more than a little help. One woman was able to invite her daughter and grandchildren for meals several times weekly. In another case, a priest took care of the extras in his brother's family, such as medicine, toys at Christmas, and the like. Clothes were frequently handed down.

Some families, like the Atkinsons, felt badly about the treatment they received from their relatives. "Mrs. Atkinson has very little to do with her relatives. She says that when people are down and out, strangers are frequently kinder than one's own people. She is glad that she has been able to get along without help from her brothers, and added that she has little desire to see them." Mr. Gilbert was even more morose. "In the situation in which they find themselves, they can expect no help from anyone. Relatives tell you, before you ask, that they are unable to help."

If relatives frequently failed one in time of need, many unemployed seeking to hide their Relief status broke all social ties with friends. Sometimes the breach was not of their own making. Mr. Davidowitz summed up the matter in these terms: "Their friends know their circumstances and fear to visit because they know they will be offered refreshments, which can only come out of the limited budget which the Davidowitzes have at their disposal. Hence, rather than deprive the Davidowitzes of much-needed food, they stay away and deprive them of much-needed company." Mrs. Horowitz said that one of the most difficult problems in management is "to be able to furnish light refreshments when friends call, especially the children's friends." Mrs. Burke, however, did not find refreshments a stumbling block. "They had always had a wide circle of friends and visited back and forth a great deal. Since Mr. Burke lost his job, this was almost their only source of recreation. One could always serve a cup of tea. Usually, friends would bring a cake with them. This did not hurt the family's pride because it was done in friendship."

Unemployment was more than a question of shortages in food, clothing, and amusements. Unemployment transformed the life of the man, changed the position of the woman, and left its imprint on the physical, emotional, and occupational life of the children. But it did even more. Unemployment left its mark on the thinking of people.

13.
ILLITERACY IN WORLD WAR II

There is no need to present detailed evidence to support the contention that since 1890 important changes have been made in the educational structure of the United States to insure that a basic education is available to everyone. Despite this improvement in educational facilities, however, the Census of 1940 revealed that approximately 4 million males in the working force had less than five years of schooling. Approximately 1.5 million of these poorly educated were in the age group eighteen through forty-four—the range which includes the men liable for military service.

The vast majority of these illiterate and poorly educated persons in the population had somehow adjusted to life—they were able to secure employment, discharge familial responsibilities, and participate in community activities. This contention cannot be supported positively as easily as it can be by the absence of contradictory evidence. In our democratic society extreme maladjustment is expressed in one of two ways: some individuals, unable to discharge their responsibilities through their own efforts, seek assistance from the community; others run counter to the rules and regulations of the community, which then intervenes to apprehend and punish them. There is no significant evidence to indicate that the illiterate and poorly educated presented either symptom of maladjustment. They were making an adjustment to life, as workers and citizens, however much the level of their adjustment was adversely affected by their lack of formal schooling.

A new fact of community life has developed, however, that has necessitated the evaluation of such precarious individual adjustments in a broader light. Modern wars cannot be fought and won without the total involvement of all members of a society, or without the redirection of the nation's resources to the ends of war. Among the consequences, therefore, of a national emergency is the new perspective which is placed upon many aspects of a nation's life, some of which may have escaped recognition or evaluation during a more placid period. Although the experts in education had been aware of the existence of large numbers of individuals in the population whose ability to read, write, and reckon was totally non-existent or minimal, there had been no widespread concern with the problem of illiteracy in the pre-war years. The only significant attempt to remedy the lack of schooling and the lack of literacy among young adults, even as late as the 1930's, was the basic instruction provided by the Civilian Conservation Corps and the Works Progress Administration. It was the large-scale screening of the younger male population consequent to the passage of the Selective Service Act of 1940 that turned a local and isolated fact into a national problem.

Between 1940 and the late summer of 1945, when Japan surrendered, the Selective Service System held six registrations. Men within various age brackets were required to answer a series of questions devised to aid local boards in determining whether individuals should be classified as available for military service or placed in a deferred category. There were almost 6,500 local Selective Service Boards throughout the United States and prior to V-J Day they had registered more than 22 million persons in the age group eighteen through thirty-seven. The total number registered was greatly in excess of this figure, since the third registration in February, 1942, required men through the age of forty-four to register; the fourth registration, looking forward to the possibility of a total mobilization of the nation's manpower resources, required all men between the ages of forty-five and sixty-five to register.

The basic responsibilities of the local boards were threefold: to register individuals in the liable age group, to classify the registrants, and to meet specific quotas set by the Armed Services. It is important that although early in the war the local boards did examine and reject some registrants, the vast majority were examined by the military under standards established by the Armed Services.

Although the Armed Services needed very large numbers of men, and although they were convinced that in general the younger the man the better soldier he would make, they did not consider it practical to ask the local boards to forward for induction all men of certain ages. Instead, they established a series of standards which each registrant had to meet. These standards set minimum requirements in terms of physical, mental, emotional, and moral qualifications. Illustrative of the complexities of the screening process is the fact that there were thirty general causes for rejection. Any individual who fell below the minimum standard with respect to any one of these thirty traits or qualities was rejected for military service and classified IV-F.

At the end of the war, the Selective Service System made a count, on the basis of a 20 percent sample, of all men who had been classified IV-F after their initial examination. This enumeration was for the period from the beginning of Selective Service through December, 1944. On the basis of this and other relevant data, we developed the distribution by major cause of rejection of the 5.2 million men in the IV-F pool at the end of the war shown in the accompanying table.

Selective Service registrants, 18–37, classified IV-F, August, 1945

Reason for rejection	Total	White	Negro
Mental deficiency	716,000	391,000	325,000
Mental disease	970,000	855,000	115,000
Physical defects	3,475,000	2,933,000	542,000
Administrative (moral, etc.)	87,000	71,000	16,000
Total	5,248,000	4,250,000	998,000

Our particular interest centers on the 716,000 men between the ages of eighteen and thirty-seven who were not accepted for military service during World War II because they were adjudged to be "mentally deficient." It is not easy to define even abstractly the term "mentally deficient." An easy way is to declare that an individual who fails to achieve a specified score on an intelligence test is mentally deficient in that he does not possess the intellectual ability to meet the arbitrary standard. The real question here would be the adequacy of the test and the reasonableness of the standard. It is known, however, that it is difficult, perhaps impossible, to devise a test which takes proper account of the cultural and environmental factors in the individual's background so that his response to questions reflects his intellectual ability and not his specific knowledge of certain words and circumstances.

Another definition, more useful for present purposes, is that a mentally deficient person is one who is unable to meet minimum performance standards as worker and citizen because of a lack of intellectual capacity, rather than because of a physical handicap or emotional disturbance. In our society the inadequate performance which most frequently leads to a suspicion of such mental deficiency arises in preschool years, when the child is unable to acquire the usual skills for his age, or in the early years of school, when he fails to absorb the instructional materials solely or mainly because of a lack of basic intellectual capacity. A few children are so severely deficient that they must be institutionalized. The vast majority, however, continue for some time in school, some in special classes. Once they are out of school, they merge with the population at large.

Relatively little research has been devoted to ascertaining the number of individuals in the population who cannot meet a minimum performance criterion as workers and citizens. Some authorities estimate that approximately one percent of the population can perform even unskilled work only under close supervision in a protective environment. It is believed that another one percent of the population are able to work effectively only if they have some type of special supervision. According to these estimates the percentage of persons who would not meet a minimum performance standard because of intellectual deficiency would be 2 percent. The more than 700,000 men rejected for military service under the general heading of "mental deficiency" amounted to about 4 percent of the men examined. On the surface this might be taken to mean that the screening standards used were somewhat tight but approximately correct. Again, however, a national average obscures the truth, for nearly 14 percent were rejected in some states and only one-half of one percent in others. The fact that the national rejection rate was only a little higher than the theoretical rate of true mental deficiency cannot be taken as an indication that the screening validly assessed either mental deficiency or ability to give satisfactory performance. The regional patterning of the rejections indicates that the screening assessed primarily the individual's educational background.

Since the mental screening by the Armed Services during World War II was mainly a measure of educational deprivation, the results of the large-scale examinations are helpful in determining the number and distribution of persons who were so educationally deprived that they were considered unsuitable for military service during the most important war in the country's history. In considering the results, it is important to divide totals between whites and Negroes because educational deprivation has been so much more characteristic of the Negro population. The accompanying table presents a breakdown of the total number of men rejected for mental deficiency by the end of the war.

Rejections for mental deficiency by region and race

Region	Total	White	Negro
New England	20,765	19,803	962
Middle Atlantic	71,416	49,708	21,708
Southeast	435,639	167,599	268,040
Southwest	89,881	70,661	19,220
Central	70,460	57,274	13,186
Northwest	13,089	12,530	559
Far West	15,150	13,725	1,425
Total U.S.	716,400	391,300	325,100

Several conclusions emerge from this tabulation. By far the largest number of rejectees are from the South—the Southeast and the Southwest—which together account for just under three-quarters of the total. At the opposite extreme are New England, the Northwest, and the Far West, which altogether account for only 7 percent. The Middle Atlantic and the Central States each account for about 10 percent. Furthermore, rejections were usually credited to the region of the rejectee's current residence, rather than to his place of birth or longest residence. There can be little doubt, therefore, that the totals of the Middle Atlantic and Central states were increased by migrants who had moved from the South.

With respect to the Negro population, the Southeast and the Southwest account for an even larger part of the national total—more than 88 percent. The total for whites in the Southwest includes the substantial Latin American population and the Indian population which is fairly heavily concentrated in New Mexico and Arizona.

Even more revealing than the absolute number of persons rejected are the rates per thousand examined. The accompanying table summarizes the experience by region and race.

Rejection rates per thousand registrants, by region and race

Region	Total	White	Negro
Total U.S.	40	25	152
New England	17	16	65
Middle Atlantic	15	11	67
Southeast	97	52	202
Southwest	60	54	107
Central	14	12	61
Northwest	14	13	40
Far West	10	9	50

Several striking facts are revealed by this table. First, the rate of rejection in the Southeast is almost ten times as large as that in the Far West. All of the regions of the country except two have a total rejection rate between 10 and 17 per 1,000 examined; the Southeast and the Southwest have rates of 97 and 60, respectively. Although the range is less for the white population, it is still striking. The Far West has a rejection rate of 9 while the Southeast and the Southwest each have a rate of more than 50. The Negro rate is so much larger in every region that it might appear to be a different population; the over-all Negro rate is just over six times the white rate. However, there is evidence within the Negro distribution to suggest that the population is basically parallel. One finds, for instance, that the rate of rejection for Negroes in the Northwest and the Far West is actually below the white rate in the Southeast and the Southwest. Even in the other three regions—New England, Middle Atlantic, and Central, the Negro rate is only slightly above the white rate in the South. The sixfold difference in total rates between Negroes and Whites results from the exceptionally high rejection rate for Negroes in the Southeast and the lower but still high rate in the Southwest. The most extreme regional and racial differences are between the rejection rate for Whites in the Far West of 9 per 1,000, or less than one percent, and the rate of 202 per 1,000, or more than 20 percent, for Negroes in the Southeast. Unless there were evidence that there are gross differences in mental capacity among various racial and ethnic groups, here is an overwhelming demonstration that the results of the screening examination reflected primarily differences in the educational and environmental opportunities in different regions.

Although similar rejection rates have been tabulated and analyzed by various experts, all of the analyses to date have been limited either to national totals, regional comparisons, or state comparisons. These comparisons shed considerable light upon the problem of the illiterate and the poorly educated youth of the country, but a more thorough understanding of the problem awaited an analysis of smaller geographic units which might bring out the range of specific factors likely to contribute to high or low rejection rates.

On the basis of Selective Service sample data, we prepared two detailed maps. The first presents the rate of rejections for mental deficiency for white registrants in each of the more than 3,000 counties throughout the United States. The second map is necessarily less extensive; it shows the Negro rejection rates for Eastern counties having at least 100 Negroes in our sample. Nearly all other counties in the nation had too few Negroes examined to compute a rate. Exceptions were a few large urban counties.

The county map of white rejections facilitates an identification of the major areas of the country in which the rejection rates were at either extreme. The highest rates are found in five regions: the Appalachian Mountains, the Ozarks, counties bordering the Gulf of Mexico, counties bordering the Rio Grande, and the northern parts of Arizona and New Mexico. As we have pointed out, Latin Americans and Indians, being non-Negro, are counted among the white population, which helps to explain the last three areas of high rejection rates.

This map also calls attention to relatively high rates in several other parts of the country. These are the northern parts of Maine, New Hampshire, and Vermont which can probably be explained by the considerable numbers of French Canadians resident there; their inability to speak and understand English might have led them to be labeled "mentally deficient." There are several counties in northern Michigan, Wisconsin, North Dakota, and Montana which had high rates. We found that many of these counties were in cut-over timberland country, former mining centers where the ore had thinned out, or isolated, poor farming country.

In the South, which produced by far the greatest number of rejections, a careful inspection of the map indicates the following distinguishing characteristics. The large urban centers, even in a high rejection area, show a considerably lower rejection rate than the adjacent rural areas. The Atlantic coastal region has considerably lower rates than the inland mountain regions. Among the Southeastern states, Mississippi and Florida stand out with conspicuously lower rejection rates. In several states there are sharp distinctions between one section and another, as, for instance, between southern Louisiana (probably because of the Cajuns) and northern Louisiana. Northern and southern Missouri also show a sharp difference, as do eastern and western Oklahoma. Perhaps the most striking intra-state difference is between the north and south of Texas, doubtless because of the concentration of the Latin American group in the southern section.

The most general finding that emerges from the study of rejection rates on a county basis is the general gradation from low to high rates

rather than abrupt changes. In a large number of cases this gradual-
ness ignores state boundaries, suggesting that local factors play the
predominant part in determining the differential rates. There is, however, contrary evidence which suggests that in some instances state
policies are determining. Sharp differences are conspicuous between
Mississippi and the bordering states, and between the western and
northwestern counties of Texas and the much higher rates in the neighboring states. Much the same contrast is observed between the higher
rates in West Virginia and those in the border counties of Ohio and
Pennsylvania, and in the border counties of Kentucky and Virginia.

The map of county rejection rates for Negro registrants in the Southeast helps to bring certain generalizations to the surface. An outstanding fact is that every county in South Carolina, without exception, had
a Negro rejection rate of 175 per 1,000 or more. The situation in Alabama was little better. The counties in which the cities of Birmingham
and Mobile are located show, however, relatively low rates. The other
states show greater variation between high, medium, and low county
rejection rates. There is no doubt that the degree of urbanization is a
major factor related to lower rejection rates of Negroes, just as for
whites. On the basis of sample studies, the other two factors which
seem frequently to be connected with relatively low rejection rates for
Negroes are the economic prosperity of the county and a relatively low
proportion of Negroes in the total population. There are, however, a considerable number of counties where such specific factors as local white
or Negro leadership, or special efforts by outside groups, such as foundations interested in Negro education, apparently are important. Such
factors may be at work where the rejection rate for a particular county
or group of counties is low in comparison to others which are broadly
similar on an economic and demographic basis.

The broad regional and county outlines of the rates of rejection for
"mental deficiency" have been presented. It is now desirable to turn
to a state analysis, since some policy actions fall specifically within
the scope and competence of states rather than any other unit of government. The map of the country supports the data presented earlier
by emphasizing the extent to which high rejection rates for white males
were so heavily concentrated in the Southeast and Southwest. In addition, it introduces several new findings. First, it indicates that Florida
is a thoroughly atypical Southern state: its rates are similar to many
Northern and Central states. Perhaps more significant is the finding
that rates for Oklahoma and Mississippi more nearly approximate those
which prevail in a number of Northern and Central states than those
typical of the Southern states. Kentucky, Tennessee, Texas, and North
Carolina have, on the other hand, very high rates. The table on page
183 gives the number of white rejectees and the rejection rate per
1,000 whites examined.

A comparison of the state figures on the rejection of Negro registrants with the map indicates that interesting differences are discernible within the broad generalization that high rejection rates are con-

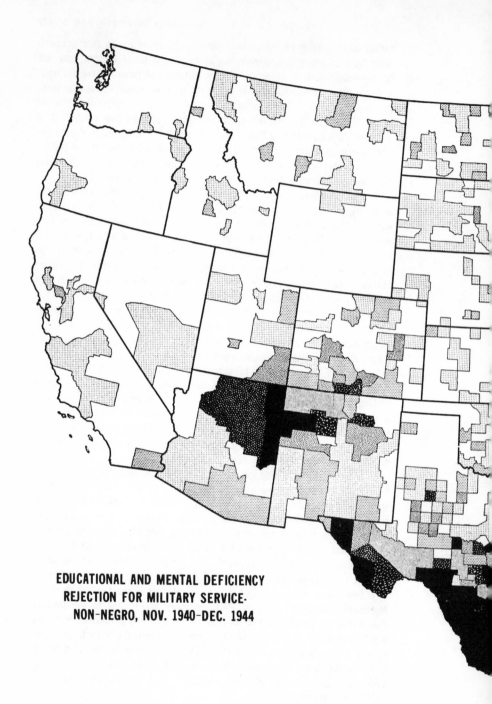

EDUCATIONAL AND MENTAL DEFICIENCY
REJECTION FOR MILITARY SERVICE-
NON-NEGRO, NOV. 1940-DEC. 1944

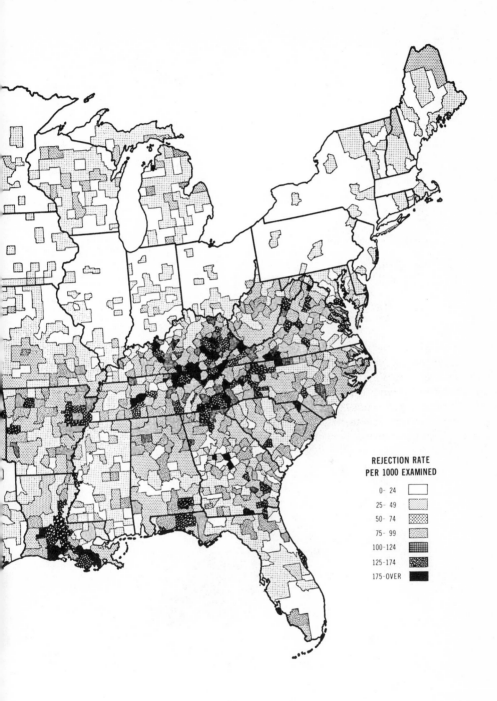

REJECTION RATE
PER 1000 EXAMINED

0- 24	
25- 49	
50- 74	
75- 99	
100-124	
125-174	
175-OVER	

181

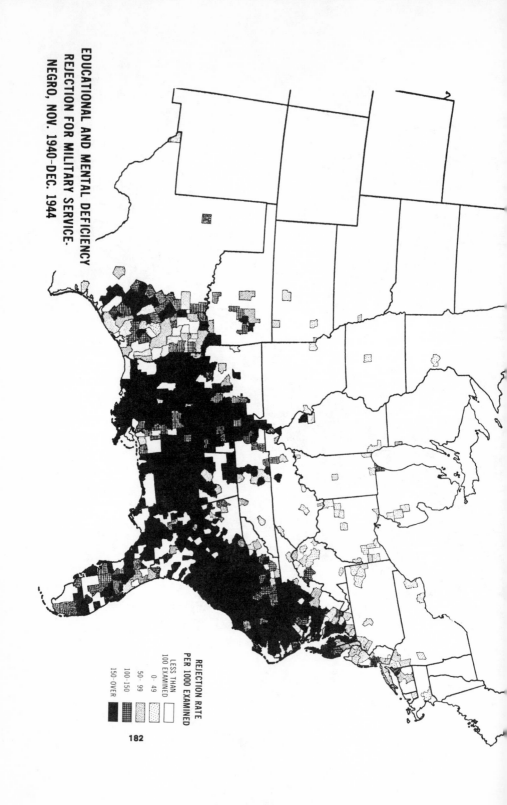

EDUCATIONAL AND MENTAL DEFICIENCY
REJECTION FOR MILITARY SERVICE:
NEGRO, NOV. 1940–DEC. 1944

REJECTION RATE
PER 1000 EXAMINED

LESS THAN
100 EXAMINED

0 - 49

50 - 99

100-150

150-OVER

182

Number of white registrants rejected for mental
deficiency and rate per thousand examined, by
region and state

Locality	Number	Rate per thousand
New England	19,800	16
Connecticut	3,500	14
Maine	2,500	20
Massachusetts	9,700	15
New Hampshire	1,400	20
Rhode Island	1,600	15
Vermont	1,100	21
Middle Atlantic	49,700	11
Delaware	600	18
District of Columbia	300	4
Maryland	4,500	17
New Jersey	5,700	10
New York	15,700	9
Pennsylvania	10,900	8
West Virginia	12,000	42
Southeast	167,600	52
Alabama	13,900	47
Arkansas	14,300	59
Florida	4,800	21
Georgia	12,700	41
Kentucky	24,600	64
Louisiana	14,100	55
Mississippi	4,700	28
North Carolina	26,700	62
South Carolina	8,300	43
Tennessee	23,400	64
Virginia	20,100	59
Central	57,300	12
Illinois	9,100	9
Indiana	6,600	14
Iowa	3,600	11
Michigan	9,000	13
Minnesota	3,900	11
Missouri	10,300	20
Ohio	8,300	8
Wisconsin	6,500	17
Northwest	12,500	13
Colorado	2,900	19
Idaho	700	9
Kansas	3,000	14
Montana	900	12
Nebraska	1,800	11
North Dakota	1,200	16
South Dakota	1,100	14
Utah	600	8
Wyoming	300	10

Number of white registrants rejected for mental
deficiency and rate per thousand examined, by
region and state (Continued)

Locality	Number	Rate per thou- sand
Southwest	70,700	54
Arizona	4,000	53
New Mexico	4,000	50
Oklahoma	9,000	29
Texas	53,700	63
Far West	13,700	9
California	11,500	11
Nevada	200	8
Oregon	800	5
Washington	1,200	5

centrated in the Southeast and Southwest. For instance, the rejection
rates for Oklahoma, Texas, and Kentucky are generally similar to those
of important Northern and Central states to which considerable numbers of Negroes have migrated. Two other Southern states, Florida and
Tennessee, have rates that more nearly approximate the rates of Northern states than the very high rates which are found to exist in South
Carolina and Louisiana. The accompanying table presents the data both
in absolute numbers and in rates.

The rejection rates for "mental deficiency" were, in general, the result of the quantity and quality of education available in the 1920's
and early 1930's. As we shall see later, important changes have taken
place since that time in the economic, social, and educational struc-

Number of non-white registrants rejected for
mental deficiency and rate per thousand examined, by region and state

Locality	Number	Rate per thou- sand
New England	1,000	65
Connecticut	600	96
Maine	*	..
Massachusetts	300	47
New Hampshire	*	..
Rhode Island	*	..
Vermont	*	..
Middle Atlantic	21,000	67
Delaware	700	96
District of Columbia	2,100	58
Maryland	8,200	133
New Jersey	2,800	74
New York	3,300	36
Pennsylvania	3,500	50
West Virginia	1,100	58

Number of non-white registrants rejected for mental deficieny and rate per thousand examined, by region and state (Continued)

Locality	Number	Rate per thousand
Southeast	268,000	202
Alabama	31,500	214
Arkansas	15,900	212
Florida	16,400	148
Georgia	30,500	206
Kentucky	2,500	73
Louisiana	37,500	247
Mississippi	33,400	205
North Carolina	36,100	209
South Carolina	34,100	277
Tennessee	9,800	120
Virginia	20,300	178
Central	13,200	61
Illinois	4,100	70
Indiana	1,000	47
Iowa	100	52
Michigan	2,900	94
Minnesota	*	..
Missouri	2,900	64
Ohio	2,000	38
Wisconsin	200	84
Northwest	600	40
Colorado	*	..
Idaho	*	..
Kansas	400	42
Montana	*	..
Nebraska	*	..
North Dakota	*	..
South Dakota	*	..
Utah	*	..
Wyoming	*	..
Southwest	19,200	107
Arizona	300	94
New Mexico	100	99
Oklahoma	2,600	112
Texas	16,200	106
Far West	1,400	50
California	1,300	50
Nevada	*	..
Oregon	*	..
Washington	*	..

* Under 100 rejected.

ture of the South, the source of most of the rejections. Hence, there is little but an historical justification for an exhaustive analysis of the World War II tables of educational rejections. We must, nevertheless, consider at least the major factors underlying the educational inadequacy of three-quarters of a million young men.

In this connection we must note that in 1930 there were between two and three out of every hundred white children between the ages of ten and fourteen no longer in school; the similar ratio for Negro children was eleven out of every hundred. Unless they had been especially good scholars or had had opportunities after leaving school to acquire certain rudimentary skills, a large percentage of these individuals would have failed the Armed Forces' mental test and been rejected. The foregoing ratios relate to the country as a whole. We know, however, that it was the Southeast that produced the largest number of rejections. In that region, in 1930, there were six white and thirteen Negro children out of every hundred in this age group no longer in school.

A first approximation, and it is only that, of the amount and quality of schooling available in different regions of the country can be obtained by reviewing the annual educational expenditures per pupil. For 1929–30, the range of expenditures of the forty-eight states and the District of Columbia was from just under $32 per pupil to over $137 per pupil. The twelve states with the lowest educational expenditures, up to $55 per pupil, accounted for five out of every seven rejectees. The relation between annual educational expenditures and the rejection rate per thousand examined during World War II is presented in the accompanying table.

This table indicates that the total rejection rate for the states in the fourth quartile was seven times as large as the rate for those in the first quartile. Perhaps the most striking single fact which is revealed by the table is the finding that the rejection rate for Negroes in the twelve states with the lowest educational expenditures was eighteen times as great as that for whites in the states with the highest expenditures. In order not to overelaborate this analysis, no distinction was

Rejection rate per 1,000 examined by states, classified according to educational expenditures per pupil, 1929–30

Division	Total	White	Negro
Total	37	22	155
12 states * and D.C. with high educational expenditures ($102.57–$137.55)	13	11	57
12 states † with medium high educational expenditures ($92.80–$102.56)	12	11	55
12 states ‡ with medium low educational expenditures ($60.00–$92.77)	21	11	80
12 states § with low educational expenditures ($31.89–$59.99)	91	54	192

* New York, Nevada, California, District of Columbia, Wyoming, New Jersey, Michigan, Colorado, Montana, Massachusetts, Arizona, Oregon, Connecticut.
† Illinois, Minnesota, Washington, North Dakota, Iowa, Rhode Island, Ohio, South Dakota, Delaware, Wisconsin, Nebraska, Kansas.
‡ New Hampshire, Indiana, Pennsylvania, Idaho, Vermont, Maryland, New Mexico, Utah, West Virginia, Missouri, Maine, Oklahoma.
§ Texas, Florida, Louisiana, Kentucky, Virginia, North Carolina, Tennessee, South Carolina, Alabama, Mississippi, Arkansas, Georgia.

made between the amount of money spent on white and Negro pupils. There are, however, marked differences in this ratio, even for states in the same class.

Many studies have pointed to the conclusion that there is a close relationship between expenditures for education and per capita income. The relationship does not, however, always obtain. The twelve states with the lowest per capita income in 1929 ($252 to $417) accounted for 380,000 out of the 716,000 total rejections during World War II. This was a smaller percentage than the twelve states with the lowest expenditures on education. As one would expect, the amount of money spent on education is more directly relevant than the average income of the state. It is interesting to note that North Dakota and South Dakota, which ranked in the lowest quartile on a per capita income basis, were in the second quartile in terms of educational expenditures. The following table summarizes the relationship between rejection rates and per capita income. Once again there are tremendous differences between Negro rejection rates in the poorest states and white rejection rates in the richest. This time the ratio is 21 to one.

Rejection rate per 1,000 examined by states, classified according to per capita income, 1930

Division	Total	White	Negro
Total	37	22	155
12 states * and D.C. with high per capita income ($745–$1,191)	12	10	56
12 states † with medium high per capita income ($574–$713)	20	16	93
12 states ‡ with medium low per capita income ($422–$566)	46	35	131
12 states § with low per capita income ($252–$417)	96	52	210

* District of Columbia, New York, New Jersey, California, Illinois, Delaware, Connecticut, Massachusetts, Rhode Island, Nevada, Pennsylvania, Ohio, Michigan.
† Washington, Maryland, Wyoming, New Hampshire, Oregon, Wisconsin, Colorado, Missouri, Montana, Vermont, Indiana, Arizona.
‡ Maine, Minnesota, Nebraska, Iowa, Utah, Kansas, Idaho, Florida, Texas, West Virginia, Oklahoma, Virginia.
§ South Dakota, Louisiana, North Dakota, New Mexico, Kentucky, Tennessee, Georgia, North Carolina, Alabama, Arkansas, Mississippi, South Carolina.

In discussing the county data presented earlier, reference was made to the obvious relation which existed between the degree of urbanization of a region and the rate of rejection because of educational handicaps. In order to test this relationship, the states were again grouped into four categories. The twelve states with the highest percent of rural population accounted for 309,000 out of the 716,000 total rejections. This is a less distinct relationship than was found to exist between rejection rates and educational expenditures and between the rates and income, but still a substantial one. The following table shows a clear relationship between rurality and rejection rates. Once again the most extreme difference between urbanized whites and the most rural Negroes presents a ratio of 21 to one.

Rejection rate per 1,000 examined by states,
classified according to percent rural, 1930

Division	Total	White	Negro
Total	37	22	155
12 states * and D.C. with low percent rural (0%–42.9%)	13	10	65
12 states † with medium low percent rural (43%–59.9%)	34	26	109
12 states ‡ with medium high percent rural (60%–68.9%)	58	36	183
12 states § with high percent rural (69%–100%)	88	48	209

* District of Columbia, Rhode Island, Massachusetts, New York, New Jersey, Illinois, California, Connecticut, Michigan, Ohio, Pennsylvania, Maryland, New Hampshire.
† Washington, Indiana, Wisconsin, Utah, Delaware, Florida, Oregon, Missouri, Colorado, Minnesota, Texas, Maine.
‡ Louisiana, Iowa, Kansas, Nevada, Nebraska, Arizona, Tennessee, Oklahoma, Montana, Vermont, Virginia, Wyoming.
§ Georgia, Kentucky, Idaho, West Virginia, Alabama, North Carolina, New Mexico, South Carolina, Arkansas, South Dakota, Mississippi, North Dakota.

The extent to which multiple factors determine the educational achievement of a population, rather than any single determinant, even one so important as the financial well-being of the community, is brought out by the following table. In this instance, rejection rates are shown by income level and by region of the country. It is apparent that there are sizable differences in rejection rates from region to region, even when income differences are taken into account. A part of these differences is doubtless due to such factors as the uneven apportionment of school expenditures in some states between whites and Negroes.

Rejection rate per 1,000 examined by region and 1929 per capita income

Region	High ($1,191–$745)	Medium-high ($713–$574)	Medium-low ($566–$422)	Low ($417–$252)
New England	15	21	20	..
Middle Atlantic	11	39	43	..
Southeast	..	..	77	100
Southwest	..	54	61	50
Central	12	19	11	..
Northwest	..	16	12	15
Far West	11	5	..	..

There is one concluding observation suggested by this table. In wealthy states a very high percentage of individuals will achieve at least a basic education. The converse is, however, not always true. Some states with low per capita income show a rejection rate comparable to much richer areas. It is clear, nevertheless, that economics has much to do with the conditions underlying the World War II rejections and their alleviation, even though there are important non-economic factors at work.

14.

WASTED MANPOWER

Four major conditions account for much, but not all, of our squandering of our human-resource capital: unemployment, underemployment, inadequate training, and arbitrary barriers to employment. The first is the waste that arises in a period of depression when there is a shortage of jobs so that men accustomed to working must sit in idleness. The next, underemployment, is a word of many meanings. We will use it to describe situations where individuals are unable to find a satisfactory, productive job in their community that pays at least the minimum wage prescribed by Federal or state law.

The third waste arises when the community fails to invest adequately in the education and training of people so that many fail to develop their full potentialities, with the result that their productivity in later life is far below what it could have been had they received better preparation. Fourthly, there is the waste which, in the language of the economists, reflects imperfections in the market. Men stay in jobs where their contribution is much less than it would be if they were able to move to where there is greater need for their skills.

Let us examine each cause of waste in turn in order to appraise the magnitude of the losses and the prospects for remedial action. Over thirty years have passed since the last major decline in business occurred, a decline marked by a sharp fall in output and employment. At the depth of the depression, early in 1933, probably as many as fifteen million were unemployed out of a work force of about fifty-two million, and many others were working only part time. Many observers feel that the long intervening period of prosperity, marred only by minor periods of recession, augurs an optimistic outlook. They believe that the worst scourge of industrial capitalism—large-scale unemployment—has now been brought under effective social control.

But a minority of informed opinion is more cautious. Most economists take cognizance of the fact that the Employment Act of 1946 gave legislative sanction to the Roosevelt revolution by acknowledging the obligation of the Federal Government to use its great powers to prevent if possible, and to counteract if necessary, any substantial decline in employment. Hopefully, the Federal Government will be able to meet its responsibilities when the challenge comes. But it may be too early to conclude that this country will never again be faced with a major depression, with its dreadful concomitant of widespread unemployment. Mounting concern at the beginning of the 1960s with the increasing number of unemployed is evidence of this latent fear. Our allies, as well as our enemies, pay close attention to our economic indicators, for they realize that a depression in the United States would have a significant impact on the rest of the world.

We know what widespread unemployment means in terms of human misery; we must not overlook its contributions to social upheaval. The evil that was Hitler's and the destruction which he wrought on Western civilization had many roots, but none more important than the desperation of the German masses growing out of their prolonged unemployment. They were willing to follow any man who promised them work— even if the work was in munitions and aircraft factories. Much as they feared war, the Germans feared unemployment more.

Another poignant example was the slow recovery of Great Britain after World War II, due in part to the earlier mishandling of chronic unemployment in the valleys of South Wales. The memories of men are long, especially the memories of those who, like the Welsh miner, suffered grievously. The Welsh were forced to live on the dole, not for one or even two years but for an entire decade—and some even longer. As I wrote in *Grass on the Slag Heaps; The Story of the Welsh Miners,* the towns appeared to be asleep. Men no longer knew what day of the week it was, for it did not matter. And they stayed in bed until noon in order to save one meal. It was inevitable that men forced to trade work for idleness, self-support for a pensioner's status, and adequate wages for paltry allowances would deteriorate physically and emotionally. And the wives of such men could not escape deterioration. Most serious, however, was the influence of unemployment upon the children. As the Commissioner for the Special Areas stated in his report on South Wales:

I am alarmed when I think of the future of those unemployed youth, whose disastrous start in life is to be consigned to idleness, and who are consequently early enmeshed in its attendant evils. Many of these youths are brought up in homes where no member of the family has worked for many years, where the daily bread is not won, but provided by assistance from the State, a position often so long established that it comes to be looked upon as a normal feature of life. It is difficult for the best instincts to survive in such atmosphere; all sense of independence and enterprise is lost. An unhealthy outlook subtly grows at a period when character is most easily formed. Life drifts on without experience of work. Lack of inclination to work is followed by complete indifference either as to its procuration or its performance when secured. Practical experience shows that many such youths fail to hold their jobs. Rejected from industry, they again find themselves in the ranks of the unemployed, but with even worse prospects than before. Under these conditions future citizens are being created, who can but become a burden to themselves and to the State. These youths must be saved from the dread consequences of idleness, quickly and at all costs. Their circumstances are particularly intolerable in a prosperous state with high ideals as to the social welfare of its citizens. However pressing other reforms may be, here is one which brooks no delay and to which precedence should be given.

The fact that the Welsh miners have been recalcitrant during the postwar years, that they have made difficulties when the government sought to bring over Italians, Germans and others to work in the mines, that they have pressed hard for advances in wages and improvements in working conditions, that they did not turn a sensitive ear to their country's need for more coal nor see the nation's crisis as their particular problem is less surprising, in light of their depression experiences, than that they and their sons went back to coal mining at the beginning of World War II and have stayed on the job since then doing a reasonable day's work for reasonable pay.

We can look at the subject closer to home. At the end of the 1930s my associates and I undertook a large-scale investigation into the long-term unemployed in New York City. On the basis of this study, participated in by a psychiatrist and several social workers, we concluded that

our evidence disclosed widespread deterioration in the physical, emotional and occupational condition of the children of the unemployed. If the plight of the present generation were not proof enough of the need for the utmost exertion of the body politic to cope with unemployment, the threat to the next generation dare not be brushed aside. In the last analysis the wealth of a nation is the quality of its human resources. Only if every individual has the right to work can the United States be true to its heritage and fulfill its promise.

Since 1946, which saw the passage of the Employment Act, the responsibility has rested squarely with the Federal Government to prevent a repetition of such human and economic devastation or at the least to use all of its power to counteract the forces of depression if they should be unleashed. But while this responsibility is unequivocally the Federal Government's, only time will tell whether our leadership has the intelligence, the imagination, and the resources to reverse a depression, if it fails to prevent its onset.

No quantitative measures can convey the cost in human suffering that the large-scale unemployment of the nineteen thirties brought in its wake. Men selling apples at street corners, rummaging in garbage cans for food, taking to the road without plan or purpose, women receiving fifty cents for a day's domestic labor or working in a factory for seven cents an hour—these illustrations could be multiplied many times over. And still they would not reveal the greatest cost of all—the hopes that foundered after a lifetime of striving and saving, particularly that one's children could look forward to a happier and more prosperous America. The depression denied the past as it did the future.

We tend to repress the unpleasant, and understandably so. Yet it is well to recall how close to anarchy the United States came early in 1933. Farm communities were threatening to hang sheriffs who sought to enforce the law. I recall one professor telling us late in February that if the banks closed and farmers refused to send their produce to the city, New York would suffer a famine by the end of the week.

The second major cause of waste—underemployment—is more difficult to illustrate. Let us start by considering what the concept does not include. When millions of young people in high school and college hold down part-time jobs, they are not underemployed any more than are the millions of women who work out of personal preference for only part of the year. Many older women take jobs for the two months before Christmas to add to their spending money at the holiday season. They do not want to work longer.

Who then are the underemployed? They are in the first instance men and women on farms who are busy when there is planting or harvesting to do but who have little opportunity to use their time productively during the rest of the year. Although the agricultural labor force declined from about 9,500,000 in 1940 to 6,600,000 in 1956—a decline of more than one-half over the quarter century during a period when the population it has been feeding has increased by 62,000,000, or 47 per cent—apparently considerable underemployment continues. We can overlook the wealthy Iowa farmers who close up their homes at the end of November to spend the winter in Florida; and we can disregard the exceptional case of wheat farmers who have moved to the city where they have full-time jobs but who return to their farms in the spring for two weeks to plant and again for two weeks in the fall to harvest.

More directly relevant to an understanding of underemployment in agriculture is the typical experience when a company opens a new plant in rural Georgia or Tennessee. As many as five or ten thousand applicants may be lined up at the plant gate on the day hiring begins. Some have come as far as five hundred miles. And the reason is that if husband and wife in a farm family should be lucky enough to get jobs, even at minimum pay, they will earn more than $4,000 in cash during the course of a year while they would probably net little more than $1,500 cash from their farm operations. Moreover, by working a little harder—in the early morning and in the evening—and by being absent for a day from the factory now and again, they can continue to run their farm and handle their new jobs as well.

In southeastern Ohio the leaders of the business community are actively recruiting industry to insure that the farm population does not desert the countryside for the city, and the rich farm states of the Middle West are engaged in similar promotion for the same reason. In many parts of the country farming is becoming a part-time occupation. A decade ago, only one out of every four families living on a farm supported themselves solely from agriculture. As the average length of the industrial work week continues to decline and as the technology of agriculture further advances, this trend of mixed agricultural-industrial employment is likely to be accelerated wherever family-size farms continue to be an economic unit. The necessary correlative trend of locating new plants in predominately agricultural regions is favored by many companies, because among other reasons it fits in with their plans to decentralize and promises escape from intense trade-union pressure.

World War II saw a tremendous increase in the number of women in paid employment, including approximately 4 million housewives who had not been in the labor force in 1940. Since the turn of the century the trend in women's employment has been up, but World War II represented an important breakthrough in that it became respectable for married women, even those with children, to work out of the home. This trend has continued in the postwar years; during 1964, over three-fifths of the thirty-three million women who worked sometime during the year were married, and more than two out of every five mothers in the country with children of school age worked.

These figures are startling, but even more so are the wide differences among various regions of the country in the proportion of women who work. In Durham, North Carolina, more than 45 per cent of women who are fourteen years of age or older were in the labor force in 1960. In Johnstown, Pennsylvania, the proportion was only one out of four. Although there are several factors responsible for this variation, including the percentage of Negroes in the local population (Negro women are more likely to work), as well as age and marital distribution (single girls are more likely to work and married women in their twenties are less likely to), the key factor is the labor market. Are suitable jobs for women available?

A related consideration is the tradition in the community—is it the custom for women, especially married women, to work? The city with one of the highest female-participation rates in the country is Fall River, Massachusetts, a community with a heavy Catholic population. The negative attitude of the Church toward married women working out of the home has not been an effective counterweight against the tradition of married women working in New England textile towns. The fact that mill workers are likely to be related to one another facilitates caring for the children while the mother works.

Although many women who now spend their time at home and in voluntary activities do so out of preference and would not take a job even if one became available, there are undoubtedly many who would welcome an opportunity to work in paid employment. There is no way of determining what percentage of the twenty million women between the ages of eighteen and sixty-four with no work experience during the year would be interested in a part- or full-time job if the opportunity presented itself. A conservative estimate might place five million of these women as "underemployed" in the sense that they would like a paid job.

Another large group of the underemployed which is also difficult to estimate in statistical terms, is the physically handicapped who are either not working or have only makeshift jobs. Some are so severely handicapped that they cannot do a full day's work, but there are many others who, with some rehabilitative help, could be regularly employed. One government committee recently estimated that there are two million persons of employable age who with rehabilitation could and would work.

An interesting sidelight of the subtle relations between employment and illness is what transpired during the peak of World War II when industry was desperate for workers. For the first time in the recent history of the mental-hospital system of the state of New York the annual patient census failed to increase. In part, this occurred because many persons capable of making only a borderline adjustment in a normal environment were hired or kept on their jobs because there was no one else available; in part it reflected the change in hospital discharge policies, which were liberalized because the doctors knew that convalescent patients have a better chance to readjust when they are more likely to find jobs.

It is also difficult to appraise the amount of underemployment that is masked by the rise in school enrollment. Although in most states sixteen is the age at which young people can get working papers, by 1963–64 four states had advanced the school-leaving age to eighteen or high-school graduation. Although the prolongation of schooling must be viewed as a social gain, it is not without drawbacks. Many adolescents attend school but fail to profit from the experience. In fact, they would be better off if they could work. The high percentage of youngsters who leave school just as soon as they reach the legal age points up that they have been straining at the leash for some time—a fact that can be attested to by any high-school teacher.

The contemporary concern with juvenile delinquency has led some informed people to reconsider the wisdom of compulsory school attendance for certain groups of adolescents. The real dilemma is the absence of adequate alternatives. A pressing need in metropolitan communities is to find constructive activities for emotionally disturbed and recalcitrant young people to whom the conventional school, academic or vocational, has little to offer.

Many college students are little more than time servers, waiting to grow up so that they can marry or get a job. Until recently, middle-class parents did not expect their daughters to marry before twenty-two. Today more and more young women are getting married while at college. One young lady recently withdrew at the end of her sopho-more year because most of her intimate friends had married and she found herself socially isolated. As far as the young men are concerned, many companies will not take them on for executive training until they have their college sheepskins. At what age young people begin to work has as much to do with social convention as with the require-ments for formal training.

Older persons represent still another important group among whom underemployment is typical. In a farming community a man keeps on working as long as his strength holds out, but compulsory retirement is characteristic of an industrial society. Until recently revised, the Social Security Act served to deter older people from working. A man who kept working gained little; his benefits were suspended and his taxes increased. The extent of the decline in the percentage of older persons in the labor force can be illustrated by comparing 1920 and 1960. In the former year three out of five men sixty-five years of ago or above were gainfully employed; in the latter year only one out of three were in the labor force. The participation rates for older women are particularly low; currently one in ten women over sixty-five works. Considering the fact that on the average women live six years longer than their husbands and that they usually marry men three years older than themselves, they must anticipate a long period of widow-hood. More than half of all women over sixty-five are widows and nearly half of all women who become widows can expect to live for twenty years after their husbands die. For economic as well as psychological reasons many of these older women need to work.

There is no simple way of determining the extent of underemploy-ment among each of the five groups—farmers, housewives, the handi-capped, youth, and older persons—and still less of developing a sound aggregate figure. But the total waste of human resources arising out of the inability of members of these several groups who want to work to secure jobs is substantial.

This brings us to the third major cause of waste, that growing out of the failure of our society to invest adequately in the development of its people, particularly its young people during their formative years. A comprehensive treatment of society's investment in its human re-sources would necessitate consideration of such basic desiderata as higher incomes for families which are still below a decent minimum; improved housing and recreational facilities, particularly in metro-politan centers; expanded health services; and more special services to help young people to meet their emotional and behavior problems. However, here we will illuminate the problem by concentrating on a single aspect—investment in education. While people may disagree about the responsibility of government to realize all of these desid-erata, there is agreement that it is government's obligation to provide adequate schooling for all—at least through high school.

World War II threw a searchlight on the deficiencies in the educa-tional preparation of the young. More than 700,000 young men were rejected for military service because of illiteracy; another 500,000 illiterates were taken into the armed services. Most of these were sent to special training units where they were taught how to read and write before they were permitted to start their basic military training. The record also shows that another 700,000 who served had had only the barest education. In short, almost two million men out of the eighteen million who were screened—one out of every nine—were total or borderline illiterates.

Not long ago in certain regions of the country it mattered little whether a man could read or not. What he needed to know to take care of himself and his family he learned by word of mouth. But developments after World War I doomed these isolated and self-sufficient communities. The automobile was the most important disruptive factor. The steady advance of industrialization also contributed to making the uneducated very vulnerable as regards their employability. Not only the large corporation but the small business firm moved to establish hiring standards. With most of the population able to read and write, employers were disinclined to add illiterates to their work force. Even the night watchman must keep records which the insurance company will accept in case of a claim. A Detroit manufacturer who installed an electric time clock found that his anticipated gains failed to materialize because illiterate workers, unable to locate their cards, defaced them so as to be able to recognize them. Unfortunately, the machine would not stamp a defaced card.

There is no place in modern American industry for the illiterate. There will soon be no place for him anywhere in the economy. Even in the face of a severe shortage of domestic help, a woman of means will hesitate to hire a maid who is unable to write down the names of people who telephone during the course of the day. A major escape route to economic emancipation is being closed for the many uneducated persons now living in the impoverished rural areas of the Southeast. Because they encounter increased difficulty in finding work in the larger urban centers of the South or the North, they hesitate to migrate.

Large-scale illiteracy remains a major national deficiency even when considered solely within the context of our defense preparations. Although the present manpower needs of the armed services can be met without dipping into the pool of the poorly educated, this country would be in a serious plight if major hostilities should develop. Its mobilization time will be in terms of hours, possibly minutes, not years or months as in earlier wars. We would not again be able to devote time and resources to training illiterates if war came again.

But there is more to illiteracy than the threat which it represents to our national security and economic progress. What does it imply for the quality of life of the individual citizen? How can a man who is unable to read and write take proper care of his family and himself, safeguard his health and theirs, keep in contact with relatives and friends, guide his children in the choices which they face, and take advantage of the privileges and responsibilities of citizenship?

Small wonder that the Russians have begun to exploit this social blight on American democracy by pointing out, among other things, that we "spend more on migratory birds than on migratory people" among whom illiteracy is rampant. With illiteracy a major barrier to progress in both Asia and Africa, the Russians are profiting greatly from a propaganda effort which stresses their own phenomenal progress in its eradication. At the same time they are calling attention to the shocking number of illiterates still to be found in the United States. The less prosperous nations cannot conceive how the wealthy United States, with its long tradition of public education, has not eliminated the scourge of illiteracy.

Inadequate investment in the educational preparation of Americans is not limited to illiteracy, which is only an extreme example of neglect. Other evidence of glaring deficiencies is at hand. As was pointed out in a presentation to the President's Cabinet some years ago (*The Skilled Work Force of the United States*), one third of all young men screened for military service at the end of the Korean hostilities were placed in Mental Groups IV or V, which means that because of their low intellectual achievement they were either rejected for service (V) or found unacceptable for advanced training (IV). Only 23 per cent of the men from the western states were in these two lowest classes, while almost 53 per cent of the selectees from the southeastern states were so classified. The serious implications of these findings are suggested by the following quotation from the presentation:

Men acquire skill by building on what they learn in school. The experience of the Armed Forces illustrates the high percentage of the population that cannot readily profit from advanced training for skills.

The number and percentage of men who scored high on the test also reflected significant regional differentials. For the country as a whole, about one out of every three men scored in Groups I or II. The ratio for the West was two out of five; for the Southeast only one out of six. While part of this difference was due to the larger number of poorly educated Negroes in the South, the greater part reflects the fact that the West has twice as many high-school graduates among men of military age as does the Southeast—61 per cent compared to the South's 30 per cent.

A further distinction is suggested by these figures. Not only does the South have fewer high-school graduates, but the quality of their schooling is inferior. In an equal number of high-school graduates, those from the West accounted for more than twice as many in Groups I and II as those from the South.

Our study of the Negro (*The Negro Potential*) throws some additional light on underinvestment in education. The glaring deficiencies in the educational preparation of the Negro can be underscored by pointing out that if every Negro received the same education as did the average white child living outside the South, there would be an annual increase of Negro high-school graduates, according to the census of 1950, of about 65,000 to 158,000; of college graduates from less than 10,000 to more than 23,000.

The fourth important area of waste grows out of various imperfections in the market place. The American economy derives much of its strength from its reliance upon the operations of the "free market," but, as we shall soon see, the market is not always free. The job does not always go to the best qualified. Discrimination on the basis of race or sex takes a heavy toll.

Although the Negro represented in 1960 21 per cent of the population of the South, he is still almost completely barred from production jobs, which means that he is cut off from the opportunity to acquire industrial skills and to be promoted to preferred positions. In southern industry he is relegated to the dead-end job of common laborer. Aside from a few breakthroughs on the periphery of the region—in North Carolina, Tennessee, and Texas—his only opportunities for skilled industrial work are found in plants that employ only Negro labor. Many southern Negroes who have had the opportunity to acquire a skill in the armed services cannot find skilled jobs on their return home, and they are likely to be off before long to the North or West, sped on their way by the Federal-State Employment Service. To protect its folkways, the South has been willing deliberately to reduce its skill capital at a time when it needs all that it has and more to accelerate its industrial expansion.

But it would be wrong to single out the South as the only area which fosters discrimination. Negroes can now obtain employment outside of the South in many different fields from which they had long been excluded. Many national companies have begun to recruit Negroes trained in engineering, chemistry, and mathematics. However, only recently large companies have begun to accept Negroes in the executive-trainee programs out of which future management will be developed.

Once again, the experience of the armed forces is illuminating. In World War II, one out of every four white soldiers in Mental Groups I and II became officers. In the case of Negroes the proportion was one in ten. The Army preferred a less capable man with white skin, just as the South and North do today, to a more capable man whose skin is black. The cost not only to the individual who was discriminated against but to our entire society must not be minimized. How could one expect a Negro to do his best for his country in its war against fascism when he himself was victimized by a system of racial segregation?

The extent to which racial discrimination perverts the free market is illustrated by recent census data. A white male graduate from an elementary school earns more than the Negro high-school graduate;

a white male high-school graduate has earnings greater than those brought home by a Negro male college graduate. Discrimination erases the advantages of four years' additional training for the Negro.

In its study of *Womanpower*, the National Manpower Council found that the labor market was still sharply differentiated into men's and women's jobs. Many of the better-paying jobs are classified as "men's jobs" and women are automatically excluded from them. While the Council did not find many clear-cut instances of women being paid less than men for identical work, it recognized the widespread practice of subtly differentiating jobs held by men and women in order to justify what amounted to a substantially higher wage for men.

Discriminatory practices are even more pronounced in higher-level jobs. With the single exception of department stores no important sector of American business normally advances women into executive positions. As so frequently happens when discrimination is rife, there is an easy rationale at hand. It is that women do not possess the requisite skills and competences. But that only pushes the matter back one stage. Investigation disclosed that even today women are seldom hired for executive-trainee positions, and that they do not have easy entree to the wide variety of training programs that are available in most large corporations even after they have proved by a good work record that they are seriously interested in their jobs.

When challenged, employers insist that women are not really interested in working very hard; they will not travel; and in any case their turnover rate is so high that it is unprofitable to train them. There is considerable merit to each of these points but not nearly as much as most employers apparently believe. Many men also are work-shy. Many business firms are hard pressed to find or keep good men who are willing to travel. But most important, a careful review of the statistics reveals that the difference in turnover rates between men and women is much less than is commonly assumed. Young women leave an employer to get married and have children; young men go into the armed services or leave one job to seek a better one. By thirty, each tends to become more stable. The differences in turnover rates for the same kind of jobs are not nearly sufficient to justify industry's training men and failing to train women.

It is true that some changes are under way to insure the more effective utilization of womanpower. But male employers and male employees are altering their attitudes and behavior very slowly and usually only under the pressure of necessity. Discriminatory practices survive because the in-group seeks to protect its preferred position. It will give way, as already suggested, only under the pressure of necessity. There may be a slowly growing realization that, although discrimination may yield some short-run gains to the incumbents, the long-run consequences are costly to all. American society has finally decided that it has a moral obligation to put into practice the principles on which this democracy rests—that individuals must be judged on their performance, not on irrelevant considerations of sex, race, religion, or ethnic origin. The question remains: how long will it be before it puts its principles into action?

We have seen that discrimination is important in the underutilization of human resources, but it is only one manifestation of malfunctioning of the market place. The fact that there are three distinct markets for manpower is another source of trouble. The largest market is the business sector, where profit-making predominates. Then there is the market wherein professional people sell their services directly to the consumer, as, for instance, the physician. Finally there is the important market within which government and voluntary agencies provide important services but do not sell them for a profit. The strength of these respective markets to attract and retain manpower is very uneven, with the result that serious waste frequently results.

During the past several years it has not been exceptional for a well-trained young man who has earned his doctorate in one of the sciences to receive an offer of employment by private industry at a salary above that earned by his professor who has been at the university for twenty years. One need not be at home in the esoteric realm of economic theory to realize that something is seriously awry in the market when the recent graduate is paid more than the teacher who has trained him. But the company that offered the young man $1,000 a month is likely to be able to recapture this high cost in the price it charges the consumer or the government. The university, on the other hand, has been slow to learn how to charge adequate tuition—or to secure adequate subventions from state legislatures or adequate gifts from private donors—so as to be able to adjust teachers' salaries to the changes that have been taking place in the economy. One need not accept the extreme doctrine that our future depends primarily on our scientists and engineers to be disturbed by the fact that a few years ago a master plumber earned more than an associate professor of physics who has charge of a major defense project!

Einstein, in bitter reaction to the unconscionable way in which our security laws were enforced, stated that if he had to live his life over again, he would become a plumber. But it augurs ill for a society that has regained its emotional balance to continue to permit its incentive system to remain so distorted that there is a net economic advantage for a man to become a plumber rather than a physicist! The pulling power of business was so strong until recently that many were deflected from working in non-profit sectors of the economy, despite their desire to do so.

There is a growing interest among the American public in the control of mental disease. Most mental hospitals, however, encounter great difficulties in recruiting psychiatrists. A young doctor who has finished his resident training and has completed his didactic analysis is in a position to earn in private practice an average of between fifteen and twenty dollars an hour. Even when he devotes some time to hospital work or to teaching, he can quickly bring his income to

$35,000 or $40,000 a year if he is helped by older colleagues who have more work than they can handle. No state legislature, no matter how deep its concern with mental illness can establish a salary structure that is even reasonably competitive with private practice, for it must always consider the impact of raising salaries for one group on all other groups on the payroll. The mental hospitals of the country are grossly understaffed and will so remain as long as the number of young doctors able and willing to undergo the long cycle of training in psychiatry remains small and the consumer demand for their services remains high. Some may question whether any underutilization exists in this field, since the psychiatrist in private practice is busy taking care of patients. However, while the psychoanalyst in private practice may be able to complete the treatment of five patients during the course of a year, the psychiatrist in a state mental hospital is usually responsible for the care of more than two hundred patients—all of whom are seriously ill, though many may no longer be amenable to treatment.

No one who has watched the efforts of repeated administrations to recruit competent men from business and retain them in government service can be oblivious to the faulty allocation and waste of manpower growing out of gross discrepancies in rewards in different markets. Surely an able man who holds down an important position in the Department of State, the Department of Defense, or on the President's own staff is likely to make a greater contribution in government than in business. But, as the Hoover Commission was amazed to learn, the average term of an assistant secretary of the Department of Defense has been less than two years! Senior career officials, both civilian and military, leave the Federal service constantly, not because they want to become rich but because they are not able to earn enough to send their children through college. Congress and the American public, by their failure to make government employment reasonably attractive (no one suggests that it be fully competitive with private industry), are insuring that many important programs are handled by mediocre personnel. Surely it is foolish to continue a personnel system that insures weakness at the top of a government on whose wisdom and efficiency rests not only the nation's welfare and security but that of the entire free world. With the next Federal budget totaling over $110 billion, such a policy is preposterous.

In addition to the four major orders of waste outlined above, underutilization occurs in many sectors of the economy for a host of different reasons. When manpower policy is poorly designed or poorly implemented underutilization results. A spectacular example of this type of waste occurred in World War II. In the initial stages of mobilization any man who was usefully engaged in study or in work was deferred. Those drafted were either the unemployed or those with the least important jobs. After Pearl Harbor the rules were altered, but married men, especially those with children, were still deferred. It was not until 1943 that fathers were called to active duty. One unforeseen but important consequence of this method of call-up was the selection of future officers from among the least talented—those drafted early. Many immature youngsters were rushed through officer-candidate schools early in the war. When mature and talented men became available, the officer quotas had been largely filled. If the need for large-scale mobilization should arise again, we must avoid such an unbalanced call-up.

Another waste in human resources results from the lack of flexibility in promotion policies in both civilian and military life. Fortunately, General Pershing was still alive in 1939 and was able to encourage President Roosevelt to ignore seniority and select General Marshall as Chief of Staff even though he was far down on the list of eligibles. But seniority plays an important role in most large organizations, and though it doubtless contributes to stability it takes a heavy toll. The problem is compounded because the more a man has at stake in pension and retirement rights, the less likely that he will strike out in search of another job where he may have greater opportunity to utilize his skills. For men who have acquired substantial deferred benefits, the costs of moving are too high.

Malutilization also occurs through the arbitrary use of power by strongly organized groups. Everybody is acquainted with examples of featherbedding, where unions force employers to hire more men than are required to get the work done. But not everyone recognizes that when teachers fight the hiring of assistants, when registered nurses view askance the assignment of responsibilities to practical nurses, or when physicians hesitate to transfer functions to the technicians who assist them, the protection of a preferred market position is resulting in the wasteful use of manpower resources. I once asked my ophthalmologist, who is an exceedingly busy doctor, whether his nurse could do refractions for him. He answered that she could do them better than he because she is more patient and would not get bored so easily. "Why, then, don't you let her do them?" "Oh, that's very simple: you wouldn't pay twenty-five dollars for the examination, and in any case I wouldn't get the fee!"

Some months ago I asked a high-school principal why all students had to attend class for five or six sessions a day. Since he was the head of a school where pupils were specially selected for their intellectual ability, I asked him why he did not ease his staffing problems by putting more responsibility on students to study by themselves. For example, they could attend class for three or four periods a day and spend the rest of the time in the library or the laboratory. He told me that he had made this specific proposal to his faculty but they were overwhelmingly opposed to it, as was their teachers' association, for fear that if the proposal were adopted boards of education might decide to reduce the budget for teaching.

The foregoing examples suggest only a few of the ways in which organizational structure, management policies, and, above all, the functioning of different labor markets contribute to the underutilization of the nation's manpower resources. In periods of manpower stringency, such as occurred in World War II, and to a lesser degree during the Korean hostilities, our economy and society were able to develop the incentive and energy to break through tradition and structure improved patterns of utilization. Since the pressure for change is seldom so intense, the order of waste from underutilization remains high.

While the last decade offers ground for hope that in the future our economy may be spared the devastating losses that resulted from the major depression of 1929–33 and its aftermath, public policy must be designed with constant attention paid to preventing such a recurrence if possible and to alleviating it as quickly as possible if it cannot be prevented. So destructive is the loss of work to men that few modern societies are likely to survive a prolonged period of large-scale unemployment. Men will willingly gamble their own lives and the future of their society on radical change if their only alternative is to sit in idleness and see their hopes and dreams ground into nothingness.

Less dangerous than a complete economic slowdown but still very costly are the losses that a society suffers when it fails to provide adequate work for millions who have need of it and for other millions who would prefer work to idleness. Underemployment takes its toll, every day and every year, and the cumulative costs are tremendous. The solutions will not be easy to come by. They involve a wide range of actions from assisting people to leave depressed areas to rehabilitating the physically handicapped. Government—Federal, state, and local—has important responsibilities in these regards, but in our type of society, where private industry largely determines the level of demand for labor and where trade-unions and voluntary organizations exercise an important influence on the functioning of the labor market, there is need for active participation of these several groups in developing constructive solutions. The American people must recognize that the right to work is a moral as well as an economic imperative.

Although all signs point to the increasing dependence of our economy on people with high orders of skill and competence, we have been very slow to increase the share of our national income devoted to education. We have not understood the extent to which the future of our society will be determined primarily by our success in raising the quality of our human resources. We can no longer ignore the fact that children, wherever they are born, are a national resource, not only a local and state responsibility. The Northern, more industrialized states cannot ignore this problem, for it is their problem too. They will need additional workers most of whom will necessarily have to be drawn from the poorer regions of the country. We are sorely in need of a realistic accounting system that would set out clearly the costs and gains from additional investment in the preparation of the young—a balance sheet for the United States.

No matter how much we admire the workings and achievements of the free market, we must recognize that it is frequently not free enough to prevent the malutilization of the nation's human resources. Discrimination, which the free market tolerates and sometimes encourages, takes a heavy toll. So, too, does the imbalance in rewards, which has been accentuated of late, between the profit and the non-profit sectors. And, finally, there are many managerial policies that operate to waste human potential by preferring the traditional to the efficient, the established to the creative.

All of these wastes exist; some are chronic, others intermittent. But of their seriousness there can be little question. They slow our economic progress and weaken our national security. Even more, they deny to untold millions the promise of our democracy, which is to give each man a fair start in life and to reward him according to his performance.

15.

THE MANAGEMENT
OF MEN

Understanding is a prerequisite for effective action. In Chapter 10
we considered the relationships between personality and performance
with regard to the individual's assets and liabilities, the impact of
organizational policy and of environmental factors, and the level,
range, and continuity in performance. In this chapter we shall search
out the more important actions that can be taken by the various
sectors of our society to control and reduce ineffectiveness.

Since ours is a pluralistic society, no single institution—not business, not government, nor community agency—can exert more than a
limited influence on the performance of individuals and groups. No
matter how hard it strives, no matter how powerful it may be, the
fact remains that the power and influence of any institution is limited. Its actions alone can never fully determine the outcome. This
limitation on the scale and scope of action which attaches to even
the most powerful institutions in our society means that a comprehensive consideration of policy must make provision for at least three
major sectors—the organizational, the governmental, and the societal.
Individually, each sector can do much to improve the level of performance, but the greatest gains can come about when the three reinforce one another.

The Organizational Sector

We will begin our consideration of how policy can contribute to the
more effective performance of men by setting out the problems and potentialities for action that confront management in large organizations.

As we had occasion to note earlier, more and more of the activities of modern man take place in large organizational structures where the element of size presents both opportunities and limitations.

The range of actions which the management of large organizations can take to control ineffective performance can be reviewed in terms of the need to plan, the stability of policies, and the specifics of policies and procedures. Large organizations have a clear need to plan ahead, for their very size means that they face serious costs if they are forced to improvise. One of the major advantages of largeness is the opportunity that it provides for decentralization and specialization of function. However, changes can be effected only within a framework of organizational objectives, policies, and procedures that are well understood and accepted by all echelons. In attempting to effect change without long-range plans, a company will be forced to solve each problem as it arises. Those at the top may have a sufficient overview of a reorganization but lower levels of management will be confused and uncertain during any change, and this can only result in a serious reduction in their own effectiveness and that of their subordinates.

But long-range planning alone is not enough: the key to success is the quality of these plans. The more management can at least delineate the range of its future requirements, the more likely that its long-range plans will be sound. In recent years more and more large corporations as well as voluntary organizations have sought to forecast their future personnel requirements, especially for key people, by developing replacement schedules which identify the important positions that are likely to become available as a result of death, retirement, and other losses. But for every instance where the analysis of future requirements has been ventured, there are tens and hundreds of illustrations of a failure to act until pressure or even a crisis has arisen. While some sort of a solution can always be worked out in an emergency, an improvised solution will generally be inferior to one which has been worked out over time. Alternatives tend to disappear as deadlines approach.

One major reason underlying the need of large organizations to plan ahead in light of their future requirements is that they are likely to encounter difficulties if they rely exclusively on the market for meeting their personnel requirements. Their very size makes it likely that the market will not have the numbers and more particularly the types of individuals that the organization will require if it is forced to replace within a short period many of its key personnel or if it must expand rapidly. The only buttress for the market is the constructive use of time when time is still available to recruit and train so that future requirements can be met more nearly from within the organization.

The extent to which planning is successful depends in large measure on the quality of the people assigned to the planning functions.

Historically, the Army and the Navy assigned its staff personnel in the following descending order—the best to operations, followed by supply, intelligence, and finally personnel. Business and voluntary organizations have followed a somewhat similar practice; they pay much less attention to their manpower and personnel posts than to such functions as finance and production.

As President Eisenhower remarked during one of his 1958 press conferences, no plans are likely to prove adequate in a world characterized by constant and unexpected changes, but the fact that an effort is made to plan will usually result in a better outcome than if no effort is ventured. It is not possible for a planning group to forecast the future, but it is often possible for them to take into consideration some of the more important contingencies that may arise. The more experience they have in planning, the more sensitive they will be in recognizing the contingencies that they must include in their future plans.

The better the quality of planning the better the level of future performance. If an organization has the foresight to take action in time to acquire resources essential to its future work, if it avoids making commitments that are likely to reduce its future flexibility unduly, if it has considered and weighed the relative advantages of responding to possible emergencies, its level of performance will be noticeably better than if it has failed to do any of these things.

A second way in which organizational action bears directly on effective performance is through stability of policy. To illustrate this point, let us consider for a moment the results that are likely to flow from a marked instability in policy. We noted earlier that one of the major advantages of large organizations is their opportunity to rely on specialization and decentralization in order to integrate the work of large numbers of people for a common purpose. But this can be done effectively only through established plans and procedures. It is not possible to rely on the personal direction and relationships which can exist in small organizations. When members of a large organization, frequently stationed hundreds or thousands of miles from headquarters and with little or no personal knowledge of the leadership, are confronted with frequent changes in policy, they are likely to conclude that the top executives do not know what they want. Such a deduction, justified or not, will be certain to have an adverse effect on their own performance and in turn on the performance of those who report to them. Having seen a radical shift in policy first in one direction and then in another within a short period of time, they are likely not to respond to the next shift, assuming that it, too, will be reversed before long.

The crucial importance of a basic stability in policy can be further illustrated by noting the impact of an organization's policy on the individual's expectations and motivation. When men know what to expect, when they understand what management considers important and what unimportant, when it will reward and when it will discipline, they will make an effort to perform as management would like them to perform. They stand to gain from this and to lose if they fail to comply. However, if the policy emanating from the top is subject to frequent change, individuals in the lower echelons cannot know what is wanted of them, and even less how they can gain favor, and therefore they do not put forth special effort. In fact, if they work for long in a situation where the objectives and standards are constantly being altered, they are likely to become indifferent, which in turn will be reflected in poorer performance.

Another important reason why management must avoid too frequent major changes is the difficulty, even in the absence of the resentment and hostility mentioned above, of conveying to the many different groups in a large organization the aim of the new policy and the plan for its implementation. To be effective, policy changes must lead to changes in behavior. These in turn can come about only if the individuals who are to learn a new technique, a new approach, have sufficient time to learn and to practice the new. A management that changes its policies too often cannot be in effective control of the organization for the simple reason that the people who are to carry out the new policies will never be able to keep up with them. As we pointed out in an earlier study, *Effecting Change in Large Organizations,* this underestimation of the time required to understand new policies and to implement them is among the most serious errors that management tends to make in instituting programs of change.

There is still another reason why management should avoid frequent changes in policy. No one can ever know all the consequences that are likely to result from replacing an established policy with a new one. The responses of the members of the organization can only be estimated. One way that management can reduce undesirable repercussions to a new policy is to take the time and effort to explore in advance how different groups are likely to receive it. There is, of course, a limit to how often and how thoroughly management can engage in such pre-testing.

Thus, management can achieve and maintain effective performance throughout the organization by introducing effective personnel planning and maintaining stability of policy. In addition to these general approaches there are specific approaches. These will be briefly considered. With regard to selection, there is a danger in establishing minimum standards which are either too high or too low or which are purely arbitrary. There is a natural inclination on the part of management to establish standards as high as possible, but this is usually an error. If the requirements which are established have no realistic relationship to the work that needs to be done, now or in the future, as when a large department store in the depression of the early 1930s hired only Ph.D.s for salesmen, the outcome is likely to be a low level of performance. Frustration and resentment are the inevitable results when people cannot make use of their training and skills.

The obverse is easier to recognize. Management stands to gain if it sets its standards sufficiently high that it rejects the less capable among those who are seeking employment.

Yet the selection process is frequently faulty because management often knows little about the true requirements of the jobs which it is seeking to fill or about the abilities and limitations that characterize the potential supply of manpower. In recent years it has sought to avoid this problem by contending that since it is concerned not only with the employee's capacity on the entry job but with his capacity for growth, there is little or no danger in setting high standards. But if the opportunities to move ahead are limited, as they must inevitably be in any organization, large as well as small, disappointment and frustration, leading to lowered effectiveness, are likely to develop when the gap between potentialities and requirements is wide.

Closely related but still distinguishable from the foregoing is the establishment of arbitrary standards which bear no relationship to the requirements of the job. It is easy for management in this as in the earlier instance to rationalize such arbitrary standards, especially if they have widespread acceptance in the community or the industry. But unless the costs of deviating from established patterns entail serious and manifold consequences—which they seldom do—the advantage is likely to be with the employer who refuses to be bound by tradition and who will consider in setting his selection standards only relevant factors such as skill and experience and not, as so frequently happens, those which more often than not are likely to be irrelevant such as age, sex, or racial or ethnic origin.

Another misconception that permeates many selection procedures should be pointed out. Many managements search for individuals who are free of any disability. As we have stated, a particular advantage of a large organization is its ability to break down its principal functions into many specialized subdivisions so that it is easier to match men who are available with the work that needs doing. But the personnel staffs in many organizations are loath to employ anybody with a clearly recognizable handicap; this policy ignores the fact that no man is free of shortcomings and that the real challenge is to know both the job and the man so as to be able to decide whether a particular disability is relevant or not.

Even if selection were more scientific and reliable than in point of fact it is, management would still have to direct considerable resources to training. The larger the organization and the more specialized its functions—and the two tend to go together—the less likelihood there is that the market will be able to supply people with all of the types of skill that are required. During the past decade, an increasing number of large business organizations have recognized this fact and have expanded and improved their training. And more effort is now being made by large voluntary organizations to do likewise since only thus can they hope to secure the number of qualified people they require.

Many of the recent efforts in training have been concentrated on formal programs, both intramural and extramural, and it is likely that much of this has been of sufficiently good quality under sufficiently favorable conditions that the effort has been justified by the results. But there is ground for believing that in the first flush of enthusiasm insufficient attention has been paid to such basic questions as who should be selected for training, how he should be trained, and for how long, and what standards can be used to measure the effectiveness of the training which he has received.

The stress on formal classroom training has also tended to divert attention from the inevitably close relations among work assignments, the quality of supervision, and training. A man is most likely to learn by doing. To learn he must have both the responsibility for a specific assignment and the authority to make the requisite decisions. Unless he can make mistakes and be held to account, he is unlikely to learn any more than a child could learn to walk without being permitted to fall. And if a man is kept at his assignment long after he has thoroughly mastered it, his acquisition of new knowledge and skill will inevitably be retarded. Thus, effective training depends on the overall effectiveness of the personnel system in which formal training can at best play only a small part.

This brings us to the next consideration—the way in which the assignment system can contribute more to effective performance. We have just pointed out the close connections between training and assignments. Here we must note the dilemma that organizations frequently face in balancing the additional training that they would like their staffs to acquire and their need to get their present work out speedily and efficiently. There is no simple resolution of this conflict between the present and the future, but a wise management knows that the price of making the most productive use of its people in the present is too high if it will lead to a weakened organization in the future. It must stand ready to remove men who are performing excellently in their present positions sometimes to give them, sometimes to give others, a chance to grow.

The assignment process can also contribute to effective performance by insuring that a reasonable balance is established and maintained between the organization's needs for generalists and specialists. One of the consequences of the continuing technological advances is the inevitably larger number of specialists that every large organization requires. But at the same time the men at the helm of a large organization can manage successfully only if they have a real understanding of many different sectors of the organization. They can have this only if they are periodically moved from one to another assignment rather than being left to become expert in one.

There is another aspect of this problem that goes beyond establishing and maintaining a proper balance between the generalist and the specialist. Since many men by inclination or necessity will have to remain specialists, and since many of them will frequently make very important contributions to the success of the organization out of their specialized knowledge, it is important for management to keep under constant review whether the incentive and reward structure has been appropriately adjusted to take cognizance of the growing importance of the specialist.

Assignments can also be used to motivate men to do better work and thus contribute to the overall management objective of effective performance. It is well known, although management frequently fails to act on the knowledge, that some men are strongly motivated to work, others only slightly. A large organization is particularly able to learn more about the motivation of its work force and then to make use of its wide range of assignments to exploit this knowledge. While the performance of men over time will usually enable management to differentiate between the strongly and the poorly motivated, this knowledge can be secured more quickly and with less expense if an organization permits men to choose from among different types of jobs that fall within their competence. There is much more room for self-selection than most managements are willing to grant.

No organization, surely no large organization, can hope to prosper unless it establishes and adheres to a set of rules governing discipline, promotion, and discharge. Large organizations are under the special necessity to govern through policy rather than through persons. Whatever actions it takes or fails to take with respect to a specific individual must be considered and weighed in the larger context, that is, with regard to how its action will be interpreted by the whole group. Since in a large organization, there cannot be personal relations between most of the work force and the management, the integrity of the people in responsible positions can be tested only by the way they act in the face of concrete situations involving members who have performed well or poorly. If promotions do not go to those who have earned them, or if punishment is not meted out to those who have broken the rules, others in the organization are not motivated either to strive to perform effectively or to abide by the regulations. They have nothing to gain and nothing to lose—at least nothing that they can count on. The fact that management reveals itself to the members of the organization only through the policies which it establishes and enforces makes equity that much more important. For policies and practices grounded in equity instill confidence—and confidence, or the lack of it, will surely be reflected in performance.

It is particularly difficult to establish sound promotion policies. Many large organizations tend to rely heavily if not exclusively on seniority, in the hope of gaining at least the advantage of following an objective criterion—of moving men ahead in terms of length of service. But few organizations have found it possible to rely solely on seniority or any equivalent objective factor. The nub of the difficulty here is the need to provide more incentive for men who are capable of and willing to perform above the average. While some men will do their best in the absence of special recognition and reward, many need the spur of knowing that their efforts will be singled out for special rewards.

It is not easy to reconcile the necessity to handle promotions objectively with the necessity to identify and reward those whose performance has been above average. The fact that it is very difficult to assess performance objectively and that, in a large organization, it is very hard for those at the top to have adequate personal knowledge of the people scattered throughout the organization only compounds the difficulties. But there is no escaping the problem: effective performance depends on a system of promotion that can soundly and objectively relate effort to reward with proper weight given to length and faithfulness of service.

Associated with this problem is management's need to establish and maintain reasonable discipline; supervisors must see to it that men do their jobs and on time and that they suffer penalties and even discharge if their performance remains unsatisfactory. Management must take corrective action when individuals perform poorly, for otherwise ever larger numbers in the organization will disregard established standards and try to "get away with" as much as or more than the next man. While management must avoid arbitrary or punitive actions which are likely to lead to disturbance that will be reflected in lowered performance, proper enforcement of discipline is an essential function of management.

This brief consideration of the several approaches through which large organizations can influence performance has called attention to the positive contributions possible in personnel planning, stability of policy, and general principles in the selection, training, assignment and promotion of personnel. Much is known about the way in which these several approaches can contribute to effective performance, but much remains to be learned. For instance, the proper balancing of the rate of technological improvement with additional efforts to raise the skill level of those who must manage, operate, and maintain the increasingly complex structures warrants further study. So too does the problem of work motivation. We are only at the beginning of understanding the marked differences between the strongly and the poorly motivated in the world of work. We also need new knowledge about how the individual, his immediate work group, and the larger organization can be more effectively integrated so that performance can be improved.

Government

Although ours is a society that has long prided itself on getting most of its essential work done through the voluntary efforts of individuals, from the beginning of its history it has relied to a considerable degree on the intermediary of government—local, state, and federal—to undertake directly or to assist indirectly in accomplishing many important social objectives. Today government spends about one-quarter of our national income and provides direct employment for almost one-sixth of the labor force.

There are two ways of looking at government from the point of view of manpower. Government is by far the largest employer in the nation and as such shares many of the problems of other large employers. This means that the approach in the preceding section is specifically relevant to government. But government also exerts a unique influence through its many different programs and policies on the development and utilization of the nation's human resources. To this we now turn.

In our tradition government has long assumed the principal responsibility for providing adequate educational opportunities which are essential if people are to develop their potentialities. Over the decades government has constantly broadened the scale and scope of its educational program, recognizing that elementary instruction is no longer adequate preparation for work and life in a modern age. While more than 7 out of every 10 young people currently graduate from high school, state governments are constantly expanding their support for post-high-school education with the result that about 36 percent of the men eighteen and nineteen years of age are now attending college, and about 63 percent of these are in public institutions.

Education until very recently has been the responsibility of local and state governments, although the federal government became increasingly involved through the G.I. Bill, construction loans for college dormitories, fellowship programs, research grants, the National Defense Education Act, and still other ways before entering upon a general program of financial support.

Education and performance are related in several important ways. We have seen that this nation's security is jeopardized when localities and states fail to support their schools adequately. Large numbers of men must be rejected for military service or they will fail to perform adequately because they lack an adequate educational background. Since many men, if they are to find work, must leave the localities where they were born and brought up, they carry their educational deficiencies to other regions. This means that they can be at best only marginal members of the labor force in the communities to which they have migrated. The entire nation pays a considerable part of the price of inadequate education in particular states and regions.

The third important tie between education and performance derives from enforced education: the prolongation of schooling is no nostrum. If an adolescent is uninterested in what is going on in the classroom and remains there only because he is forced to, he will not be properly prepared for work and life. Compulsory schooling beyond the middle teens can have a deleterious instead of a constructive effect on a young person's development. There is a pressing need for communities throughout the United States to experiment with new methods and approaches, such as combined work-study programs, to give these young people a better start in life so that they will be able to perform effectively as adults.

Important as education is as a prerequisite for effective performance, it frequently is not enough. A man with serious physical or emotional defects may be very well educated yet be unable to perform effectively. The past decades have seen spectacular advances in medicine with the result that many who in earlier times would have been lucky to survive can now reach maturity and function effectively as an adult.

The challenge to government here is to see that those in the population who do not have adequate financial means to secure essential medical care can obtain it nevertheless. No responsible society dares tolerate a situation where the poor, or even the improvident, are denied access to essential medical care or, even worse, where their children go without it.

In addition to making more adequate provision for medical care for the indigent and the near indigent, government has another responsibility in this connection and that is to continue to invest liberally in medical research and education. Future progress depends on research; and adequate medical care depends primarily on the availability of trained personnel.

These several responsibilities in the area of medical care do not rest on government alone but they cannot be adequately met without the active participation of each level of government. While progress in recent years has been notable on each front—availability of care, research, and training of personnel—and government has played an important part in the progress, still more needs to be done.

From many points of view the challenge to government to assist those with physical illness or injury is easier to meet than the challenge to contribute to the emotional health and well-being of the population which, as we have had repeated occasion to note, was so frequently responsible for ineffective performance.

The federal government has taken the lead in raising the level of psychiatric care just as it has played the leading role in recent years in many other areas affecting the nation's health and well-being. The outstanding improvement in the Veterans Administration psychiatric services, inpatient and outpatient, after World War II contributed markedly to helping many veterans get back on their feet. While some were too seriously ill to be helped, many others benefited from the psychotherapy which they received.

Undoubtedly the major efforts of the federal government to provide a high level of psychiatric care for soldiers and veterans had an impact on the community at large, with the result that state governments have in recent years been encouraged to increase their support for mental hospitals and mental hygiene clinics. At the same time voluntary groups have also become much more active in the mental health field. The monetary costs of mental illness to the American people here estimated some time ago by Rashi Fein to amount, on an annual basis, to between 2 and 3 billion dollars.

While money still remains a major lack, the problem goes deeper. Despite recent advances in chemotherapy and the earlier advances in insulin and electric shock therapy we know very little about the causes and cure for serious mental illness. And we are still seriously handicapped in treating individuals with neuroses because the origins of their difficulties are so deeply imbedded in their personalities and are reinforced by reality situations which often can be changed, if at all, only with the greatest difficulty. Despite these real limitations to psychiatric treatment, it is generally agreed that many who develop emotional difficulties can, if they receive help early, regain sufficient stability so that they are able to bring their strengths to bear on their problems and once more perform effectively.

Among the important lessons that World War II should have taught us is that most people want to perform effectively and to be self-supporting, and that in the absence of satisfactory alternatives, government should at least provide essential rehabilitative services for those in need. Sound social accounting would always justify an effort to rehabilitate even individuals who had only modest assets on which to build in the hope that some would make the grade. It is much less expensive for a society to invest liberally in rehabilitative efforts in order to help handicapped people, especially the young, to perform effectively than to conclude that there is no hope, and thus leave these people to be maintained in one way or another by the community.

There is, however, a warning in the experience of World War II that should be heeded. The supports that are made available should not be permitted to weaken the individual's motivation to recover. This is what happened as the result of the difference between the comforts, security, and relaxation of discipline that soldiers experienced in Army hospitals and the dangers and deprivations they were forced to endure at the front. It is generally agreed that a liberal annual sick-leave policy, which in essence is a sound health measure, may in organizations with poor morale be seriously abused by encouraging some workers to stay home from work when they are only slightly indisposed. The system may operate to weaken rather than strengthen motivation to work.

The foregoing recommendations concerning actions that government and other agencies of society can undertake to increase the proportion of the population who are able to perform effectively have been developed without explicit consideration of whether jobs are available for all who want to work. In our economy, however, the will to perform is not enough; a job must be available. Hence the Employment Act of 1946, which recognized the responsibility of the federal government to maintain a high level of employment, must be viewed as a major advance. It is questionable whether any national objective, other than peace itself, has a right to more consideration from a modern state. It should be a constant challenge to government to devise means of enabling all members of the community who are able and who want to work to do so, even if some of them require a protective environment. For instance, it is difficult to see how the mentally ill, or other people who may be institutionalized, can be successfully rehabilitated without the opportunity and rewards of work. Admittedly special problems must be solved before many more of them could benefit from an opportunity to work. First, care must be taken to avoid their being exploited. Next, it is exceedingly difficult in our society to provide the type of special environment which would help them to mobilize their assets without exposing them to excessive pressures. But in view of the great personal, social, and financial costs of caring for the mentally ill, efforts to help them perform effectively, even in a controlled environment, would represent a major gain.

The same holds true for prisoners. While competition between free and prison labor presents problems, they are not so serious that they should continue to prevent prisoners from engaging in useful work and adding to their skills. To confine a man behind bars and further to deprive him of the opportunity to work is cruel and inhuman punishment and can lead only to his demoralization and increase his difficulty of readjusting.

A further responsibility of government is to give all people an opportunity to develop their full potentialities. Among the principal handicaps from which large numbers suffer are those growing out of place of residence, low income, and race. With respect to each, the government has been of assistance. But it can and must do more. Many are born and grow up in regions where there is little prospect of productive employment. The best opportunity for young people who live in these areas is to migrate, but they are much more likely to make a successful readjustment if they receive proper occupational guidance and employment help.

Improved guidance is required by many others in the society, especially young people from low income homes whose parents are unable to give them good advice about the new opportunities that are opening up or how to prepare for them. Congress has taken cognizance of this need by providing through different measures for strengthening guidance and counseling services.

Another major barrier to full development and effective performance grows out of the deep-seated prejudice that still exists in American society against various minority groups, particularly Negroes. In recent years the federal government has taken the leadership to eliminate various forms of discrimination based on race, color, creed, or national origin. In this regard the record of the Armed Forces has been outstanding. While the gains have been significant the roots of discrimination are so deep and the ramifications so great that it will require sustained effort on the part of governmental and voluntary agencies before their substantial eradication can be accomplished.

Responsible under the Constitution for national defense and the general welfare, the federal government has the primary responsibility for acting on new problems growing out of the international situation and developments in science. Specifically, the nation has need for new kinds of talents and skills and for individuals who will devote themselves to work that has a high national priority. The government must see that able people are trained in sufficient numbers to meet the requirements in these new and important fields; and it also must see that there are employment and career opportunities available which will attract and hold competent individuals in these essential fields. While the federal government has been steadily expanding its support of postgraduate training, particularly in those scientific fields that are closely related to defense, and to a lesser degree in fields related to welfare, such as medical training, it has not yet responded whole-heartedly to these challenges. There is no other instrumentality of our society that has the resources necessary to initiate and support large-scale programs, though government alone cannot do the job.

One of the important responsibilities of government, especially the federal government, is to undertake logistical studies of manpower that will help the nation determine its needs and the priorities required to meet them. First of all, the government itself uses so much trained manpower that it must seek to estimate its own future needs and to relate them to the potentially available supply. Moreover, as the major collector of statistical information, it is best able to make essential information available to professional, educational, and business groups that have a direct concern with particular segments of the nation's manpower. This it has begun to discharge with increasing vigor, especially since the passage of the Manpower Development and Training Act of 1962, but many challenges remain.

Finally, government is in a unique position to study various manpower problems either by undertaking the research itself, or by facilitating, through financial grants and other means, the research efforts of outside groups. The increasing awareness that manpower sets the limit on our national strength and well-being carries with it the implication that we should seek to increase our knowledge of the characteristics and qualities of the nation's human resources in order to develop and utilize them more effectively. And in such an expanded effort government has a logical leadership role.

The Societal Sector

A democracy faces a special challenge when it comes to programs and policies that involve people directly, for they are at once the means and ends of a free society. What such a society can accomplish depends on its members; at the same time a major objective of a free society is to enrich and strengthen the lives of its citizenry. Even a totalitarian leadership cannot espouse certain programs because it knows that the masses will oppose them, passively if not openly.

A virile democracy constantly aims to remove the barriers and obstacles that remain in the paths of individuals who are seeking to develop their full potentialities, for only in that manner will it be true to its basic obligations to broaden opportunities for all. As it succeeds in eliminating its shortcomings, it provides a sounder basis for realizing its major objectives. Justice and opportunity alone provide the foundation stones for a stable social order.

The specific policies that organizations—private, voluntary, or governmental—can develop are bounded by the attitudes and values held by the citizenry who must both accept and implement them. The success or failure of new policies will be largely determined by the skill of the leadership in mobilizing the positive and overriding the negative influences embedded in the body politic.

To illustrate: a management that indicates to its employees that it has little interest in helping them to acquire additional skills and to rise in the organization will soon meet recalcitrance, for advancement as a reward of effort has become a basic expectation of men in the United States. Similar opposition will face a government that indicates to the voters that it is little interested in helping those in need of help. In fact, a lack of action to help people to help themselves can jeopardize the position of the United States in world affairs because so many nations, old and new, are now trying to help their people achieve a better life. They cannot do this alone; they need help. The United States is being weighed by most of mankind according to its willingness to help the underdeveloped nations in their struggle to emancipate their people from disease, poverty, and ignorance.

A second important value of our society that can be ignored only at the risk of failure is the need to balance efficiency with equity. Men insist on being treated fairly, or as nearly fairly as possible, in war as in peace. This means that a management which focuses solely on efficiency is likely to precipitate serious trouble. Men who have served an organization long and faithfully feel that they are entitled to special consideration. They do not believe that they should be required to meet the performance standards of the exceptionally able man, and if necessary they will act to protect themselves. These attitudes are reflected in the behavior of trade unionists and executives alike, in government and in private business. In all sectors the rule of seniority must be respected by management, even if it is not followed slavishly in promotions and layoffs. The sharing of risks and rewards as a value is deeply ingrained in a democratic society that views each man as worthy of respect and consideration for what he is as well as what he is able to do.

Closely related to the foregoing are the limitations that a wise government or management must place on itself in the enforcement of discipline. A democratic people will balk at discipline that is arbitrary or excessively severe. While restraints and punishments will be acknowledged as prerequisite for effective organizational and social performance, punitive action will be resented and will fail as policy. For people who work in fear of the exercise of arbitrary power by their leaders will become disturbed and will perform less effectively than in a more secure environment.

One other significant way in which a democracy's value structure sets limits on manpower policies is its insistence that the sick and injured be treated considerately. Illness excuses ineffective performance. However, those in control of policy must take care not to establish conditions that will encourage the sick individual to hold on to his symptoms. The advantages and rewards must always be clearly and unequivocally in favor of the man who performs effectively.

Another attitude of a democratic society is that men who fail are entitled to a second, and even a third, chance and that there is no gain in blanket condemnations. For as long as men know that even if they fail they will have another chance, to that extent will they be encouraged to draw on their latent resources and try to meet the prevailing standards. Some will not try and some who do will fail a second time—but many will succeed. But if men are not expected to perform effectively they will not even try.

These then are some of the major values characteristic of a modern democratic society that dare not be ignored in the formulation and implementation of manpower and personnel policy—broadened opportunity, the balancing of equity and efficiency in the establishing of rewards, moderation in discipline, consideration for but not indulgence of the sick, and the desirability of affording all who fail at least a second chance. The more these underlying values are respected and acted upon, the more likely it is that men will respond by performing effectively.

A democratic society is a society based on concert, not compulsion. What the majority approves, it can accomplish; what the majority disapproves will fail. Having recognized the important role that both institutions and values play in determining performance, the key question that remains open is how people can understand more clearly the connections between their own fulfillment and the general welfare. As long as these links are only dimly perceived, many will see little point to doing their best. But as men and women perceive more clearly that their own welfare—and that of their children—is indissolubly tied up with the welfare of the nation and that of the nation's with the world, many more will be willing to do their best. Understanding is antecedent to commitment and commitment is the foundation of effective performance.

5.

HUMAN POTENTIAL AND AMERICAN DEMOCRACY

Americans have long sensed, even if they did not fully understand, the links between public education, their democratic traditions, and the growth of the economy. In this century, these links have become increasingly clear. The improvement in the conditions of the working population, through the growth of trade unions as well as through other ways, is set out in Chapter 16. We see here the important role played by an independent, self-reliant working population in speeding economic development. We also know that belatedly but surely the United States is finally moving to bring the Negro from the periphery into the center of American life and in the process open to him the opportunities for self-development that have long been available to the white population. Chapter 17 shows the multiple steps that the Negro must take if he is to benefit fully from these broadened opportunities.

Chapter 18 traces the major revolution that is under way with respect to women in their relation to paid employment. Women constitute half the population and a sizable minority of the educated population. The multiplication of new opportunities for them in the world of work is fraught with significance both for them as individuals and for the larger society.

In Chapter 19 an effort is made to look ahead and point the directions that we are likely to follow as a consequence of the many changes that are under way affecting the men and women who make up the labor force and the conditions under which they work. The scale of the changes is suggested by the estimate that the time may be near when most men will be in a position to plan their lives so that their job will preempt only a part of their interests and energies and they will be able to pursue another set of objectives unrelated to their job.

16. THE AMERICAN WORKER

The thesis is advanced that even students who devote a lifetime to the analysis and evaluation of institutions and ideas find it difficult to appreciate and understand the order of change that takes place in a dynamic society of which they themselves are a part. It is difficult to see oneself or the environment in which one lives in perspective. It is even more difficult to assay the significance of changes which one does recognize. For the essence of historical change is that no one factor ever changes alone. It is always influenced by and, in turn, influences others. Therefore the meaning that attaches to larger orders of change must be sought in the transformation of broad social complexes and not in the alteration of isolated variables.

These difficulties become apparent as we face the task of deriving some broad generalizations about the American worker in the twentieth century. While we have been able to accumulate a considerable body of information, we must attempt to distill the major elements of continuity and change. Only thus can we extract from history the full measure of its contribution, which is to show how the past has influenced the present and to suggest how the future in turn may differ from the present.

Transformations

In order to delineate the more important changes that have taken place in the work and lives of American working men and women during this century, we must first provide an assessment of the changes that have occurred in the job arena itself, in employer-employee relations, in the

strength of trade unions, in the influence of government, in the standard of living of the average family, and in the position of labor in the
larger community. To each, we now turn.

No single factor exercises a more determining influence on the shape
of the lives of working people than the number of hours and days that
they must labor in order to support themselves and their dependents.
And in no aspect of life have recent changes been more spectacular.
The last three-quarters of a century has seen the working man's day
shortened to a point where he is now able increasingly to add a major
new dimension to his daily life: one part he devotes to work; the other
is his to do with as he likes—to putter around the house, to engage in
a serious hobby, to participate in trade union or political activities, or
to spend it on recreational pursuits. In every week, he has two days
for himself and in one week in five he is likely to have three days free.
During a year, workers with some continuity of employment will have
three, or even four, weeks of paid vacation. The time that working men
spend at their work had been reduced during these past seventy years
by approximately 40 per cent.

Paralleling this substantial quantitative reduction in hours spent at
work has been an almost equally important qualitative change in the
demands made on workers during the hours that they are on the job.
Poor lighting, noxious fumes, dangerous machinery, fire hazards, un-
sanitary conditions—all too prevalent at the turn of the century—have
been almost completely eliminated. While workers are still injured,
and some even lose their lives at work, the reduction in the rates of
accident and death during employment has been spectacular indeed.
Even more striking are the general improvements in the work setting
which have contributed so much to the maintenance of the health of
the work force as well as to creation of a pleasant environment for
them.

We must also mention the changes in the nature of the work performed. Here the record is more equivocal. There is no question but
that the amount of actual physical labor required of the worker has
been vastly reduced; most men and women today do not end their work
day physically spent. On the other hand, improvements in management
have led to a vast rationalization of the work process with particular
attention to improved scheduling. Less and less working time remains
unscheduled. As a consequence many more workers spend their days
under the dictation of the clock. Even here the record is confused, for
one of the important changes has been a shift from piece to day
work. We know that because of low piece wages, many workers used to
drive themselves to the very limit of their capacity in order to earn
enough for their large families. Today, they must approximate the
standard of work for the day but they are constrained from going far
above it, even if they wanted to, by pressure imposed by their fellow
workers.

On balance, workers today surely expend less physical energy than
they and their fathers were required to earlier. Whether or not they

expend more emotional energy can be assessed only after the focus is broadened to take account of changes in the relationship of employees to their employers.

Changes in this area were substantial indeed. At the turn of the century the only brake on the power of the employer to set unilaterally the terms of the labor contract was the state of the labor market. And since very large numbers of people were entering the country from abroad and equally large numbers were leaving the farm in search of industrial employment, the labor market exerted great pressure on workers to accept jobs at modest wages. These were the years when the employer had a great many special advantages; he often controlled the entire community—even judges were in his debt. He could fan internecine warfare among competing wage earners so that it would be difficult or impossible for them to combine against him. He was usually assured a friendly press if he had to fight. And the fact that workers had to live off their meager savings or exist on the small help that they might receive from friendly unionists or from charitable sources gave the employer an overwhelming tactical advantage if he engaged in a long strike or lockout.

Because of their markedly superior power, most employers were able to rule with an iron hand. They could be arbitrary, play favorites, cheat, or otherwise exploit those who worked for them. Of course, not all, not even a majority, did in fact engage in this kind of nefarious action, but even those who were scrupulously honest did not by their honesty establish the basis for a satisfactory relationship with their employees. For workers could never overlook the simple reality that if they did anything to displease their foremen, even if it was nothing overt, they might be out of a job just as quickly as they could be paid off. It is worth recalling in this connection the ways in which Henry Ford in his most expansive days saw fit to interfere with and regulate the lives of those who worked for him. He might offer them a loan to build a house, but only if he had first looked into their icebox to be sure that they were not beer drinkers!

Many factors led to the reduction in this early arbitrary power of the employer: the reduction in the flow of immigrants, the rising level of education achieved by new members of the work force who had been imbued in school with knowledge of their democratic rights, the general trends toward more liberal political and social values characteristic of the larger society, the altered views of the judiciary which acted to shift the balance between property and human rights. Of overwhelming importance was the growth of trade unionism, which provided labor with a powerful weapon of its own through which to accomplish a redistribution of costs and benefits between the employer and the employee. Among the primary objectives of unions was to cut back drastically the power of the employer to discharge workers without cause. As the years went by, the unions were able to narrow the grounds for just cause for dismissal. Recently the unions have received a major assist from the courts, which are developing the doctrine that in giving his labor to an employer over a period of years the worker is strengthening his claims to a job in the future, even if the owner relocates his plant at a new site thousands of miles distant.

We are now better able to answer the question of whether on balance the worker today is under more or less emotional stress during his day's work than previously. Even if we were to postulate that the emotional stress connected with the actual performance of one's tasks is greater today than in decades past, which is an assumption that would be hard to defend, we would still conclude that there has been an over-all easing of tension since the worker is today so much less vulnerable to arbitrary action by the employer. And in the worker's hierarchy of values job security is at the top. Moreover it usually is easier to put up with even a high order of stress if the period is not prolonged.

Let us now consider the broader implications of the expansion of trade unionism for the welfare of the working man. Some economists have argued that the union has failed on balance to obtain significant gains for its members. They argue that such gains as union members have achieved would have come to them in any case from the workings of the competitive market.

There is no need to deny the power of the market. But neither is there any reason to question that the distribution of power in our type of democratic society influences the shares of income received by various groups. Another factor is the subtle interactions that occur both in the economy and the larger society as groups take aggressive or defensive action to increase their shares or to protect them. No thoughtful employer has any serious doubts about the efficacy of a strong union to alter his profit position; and many have been willing to make substantial concessions to their work force in the belief that taking the initiative will be better than to recognize an outside union.

Even if the doctrinaire economists were correct about the relative unimportance of the trade union and could adduce proof, this position would be inaccurate because it ignores the substantial contribution that unions have made by providing the working men and women in this country with a formal institutional mechanism through which to voice their needs and desires with regard to the central challenge of their lives—their work and the income that they earn as a result of it.

It can surely be proved that many workers have been injured and exploited by the growth of unions. Members have been exploited by arbitrary or corrupt leaders; non-members have been deprived of opportunities to acquire skill or work; jurisdictional struggles have forced many non-participants to be idle—and the list of negatives could readily be extended. Despite these disadvantages the unions have been able to achieve a great deal. While some employers would be willing to attempt to undermine the unions and many more would attempt to prevent their further growth, the public's mood can best be gauged by the type of labor legislation passed by Congress. Both the Taft-Hartley and Landrum-Griffin Acts were measures aimed at correcting a limited number of specific abuses. While there remain serious differences of opinion as to whether these acts should be amended, they surely did not succeed in undermining the trade union structure, nor were they directed toward this end.

Friends of labor have been concerned about the slow growth of unionism in recent years, about the lack of inspired leadership, about the absence of a dynamic ideology. But this disquietude must be placed in proper perspective. Without question, one of the major determinants of the vast gains achieved by American labor during this century has been the trade union. It has given the working man a greater sense of dignity and self-assurance; it has added to his powers so that he could bargain more successfully with his employer; it has helped to awaken the whole society to the human waste and injustice prevalent in many sectors; it has encouraged the development of constructive public and private policies to cope with these challenges.

The relations between labor and government have been complex during the past seventy years and have undergone important changes during this period. The power of government at every level to influence the welfare of the working man has long been substantial, both when it has been used and when it was withheld. Prior to World War I, and thereafter with minor exceptions until the election of Franklin Delano Roosevelt, labor had little reason to look to the federal government for help except on very limited fronts. For the most part the men elected to the presidency as well as those elected to Congress were much more sensitive to the rights of property than to the needs of the worker. Nevertheless labor had been able to encourage the federal government to take constructive steps in establishing better working conditions for its own employees. And labor had, in association with groups of employers and other citizens, finally prevailed on Congress to take the major step of reducing the flow of immigrants.

At the level of state government, labor had pushed aggressively for many reform measures aimed at moderating the harshness of the competitive job market, especially with respect to its impact on working women and children. In these efforts, the spearhead of reform had been interested citizens, most of whom belonged to the middle or upper income classes. But the working population and its organizations, which stood to gain most from such legislation, contributed the political momentum which helped to pass constructive measures.

Labor made its greatest gains and suffered its greatest defeats at the local level. Many of its efforts were directed toward moving the local political structure from a position of overt hostility to one of at least neutrality and preferably to a more positive stance; otherwise the working population would continue to face obstacles in any and all efforts to improve its conditions of employment through union action or other means.

Although labor did seek help from the federal government when there was a prospect of receiving it, as in the case of immigration control, the overriding impression of the relation between American labor and the federal government during the first three decades of this century is that of a stand-off. Although the leaders of American labor were not satisfied with the conditions of work offered by private enterprise, they did not see much hope of help from the federal government. During these years Government was not sympathetic to labor, particularly during the twelve years from 1921 to 1933 that the Republicans controlled the White House.

The great depression of the early 1930's led to major changes in the basic assumptions of every interest group. Nowhere was the change more dramatic than in the case of the working population. There was unequivocal evidence that no working man could assure his own future and that of his family in the face of a major business decline. There was equally clear evidence that even the most sympathetic and liberal employer could do little for his workers if his market was cut back or disappeared. There was daily proof that union funds were inadequate to help their members over a prolonged period of unemployment. Philanthropy was unable to fill the breach. American workers were soon forced to realize on the basis of personal experience that there remained but one agency to which they might look for assistance and support. That was government. Many local governments were close to financial insolvency. Many state governments were in the same plight. Consequently all eyes turned to the federal government which alone had the reserve power to cope with a major national emergency such as was sweeping the land.

Conservatives are inclined to blame the major transformations which occurred between government and business on President Roosevelt and his advisors. But this conclusion ignores the more fundamental transformations which took place at that time in attitude and behavior of the major economic interest groups—farmers, businessmen, and workers—which made the New Deal possible. No group made a more complete and quicker turn-around than labor. American workers had come to realize that they had little to lose and much to gain from seeking assistance from the only agency of society still potent enough to help them.

The succeeding years witnessed a continuation and deepening of the new trend. Labor looked more and more to the federal government for help in accomplishing objectives which it could not hope to realize through collective bargaining or through the operations of the market place alone.

Nevertheless, despite this major change in attitude toward the federal government, organized labor continued to share with management a basic ambivalence about governmental power as it impinged on collective bargaining. Powerful labor leaders did not hesitate to seek presidential intervention in their disputes with management when they expected to benefit. This paralleled the behavior of industrial leaders when they saw government as a possible ally. But both groups continued to suspect that they might be forced in the long run to pay too high a price for such government intervention. Henceforth government would be able more easily to inject itself into labor-management negotiations which up to this point had been limited to the two major contestants. But it is a rare leader indeed who will willingly forego the possibility of an immediate victory because the long term costs may be too high. As so frequently happens, the inherent contradictions have not been resolved but have persisted. Labor has wanted to continue to use the offices of a friendly government on its behalf but it has realized the danger of a shift in the attitude of government more friendly to management or more aggressive in determining where the public interest lies. The dilemma persists and there is little likelihood that it will be shortly resolved.

Another dimension of the changing relation of labor and government warrants attention. Among the major advances made by the American working man during the Roosevelt years was the establishment of a social security system which provided a mechanism through which employed persons could contribute, while they were earning, to a system that would protect them and their dependents against the contingencies of unemployment, permanent disability, retirement, and death. During World War II and again during the Korean conflict when the federal government used its powers to keep a control over prices, wages, and profits, unions found that they were permitted leeway to negotiate various types of benefits with employers. Strong unions were able to secure important gains through the instrument of collective bargaining, gains that in many instances would be paid for exclusively by the employer. Many non-union employers gave their workers similar benefits in order to keep them satisfied. The development of these fringe benefits—which were the more attractive because of the power they gave many labor leaders to exercise discretion over the investment of funds accumulated as a result of these new benefits—lessened organized labor's interest in improving the social security system and related government programs. Various programs needed improvement, however, since their benefits were being eroded by inflation; many millions of workers were still not covered by social security, and the types of risk covered were far from comprehensive.

The unmistakable preference of union labor for many years to concentrate more efforts on what it could secure through collective bargaining than through an improvement in social security and other governmental programs has a further explanation. Under governmental programs, workers who receive the highest wages are likely to pay more of the total costs than are workers who earn less. Sometimes this higher cost may be returned in higher benefits but not always and not proportionately. Thus, as more and more of the total population is brought under the social security umbrella, and more and more wage earners pay taxes, the financing of governmental programs is so structured that better paid workers help to defray much of the costs incurred on behalf of lower paid workers. The increasing recognition of this fact has undoubtedly acted as a brake on the improvement of some older governmental programs and the institution of newer ones.

The enthusiasm of strong labor groups for governmental programs has not increased substantially since they have found at least a partial answer to their own needs in collective bargaining.

So far we have discussed the continuity and change in the experiences of the American worker primarily in his role as worker, member of a trade union, and citizen who is the beneficiary of governmental programs. There remains the other side of the coin—the changes in the way in which he lives—in his family life and his participation in the community and the larger society. To these we now turn.

Early in the century the typical worker's household had a large number of children, frequently including preschool children, those in school, and those who were already at work but still living at home.

The worker's wife led a very busy life trying to care for her large family. She nursed the children, who were frequently ill, she made their clothes, baked their bread, did the laundry in a washtub, and otherwise coped with the vast array of responsibilities which were considered her normal lot. In these multiple tasks she was frequently assisted by an older daughter or an unmarried female relative who lived with her. But even with such help—if she had it—her work was arduous and her days long.

She did not get much help from her husband, both because the social mores still made a sharp distinction between men's and women's work and because his own work day was so long and exhausting.

Nevertheless, except when work was slack, or on the rare occasions when there was no work because of a depression or a major strike, working class families managed to make a go of it, although many were close to the margin of subsistence. Others were able to live quite well, depending on the number and skill of those who earned money and the number of dependents among whom it had to be divided.

Throughout the years major changes have taken place. Today fewer and fewer families exist at a minimum level, although some still do. The size of the average worker's family has been substantially reduced—from five or six children or more to three or even fewer. No longer are most working class women drudges, although to bring up children on less than $5000 a year, as so many must, is still a challenge to their ingenuity and a drain on their physical and emotional energy.

No longer do children go to work at twelve—or even younger—as many did at the turn of the century. When they do enter the labor market in the seventeenth or eighteenth year, they are likely to contribute little to the household. One of the reasons for this is that so many of them go into the Army or are married within a year or two. Among the major transformations that have occurred, especially since 1940, is the extent to which married women whose children are in school have entered or reentered the labor market. Today it is the wife rather than an older child who is the important supplemental wage earner. It is the $1500 or so that she earns which helps to provide additional margins for her family.

Building on the strong desire for home ownership already manifest early in this century, a high proportion of all workers at the present time own their homes. If they have children still at home, they are more likely than not to live in suburbs and to drive a car. Their pattern of life is often not significantly different from that of other more affluent suburbanites except that they are unlikely to hold membership in a country club.

The life of the American working man and his family during the past several decades has been affected by the double impact of the increasing real income which he has available to spend and the substantial increase in the quality and quantity of governmental services to which he has access for nothing or for a relatively small fee. Both of these developments have contributed substantially to raising the standard of living of the American working class family to a level never before approximated by workers in any country. It is worth noting that the average American Negro family, and particularly the Negro family which lives in an urban community, has an annual income above that of the average Britisher. This despite the fact that the United Kingdom stands close to the top of the per capita income scale for European countries.

The last decades have also witnessed important gains obtained by the American worker that go beyond income earned or standard of living achieved. At the turn of the century, and in fact up to World War I, a significant proportion of all industrial workers were either immigrants or the children of immigrants. As such many did not consider themselves to be full-fledged members of the American society and they were not so considered by many of the native-born Americans. There was considerable difference between the pattern of life and aspirations of immigrant workers and those of native-born Americans.

Three wars, the sharp reduction of immigration, and the passage of time itself has vastly reduced this gap to a point where it scarcely exists. There are still marginal groups of workers in American society but they consist primarily of Negroes, Spanish-speaking workers, the Indians, and small groups of others who continue to live in the Appalachian range or in the Ozarks or who have recently relocated in urban communities where they have not yet been fully absorbed. But the vast majority of American workers are now an integral part of American society. Moreover they are a sufficiently large group and have sufficient income, political power, and social status that the future of American society will be in no small measure affected by how they think and what they do.

The Future

At the end of the first decade of this century almost one million immigrants entered the United States annually; a decade later the number had dropped precipitously. In the late 1920's most workers were improving their standard of living in every respect; a decade later about one out of every five was unemployed and many more were underemployed. In the decade between Pearl Harbor and the outbreak of hostilities in Korea the American worker was again able to achieve great gains. The widespread manpower shortages characteristic of the early 1950's were followed by increasing concern with automation and unemployment at the beginning of the sixties. In view of these sudden and radical shifts, a forecast of the future must be a cautious one. Nevertheless, one of the principal reasons for studying the past is to obtain some sense of the possible direction of the future.

Within the confines of the possibility of error, it may still be helpful to identify some of the major axes along which the future of the American worker will be determined. It is beyond the scope of such an effort to assess the interaction of these several axes, and this in turn makes it impossible to reach a judgment of the outcome. It may nevertheless be helpful to point directions.

Within the work arena we can identify first the likelihood of continued rapid technological change. Whether such change will be of the same or greater order of magnitude than has characterized the American economy since the beginning of this century is hard to say. But there is no reason to anticipate that it will be slower. Technological change carries with it many threats to groups of workers who currently hold good jobs as well as to many who are not yet in the labor market. Earlier in the century technological advances pushed large numbers off the farm. Men who migrated to the city found work in the burgeoning economy. In general, they improved their circumstances. They worked less and earned more. Today, automation is occasionally resulting in the displacement of workers whose earnings frequently have been in excess of $100 weekly. There may be jobs for some of these men, but probably at a lower occupational level, at less pay.

Secondly, automation is only now beginning to make headway in the fields of distribution, finance, and service, which for many years have been the fastest-growing sectors of the economy. While few employees actually lose their jobs when radical technological improvements are introduced, it is likely that jobs which otherwise would have been available for young people when they were ready to begin work will not be there. The suspiciously high unemployment rate for young people—about three times that for older age groups—suggests the validity of this hypothesis.

The less than full demand for labor which has characterized the American economy since about 1955, and which threatened for a time to worsen not only because of automation but because of the substantial increases in the number of young people becoming available for work, has inevitably set off a campaign on the part of the leaders of labor for a shorter work week. Although this drive has met oposition from management, which fears that such a reduction in the work week will lead to higher labor costs and therefore to a worsening of America's competitive position and a decline in employment, it is likely to gain momentum and to show increasing results in the years ahead. While the dangers envisioned are surely potential, they are probably exaggerated. Moreover, the opposition has failed to suggest any alternative plan for bringing about a better balance between the demand and supply of labor. Since during this century approximately two-fifths of the gains in productivity have been reflected in an equivalent increase in leisure, it is difficult to comprehend why this important mechanism should not continue to be used. Shortly after World War I, John Maynard Keynes looked forward to a reduction in the work week by the end of the century to around fifteen hours. The margin between the present work week and his forecast leaves ample room for experimentation and adjustment.

An important linkage can be made between accelerating technological change and a shorter work week. There is ample evidence already at hand which suggests that the future will differ from the past particularly with respect to the speed with which the education or training that a man receives early in life becomes obsolescent. In decades past it was reasonably assumed that during the years before one became fourteen, or eighteen, or a little older, a young man or woman would acquire all the knowledge and skill that he or she would need to hold a job and to cope with the other responsibilities of adulthood.

We know now that this no longer obtains. Steps have been taken to fulfill the need for new skill acquisition among older workers. Larger and larger expenditures have been made by corporations, the armed services, trade unions, and government to provide more and more workers with an opportunity to refurbish and broaden their skills and to add to their knowledge. We can be confident that the decades ahead will witness a need for much more continuing education and retraining, all of which will require more and more of workers' time. For those who are concerned about what people will do with their increased leisure, here is one answer. They will study to insure that they can remain productive.

Unless there is a major collapse of the economy or an outbreak of a major war—neither of which catastrophes is foreseen—the years ahead should see a substantial increase in the real income available to workers' families to spend or save. The margins between essential and discretionary expenditures should steadily widen. The fact that the practice of birth control will probably soon be adopted by most working class families and the further possibility that the trend toward larger families characteristic of our society since the end of World War II is being reversed suggest the prospect of still more rapid gains in the standard of living. Higher earnings will be divided among fewer dependents. Moreover, as social security and other governmental programs are strengthened to provide better for older persons, workers will be less responsible for contributing to the care of indigent parents.

Among the interesting transformations to which attention was called earlier was the fact that during the past several decades the gap between college-trained and professional men and those with less education has widened to a point where it has become increasingly difficult for workers with only a few years of school to move more than one or two rungs up the occupational ladder. Since our society is becoming ever more dependent on men with advanced knowledge and intricate skills this gap is likely to widen. As it does, the rigidities in our social, occupational, and economic structures will probably be increased. This places increasing importance on broadening the availability of the access of educational and training opportunities to children and adults from working class backgrounds. Only as these are available and can be utilized without crippling costs will there be much prospect for the worker to realize the American dream in the years ahead. How far a man can go in our society will increasingly be determined by his education and training. This is largely determined before he starts to work. But his initial preparation need not be the sole determinant. The United States has shown considerable imagination in pioneering in adult education and training within industry. There is scope for much more, including the establishment of broadened opportunities for mature women who want to begin or return to work in their thirties or later.

The years ahead will undoubtedly see a continuity in the ways in which the American worker will seek to realize his aspirations and goals. He will aim to better himself when the job market offers the opportunity; he will look for gains through his trade union; he will press government for benefits that he cannot obtain through his own efforts or from his employer.

But when the income of the working population reaches a level where it represents a very high percentage of the entire national income, the margins for further gains will depend increasingly on a strengthened economy which can continue to grow and compete successfully in the markets of the world.

Even more, the future of the American working man and woman will depend on the extent to which the nation shows judgment and fortitude in meeting the overwhelming challenges which it faces as the leader of the free world. To the extent that the American worker can help the nation meet these challenges successfully—to that extent, and only to that extent, can he look forward to the improvement in his own circumstances and those of his children and his children's children.

17.

BETTER PREPARATION
FOR THE NEGRO

When job opportunities are opened to all men, regardless of color, this does not mean that ability and preparation are no longer relevant in determining who gets the job. If broadened opportunities are to be realized, Negroes must add to their skills and competences. A considerable amount of community and governmental action has been devoted in recent years to increasing the opportunities of the Negro in commerce and industry, particularly in regions outside of the South. Although these efforts have met with increasing success, there is need for them to continue so that oportunities can be opened for Negroes in companies and on jobs from which they are still systematically excluded, in the North as well as in the South. Much effort has also been devoted in recent years to improving the education available to Negroes, especially in the South where the deficiencies have been greatest.

Relatively little attention, however, has been devoted to appraising the whole complex of circumstances that continue to stand in the way of large groups of Negroes assuming their full place in the American economy. Even if discrimination in employment and segregation in schools were suddenly done away with, the problem would not be fully resolved. This may be illustrated most simply by considering a young Negro who leaves his father's farm in the deep South and finds a job as a service station helper in Atlanta or as a laundry worker in New York. He is probably on the road to substantial improvement in his economic position, especially if the prosperity of the last quarter century continues. Still, there are definite limits to what this former farm laborer will be likely to accomplish in his new urban environment.

235

Poorly educated, he will probably be rejected for military service. With no particular aptitudes or skills and with little opportunity for training, he will not be able to rise above a laborer's job. The crucial question is what will happen to his children and his grandchildren. The answer will depend in no small measure on the drives and opportunities that they have to prepare themselves for work.

The Problem of
Developing Potential

Better preparation for work involves much more than a formal equalization of educational opportunities. For Negroes as for whites, basic preparation for school and for work occurs within the family, the neighborhood, and the community. The habits, the values, and the goals that the child acquires provide the basis for his later accomplishments in school and at work. Because of his history, the American Negro is not prepared in the same way as the white population to take full advantage of the economic opportunities that exist. The Negro must alter many of his values before he will be able to cope effectively with his new situation.

To appraise how Negro potential can be fully developed therefore requires consideration of a whole complex of factors, including the structure and functioning of the Negro family and community and the values and behavior of both Negroes and whites, as well as the present state of and future prospects for his educational and economic opportunities. Each facet is inseparably connected with all of the others. A deficiency in any one area will react adversely on all other areas, just as improvement in any area will lead to cumulative benefits. To speed the development of Negro potential, therefore, requires a concerted and simultaneous attack on all conditions that now impede that development.

The challenges that must be faced and some of the ways in which they can be met may be illustrated by turning again to the young Negro farmer who migrates from the deep South to a Northern city. Even the industrious man on a poor Southern farm is hard put to use his time effectively at certain periods of the year. On the other hand, the Northern worker during the past twenty-five years has had the benefit of more or less regular, full-time work. The migrant finds that steady remunerative work soon becomes a regular part of his life. His children will have a much better chance than they would have had on a Southern farm to develop values and habits that will facilitate their later adjustment to an industrial economy.

The urban Negro family in the North is likely to have three times more to spend during the year than the $1,250 income which is the approximate amount earned by the average Negro farm family. The living conditions of the Northern Negro may not be three times better, but he will have much greater scope for choosing what he buys. Moreover, directly exposed to the wide range of goods and services available, he will probably be stimulated to make greater efforts to raise his standard of living. Urban Negro families are generally much smaller than farm families. Consequently, the higher incomes of the urban families are divided among fewer family members and there is more for each. According to the 1960 Census, married nonwhite women living on farms had an average of about five children each by the time they reached the end of the childbearing period. The corresponding group of urban women had an average of only about two children each.

In a city, the Negro is no longer confined to the very narrow range of jobs available in the rural South. There he could have been a farm laborer or perhaps a lumber mill or road gang worker. The city offers him a much wider range of occupational opportunities, even though his education is limited and his skills few, and in spite of the barriers that remain because of the color of his skin.

Although he will probably have to live in a neighborhood inhabited exclusively by Negroes, during his working day he is likely to have more contact with the white population than he would have had at home. What is more, the quality of these contacts will be quite different than in the South. If he is to make his way in the larger community and if his children are to take advantage of the opportunities that have opened up, this difference is very important.

Northern schools attended by Negroes frequently leave much to be desired, but there can be no question that by moving from the rural South to the urban North, the Negro has made a major contribution to improving the educational preparation of his children. The striking differences in the proportions of Negroes accepted for military service from the North and from the South underline the better schooling available to the Northern Negro—however inferior it remains when compared to the best schooling for whites. The fact that the Northern Negro's sons will have a much better chance to be accepted by the armed forces will also help them prepare themselves more effectively for work.

Further gains of the move from rural South to urban North are the result of the improvement of the Negro's status in the community. Despite occasional outbursts of race conflict in Northern cities and many restrictions on true equality, the Negro is much closer to being a full citizen in the North than he has been or will be for many years to come in the South. It would be hard to exaggerate the importance of this factor, not only for the migrant Negro, but even more so for his children as they seek their rightful place in American society.

The rapid movement of Negroes to Northern cities represents a substantial contribution to solving the problem of developing Negro potential. This contribution is by no means confined to the advantages accruing to the Negroes who migrate. The Negro who remains in the South also benefits. His economic opportunities are improved by the draining off of part of the surplus labor supply. The more fully the Negro is integrated into Northern communities, the greater is the pressure against segregation in the South. Eventually, the reduction in the Negro population in the South will weaken segregation, for discrimination tends to be most severe where the Negro population is largest compared to the white population.

It would be idle to imagine, however, that the migration of Southern Negroes to Northern cities will provide an adequate answer to the problem. In the first place, not all Negroes can move to the North. In the second, the Negro suffers from serious inequalities of opportunity. Because inequality is so deeply imbedded in the past, it will take considerable time, even under the best of circumstances, for the Negro to gain equal status with the white population. The speed with which this goal is reached will depend on the extent to which those who seek its accomplishment become aware of the problems that must be solved. It is the responsibility of the white community to provide equality of opportunity, both educational and economic. The leaders of the Negro community, of course, must continue to press for treatment according to merit rather than color. But this is only the beginning of their responsibility. They must convince their fellow Negroes that equality cannot be bestowed; it must be earned. Negroes must learn how to utilize the opportunities now open to them. Only if they do so will they achieve the equality they seek.

The Influence of the Family

Preparation for work begins in earliest childhood. When a young Negro has an opportunity to apply for a good job, his willingness to compete for it and his prospects of securing it depend on his earlier development and preparation for work. It is hard to exaggerate the importance of the home in this connection. As the National Manpower Council pointed out, "It is not possible to acquire skill, and surely not possible to acquire a high level of skill, unless one is motivated to do so and puts forth real effort." Few become skilled workers by accident. Although relatively little is known about the growth, during the formative years, of basic values, including values connected with work, there can be no question that the child develops these values largely as a result of his relations to his parents and other key persons in his environment. If the father hates his work and the mother fails to plan for the future, these considerations will be reflected in the later work attitudes and behavior of their offspring.

The family structure of Negroes has long been subjected to serious stresses and strains. Millions of Negroes leave their home communities during their formative years and must sink roots in new and different communities. Many family units are disrupted, temporarily or permanently, by migration. Residential restrictions in the large urban centers of the North are a serious handicap to family life, for they imply poor housing, inadequate recreational facilities, and all other blights of slum areas.

Moreover, a disproportionately large number of young Negroes are brought up in homes which the father has deserted or in other situations where major responsibility for the continuance of the family unit centers around the mother and her relatives. According to the 1960 Census, 38 percent of the Negro women who had ever been married were no longer married or no longer living with their husbands. This was true of only 22 percent of the white women. The absence of the father, or the fact that he often plays a secondary role when present, makes it difficult for the young Negro male to develop a strong positive motivation for work. The father's absence also puts additional stress on the mother who must work to support herself and her children. The 1960 Census found that 58 percent of the Negro mothers with children between 6 and 17 years and 34 percent of women with children under 6 were in the labor force while this was true of only 42 and 21 percent respectively of white mothers.

This problem has been dealt with very succinctly by E. Franklin Frazier in these terms:

> The incidence of desertion on the part of the male . . . is much greater among Negroes than among other racial or ethnic elements in the population. . . . Since family disorganization is so widespread, the family environment of a large number of Negro children is precarious and fragmentary. . . . Because of the lack of discipline, the children in such homes never acquire the most elementary habits in regard to cleanliness or even as to eating. . . . They do not even acquire the domestic work skills necessary to make a living. . . .
>
> Negro children from disorganized families often exhibit little interest in the knowledge and the skills provided by the public schools because it has little or no meaning for them in terms of their family background. . . . The lack of family discipline and a failure of the disorganized family to provide models . . . of the values of the community are partly responsible at least for the irregular work habits and lack of ambition among many Negro youths. . . . The mitigation of this problem must await those changes in the Negro and American society which will enable the Negro father to play the role required of him.

But even if the Negro child grows up in a normal family and has good relationships with both parents, it is often difficult for him to develop proper attitudes and habits for the world of work. Most Negro parents have had to work hard most of their lives at jobs which command little esteem, are often extremely unpleasant, and provide no more than a subsistence wage. Many Negroes are likely to feel embittered or resigned about their work, and these attitudes will eventually carry over to their children. The Negro child, moreover, is also likely to respond to the attitudes of the dominant white population toward the work role of his race. Seeing his elders holding down poor jobs and sensing that the white community takes this for granted, the Negro child is not likely to develop high aspirations for himself. Only as increasing numbers of their own race rise in the world of work will more young Negroes develop the motivation necessary to prepare themselves properly to compete for the better jobs.

The Home and the School

The home and the family also help to determine the young Negro's performance in school. In seeking to correct the errors that were initially made in interpreting the low scores of Negroes on Army intelligence tests in World War I, psychologists emphasized that there was probably no significant difference in the genetic potential of Negroes and white persons. Insufficient attention has been paid, however, to the ways in which cumulative environmental handicaps can result in gross differences in *developed* potential between the vast majority of Negroes, who grow up under unfavorable conditions, and the many white children who grow up under more favorable circumstances.

The school and the home always stand in a reciprocal relationship to each other. When children first enter school, there are great differences in their ability to profit from it, resulting in large part from their preschool experiences. The child who begins school with a meager store of facts about the world around him, with a limited vocabulary, with no sense of the pleasures to be found in learning, is under a handicap that he is never likely to fully overcome. It is next to impossible, even for a skillful teacher, to stimulate students to develop their latent potential unless parents take a positive or at least neutral attitude toward the schooling process. Although many Negro parents are aware of the handicaps they have suffered because of poor schooling and therefore place great store on a good education for their children, there are many others who do not have a positive attitude toward their children's schooling. It is not easy for a Negro child to respond enthusiastically to school when there is nothing in his home or community environment to feed the interests that have been awakened. Books are hard to come by, but even more enervating is the absence of sympathetic understanding on the part of the elders of what goes on in school and its value for the future adjustment of the child. Many white children, especially boys, are strongly motivated to work hard in school, in part because they realize the importance of schooling for their future work. But since the Negro boy is likely to have a limited occupational objective, he is less likely to have this stimulus to do well in school.

It is too much to ask of the school that it make up for all of the deficiencies in the home and the community. Yet the fact that so many Negro children come from deprived families who live in disadvantaged neighborhoods presents a special challenge to the school. If it is to accomplish its primary mission of instruction, the school must provide special support to compensate for the major values lacking at home. Unfortunately, in most urban communities the public schools that serve Negroes have neither the physical nor the personnel resources to meet their primary responsibilities, let alone the ability to cope with these additional ones.

Still other circumstances handicap the Negro student. De facto segregation creates school classes composed exclusively of children who come from disadvantaged homes. If most students are slow learners, there is little incentive for the potentially good student to excel. A Negro student who attends an interracial school in the North may encounter other psychological obstacles. His teachers are usually white. This fact alone may inhibit the quality of his performance. The Negro student may be further inhibited by repeated failures to meet the competition of better prepared white students. The combined effects of poor homes, poor neighborhoods, and poor schools on the intellectual development of the Negro even in the North results in the early atrophy of the potential of many Negro children.

The Armed Forces and
Skill Development

How the disadvantages of home and school limit the later opportunities of Negroes to acquire skill can be dramatically illustrated by reference to the armed forces. Confronted with the necessity of using men who serve for only a short period to operate and service a highly complex military technology, the armed forces cannot make their advanced training courses available to everyone whom they induct or enlist. They must select those most likely to cope quickly and effectively with the demands of training. They have found that those who can most easily profit from advanced training are men who fall in the upper half of the test score distribution for mental aptitude. The following table shows this distribution for white and Negro men examined for military service during the Korean hostilities. Since then, data by race are no longer collected or released. Data are shown for the United States as a whole and for the Third Army Area, which consists of Alabama, Florida, Georgia, Mississippi, North Carolina, South Carolina, and Tennessee. The table shows that only 18 percent of all Negroes and less than 10 percent of the Negroes in the Third Army Area were in the upper three groups, compared to 65 and 48 percent, respectively, of the whites.

Percent distribution among mental groups of men
examined for military service, December, 1951

Mental groups	White		Negro	
	U.S.	3rd Army area	U.S.	3rd Army area
I	6.3	2.9	0.4	0.1
II	24.0	13.3	3.5	0.8
III	34.3	31.6	14.1	8.1
IV	31.3	40.8	52.3	46.8
V	4.1	11.4	29.7	44.2

Source: Adjutant General's Office, Department of the Army.

The following paragraph from the National Manpower Council's *A Policy for Skilled Manpower* points up the serious loss of opportunity that many Negroes experience because they cannot qualify for active duty or advanced training:

The elaborate training offered by the armed forces opens up areas of training and work experience to many who, in civilian life, would be barred from such training and work because of discriminatory practices. Some men, of course, are so severely handicapped by lack of proper education and training prior to their entering service that they cannot be given technical training. The fact that military training in many cases provides the impetus for new and higher occupational goals underlines its importance for men from depressed farm areas, for Negroes, and for others who do not have equal access to civilian training opportunities.

A major disability of the young Negro in the world of work is his lack of intimate knowledge of the values and behavior of the white population with whom he is in frequent contact. His ability to cope with the problems presented by working with whites depends largely on the opportunities he has had in his formative years to live in close association with members of the white race. The armed forces provide him with an excellent chance to expand such experience in living and working with whites as he has earlier acquired. Hence, rejection for service represents a much greater loss for the Negro than for the white man.

Preparation for Skilled Work

By the time the Negro youth reaches adulthood, he is likely to be triply handicapped in his preparation for work by experiences at home, in school, and in connection with service in the armed forces. But these do not exhaust his special disabilities. Preparation for work normally continues long after the individual gets his first job. For instance, the great majority of the skilled workers and foremen in our economy acquire their skills gradually, over the course of many years at work. Typically, the worker begins with a low-level job and moves up as he accumulates competence that he gains by moving from one assignment to another, frequently from one employer to another. In this process he is usually aided, at one time or another, by informal or formal training, either in the plant or at a school.

To acquire skills in this way, the worker must first be able to get the right type of job at which he can learn enough to move on to a slightly different job which is somewhat more skilled, more responsible, which pays somewhat better, and from which he can move again. Employers are becoming increasingly demanding about the educational qualifications of young people whom they hire for such break-in jobs. Especially in the North, but also increasingly in the South, high school graduation is a prerequisite. This is the natural result of the rising educational level of the population and the increasing complexity of our industrial technology. A generation or two ago, a man with negligible formal education could become a skilled worker. Today, participation in the industrial process requires of the worker not only basic literacy but a fairly high level of ability to deal with words and figures. The prospective employee must first be able to cope with a complicated application form. On the job, he must be able to follow written instructions, to read the bulletin board, to keep various kinds of records. If he advances very far, he must also be able to master considerable technical knowledge.

The inferior quantity and quality of their educational preparation makes it difficult for Negroes even to be considered for jobs from which one can later advance. Poor preparation is not the only reason why the Negro has encountered serious difficulty in breaking into the area of skilled work, but it does add to the obstacles created by racial discrimination. The informal route to skilled and supervisory work, therefore, is a rocky road for the young Negro. On the formal route, through apprenticeship training, his obstacles are perhaps even greater. Apprenticeship is most important in the building trades. Here the unions exercise a high degree of control over the admission of apprentices, which has frequently been used to exclude Negroes. In the South, many unions have excluded Negroes entirely from the union and therefore from skilled work, or have forced them into all-Negro locals, where they have limited rights and opportunities.

In spite of the important gains that the Negro has made particularly outside of the South in recent years through the opening of wider economic opportunities, his progress has been slow in the case of apprenticeship training. Many locals in the North continue in one way or another to bar Negroes from apprenticeship. Many Negroes have been able, however, to acquire skills informally. Usually a Negro is taken on as a helper and given more responsibility as he learns one facet of the job after another. Although he may become a journeyman through this pick-up process, he is not as likely to acquire the same rounded knowledge of his trade as are workers who successfully complete a formal apprenticeship.

The difficulties encountered by the Negro in gaining entrance into apprenticeship programs reflect not only overt discrimination but also his inadequate preparation. Both trade unions and employers have become concerned over the high costs involved in the heavy attrition of trainees from formal apprenticeship programs. One major reason for the failure to complete apprenticeship is the difficulty many young people find in completing their related school instruction, which generally totals at least 144 hours a year of formal classroom work. Most apprenticeship programs, therefore, will now accept only those trainees who have graduated from high school with a reasonably good record.

Once again, his poor educational preparation proves a serious handicap. Even among those Negroes who complete high school successfully, many have not taken the college preparatory course. Although it is surely not necessary for a student to take the full college preparatory program to become a skilled worker, he needs sound preparation in the fundamentals of mathematics and science if he is to cope later on with the related instruction of most apprenticeship programs. Most vocational programs attempt to provide their students with such preparation. But in those which have a high proportion of Negro students, the instruction is necessarily geared to the low learning ability of the majority. Moreover, the courses offered are very likely to be limited to the kinds of work which have been open to Negroes traditionally. Consequently, the able Negro student is not likely to get adequate high school preparation for becoming a skilled worker unless he enrolls in the academic program.

There are still other circumstances that interfere with the young Negro's becoming a skilled worker. It has been pointed out that to acquire the necessary skills and competence a man must make a real effort over a long period, both in school and later during his apprenticeship or on the job. Many young people are unwilling to make this effort because they hold manual work in low esteem. For them, white collar work has more prestige, even though it may not pay as well. This attitude is reinforced by the fact that preparation for skilled work usually requires a substantial sacrifice of immediate financial rewards. Apprentices earn less than semi-skilled production workers and frequently even less than unskilled workers. There are many laborer's jobs which lead no place but which pay more than many break-in jobs in manufacturing.

The low prestige of manual work and the necessity of postponing rewards undoubtedly deter many young people of both races from training for skill. But these factors are probably more significant for Negroes than for whites. For decades the Negro had little basis for a rational planning of his preparation for work. He set himself either no goals or badly skewed goals. As a result of his background, the ambitious young Negro is even more likely than the white youth to scorn skilled work and to overestimate the importance of achieving status through white collar or professional employment.

Preparation for the Professions

Negroes are even more poorly represented among scientists and professionals than they are among skilled workers. In 1960 the proportion of Negro men in professional and related occupations was only about one third the proportion among white men. Actually, the Negro's role in the professions is even more limited than this figure indicates. Until recently, most Negro professionals were either teachers or clergymen. This is still true of the South today. In these occupations, Negroes do not compete with whites. They provide professional services for members of their own community and are able to find employment even if their preparation and competence is below that of white professionals.

This situation is now changing rapidly. In the North, at least, the well-trained Negro can find employment in a variety of fields in the larger community. This is especially true in the sciences and engineering where, for a number of years, the demand for qualified persons has been much larger than the supply. The professionally trained Negro is still discriminated against by many employers. Yet the speed with which the professional employment of Negroes will increase in the future will depend more on the number of Negroes who complete professional training than on breaking down additional barriers to their employment. Agencies engaged in broadening the economic opportunities for Negroes have found in recent years more job openings at the professional level than fully qualified Negroes to fill them.

Increasing the number of Negroes who receive college and graduate training and improving the quality of higher education for Negroes are, therefore, the most important ways of insuring that a larger number will be employed at the professional level. But this goal, like so many others, is difficult to achieve. Very few Negroes complete high school with the necessary qualifications to enter a college which maintains reasonably high standards. In addition, many of the best graduates from Negro high schools in the South shy away from seeking admission to good interracial colleges, even when offered scholarship aid. Most of them attend one of the segregated colleges in the South. The weakness of many of these institutions is well known. They have had difficulty in finding competent faculty members and have seldom been able to maintain good libraries, laboratories, and other basic facilities. They have also been forced to gear their instruction to the abilities of their students, most of whom come from mediocre high schools and are therefore unable to pursue a rigorous college program. These institutions have done the best they can with the resources and students they have. They have performed a valuable service for the Negroes of the South, but the fact remains that their graduates are often not prepared to compete for jobs on an equal basis with white college graduates.

For a long time the well-qualified Negro high school graduate had difficulty in obtaining admission to the private colleges and universities outside the South. In recent years, however, these institutions, having become aware of the advantages of a varied student body, often seek out such Negro applicants and are even willing to accept some whose qualifications may be questionable. For the Negro to be able to compete successfully for work at the professional level involves, therefore, much more than improving his opportunities for securing a higher education. Changes are required all along the line—at home, in his community, in his elementary school and high school. Only as these changes are brought about will he be able to develop his potential and be motivated to do so.

Nevertheless there are serious problems in higher education for Negroes which can be attacked directly. One of these is the inadequate financing of Negro colleges in the South. Another is the cost of higher education to the Negro family. A college education is becoming increasingly expensive, in terms of both tuition and maintenance, and Negro parents are generally far less able to support their children through college than are white parents. Many able Negro boys and girls never plan to attend college for this reason. And many of those who do attend are severely handicapped by having to earn their full tuition and living expenses.

For the Negro who attends an interracial college, participation in extracurricular activities presents another hurdle. Much of the preparation for a professional life is derived, not from books alone, but from the abilities that one develops through experience in dealing with people in social situations. Until recently the Negro was cut off almost completely from normal relations with his white fellow students, but this pattern, too, has begun to change. The need for change in social relations points to the importance of breaking down residential segregation. The more young Negroes have an opportunity to live in close and continuing contact with the white population, the more likely they are to develop similar values. Shared experience is a prerequisite for true equality of opportunity.

The Negro Community and the Development of Negro Potential

At least three basic conclusions emerge from this chapter. One is that while expanding economic opportunities are essential, new opportunities by themselves will have little value unless Negroes are adequately prepared to take advantage of them. Another is that preparation for work is a cumulative process that begins in earliest childhood and involves the total life of the individual, not only his formal education and training. The final conclusion is that much of the responsibility for improving the Negro's preparation for work falls on the Negro community itself.

The recent growth of new employment opportunities for Negroes is important in itself and even more because of its consequences for the future. The younger generation of Negroes cannot be expected to invest heavily in developing their abilities unless they can see a reasonable chance of putting their training to use. Moreover, every improvement in the financial base for a good family life contributes in many ways to the fuller development of the innate potential of the younger generation. It is, therefore, important for Negro leaders to continue to strive against discriminatory employment practices. But, in addition to striving to remove the remaining barriers, they must allocate time and effort to make Negro youth aware of the new opportunities so that they will prepare themselves adequately to take advantage of them.

It is not easy for a group that has been so seriously discriminated against and that has been forced to exist on the periphery of society to become quickly aware of major changes in its condition. The Negro community has developed deep-seated, traditional ways of thinking about how its members can best prepare for work and life. We have noted the importance ascribed to teaching and to the ministry, and the deprecation of manual work. These are not irrational patterns, but practical adaptations to the discrimination that Negroes have long encountered. However, it would be unfortunate if these approaches continued to dominate now that conditions have begun to change. The young Negro today needs to know not only about the new opportunities which already exist, but also about those likely to be opened up by the time he completes his education. In short, there is a major challenge to be faced in the counseling and guidance of Negro youth. This challenge cannot be met through a few brief sessions with a school counselor. It requires, rather, changes in the basic attitudes of parents, teachers, and the Negro community at large.

Recognition on the part of Negroes of the need for better preparation for work will be of little avail unless better preparation can be secured. The growing importance for an individual to acquire a high school or college diploma for entrance into a better job has been repeatedly stressed. Better preparation for work means not only that more Negroes must complete high school and college, but also that the quality of education they receive must be vastly improved. Within the last twenty-five years compulsory military service has come to represent an important new institution that helps to prepare men for work and life. The importance of this development has not been fully grasped either by Negroes or whites. Military service, however, has special significance for the Negro population. Since the armed forces are fully integrated, they can provide the young Negro with a unique opportunity to gain experience in living and working as an equal with whites.

It would be a serious error, however, to think of better preparation for work solely in terms of college, high school, and the armed forces. At every stage in the development of the young person, what can still be accomplished in the future is limited by the foundations built in the past. Negro achievement in high school is poor not only because the high schools are poor but because Negro students were poorly instructed in elementary school. The achievement of Negro children during the elementary grades is low because they bring to school the handicaps growing out of a childhood characterized by poverty, family instability, inferior social status, and isolation from the white community. There is evidence that the intellectual potential of Negro children growing up in deprived neighborhoods is already seriously stunted well before they reach school age. Improving the preparation of Negroes for work involves, therefore, fundamental changes in many aspects of Negro life. By the same token, however, any improvement in the education, work, or life of the Negro will enable the present generation, and more particularly future generations, to be better prepared for work.

These considerations suggest that it is important for leaders of the Negro community to assess carefully the priorities they assign to various kinds of efforts to speed the assimilation of Negroes into American society. Since all the factors impeding the realization of this goal are closely related to each other, it is important to seek improvements at every point. Nevertheless, recent developments may call for some adjustment in emphasis. Thus, more attention should be paid to preparing young Negroes for the new employment opportunities that have been opened up and that are likely to become open in the near future. The Negro community must do more than it has in the past to help its own members adjust to changing conditions.

Negro leaders have concentrated on breaking open areas of employment from which their members have previously been barred, and have stressed high prestige jobs, such as the professions. The continued importance of these efforts cannot be denied. On the other hand, there are never many opportunities at the top of the occupational ladder, even for whites. It may be that more emphasis should be placed on helping larger numbers of Negroes to achieve more easily realizable occupational advances. The importance of such a goal is underlined by the fact that the early environment of many Negroes continues to severely restrict their later development. Even modest advances in the living conditions of Negro families may make a significant contribution to preserving the potential of their children. This suggests, in turn, that it is imperative to concentrate efforts on improving Negro education at elementary and secondary school levels. Contrary to a widespread impression, this is an important task in the North as well as the South. Because the ability of Negroes to profit from higher education is severely restricted by deficiencies in their prior preparation, such an emphasis may also be the quickest and best way to insure a substantial improvement in the accomplishments of Negroes in higher education.

Finally, it must be recognized that the Negro cannot suddenly take his proper place among whites in the adult world of work if he has never lived, played, and studied with them in childhood and young adulthood. Any type of segregation handicaps a person's preparation for work and life. The Supreme Court took cognizance of this fact in its school decision and therefore called for the elimination of segregation. Yet conditions in many Northern cities indicate that segregation does not always require legal sanction. Indeed, residential segregation is often more rigid in the North than in the South. Only when Negro and white families can live together as neighbors, when Negro children and white children can play together, study together, go to the same church—only then will the Negro grow up properly prepared for his place in the world of work.

18. WORK IN THE LIVES OF WOMEN

In this chapter, we will discuss some of our broader findings and interpretations of the role of work in the lives of women, particularly with respect to occupational choice and career development, and we will compare and contrast the experience of these women with that of educated men. We will review the parallels and differences between educated men and women by considering three stages of their lives: first, the developmental period up to entrance into college; second, young adulthood in college and graduate school; third, their early years after completing their schooling.

By the time a boy enters adolescence, he realizes that in a few years he must begin to work. Society insists that a man work after he has completed his schooling. Moreover, the prevailing social expectation is that he will work throughout the whole of his active years—which means until he reaches retirement age.

Girls also grow up with clear-cut social expectations, but these usually relate to marriage and motherhood, rather than to a career. A young girl in a middle-class family is, however, likely to grow up in a household and a social group in which there is no single model of the adult woman. Her mother may work full time, part time, or not at all. Similarly, the mothers of her relatives and close friends may or may not work. Nevertheless, a young girl growing up in these circumstances senses that it is the man who carries primary responsibility for providing for his family. As she grows older she will begin to appreciate that the status of the family, including the position of her mother in the community, is largely determined by the work that her father does and the income which he earns. This may be only dimly perceived at first, but as girls mature, these basic social realities become clearer.

Important consequences inevitably flow from these perceptions. Girls are under relatively little pressure to concern themselves with the kind of work they would like to do when they grow up. While some are strongly drawn to careers and prepare for them with mounting interest and determination—sometimes exceeding that of their brothers—they are the exceptions rather than the rule.

Despite this fundamental difference in the expectations of girls and boys, both are exposed to the same educational process. They pursue the same curricula and are generally taught in coeducational schools and classes. In fact, there is a good deal of scholastic competition between girls and boys throughout their elementary and secondary schooling. In high school, there is some differentiation in the elective courses which they select, although those bound for college study many of the same subjects. In general, the girls stress the humanities and the social sciences, the boys mathematics and sciences. Part of these differences may reflect differences in aptitude; partly they reflect custom and tradition. But they are related to the process of occupational choice.

These differences continue at the college level; the choice of the humanities and social sciences as college majors by so many girls reflects, on the one hand, their perception that these subjects may be more interesting and useful in attaining a general goal of self-development, and on the other, that they will provide better access to traditional women's fields of employment, such as teaching and social work.

There is no reason to question that girls, like boys, make curriculum choices in terms of deepening awareness of their interests, capacities, and emerging values. However, while some girls select their colleges and curricula in terms of long-range plans of preparation for adult life, the majority are not deeply concerned with their future work or careers. But such a concern is an increasingly prominent element in the planning of young men, not only in their choice of college, but also in their choices after they enter college.

A considerably lower proportion of qualified young women than qualified young men go to college, which is a reflection of the widespread belief that additional education will be less valuable for them than for their brothers. And among those who do go to college, more and more become increasingly concerned with finding husbands. Many young men also become preoccupied with their relations with the other sex, but the typical spread of three years in the age of marriage between men and women implies that more men than women are likely to have finished college before they marry.

The earlier and more intense preoccupation of many young women with the choice of mates means that their planning for their immediate future is much more centered about husbands and families than it is about education and careers. Most young women, especially those from middle- and upper-income families, do not feel under severe pressure to study hard in college or to relate the choices which they confront to alternative occupational roles they might later pursue.

But although most young women are more husband- than career-oriented, not all of them are indifferent students. Many become deeply interested in a field and willingly invest much time and energy in study. They find stimulation in their studies and are genuinely concerned with the pursuit of knowledge without concern about how to put it to use later on. Their educational horizons are also likely to be limited: many can see to the end of college but not beyond. Those who have such a foreshortened view are less likely to take steps to acquire the broad set of tools which they might need if they choose to pursue graduate studies.

However, some young women do have career objectives even in college. They have set their sights on graduate studies: they avoid early marriage as an obstruction to their occupational planning, and they are thoughtful and deliberate about their college courses, weighing their alternatives in light of their future educational and career plans. The approach of this minority to education, work, and life is much closer to that of college men.

The majority of young men, on the other hand, often become more involved in their studies because of the increasingly clear connections which they perceive between their educational opportunities and their emerging occupational choices. Some young men, of course, go through college with short-range educational plans, loosely linked, if at all, to what they want to do after college. These young men often invest much of their energies and emotions in social relations, or they may be more concerned with self-development than vocational planning. There is considerable overlapping, then, between the sexes: some women follow a pattern characteristic of most men, and some men follow the pattern generally pursued by most women.

We have described briefly the similarities and differences between the sexes during the developmental period and young adulthood. The divergence in patterns becomes more marked after they reach maturity. Men can delay marrying without social opprobrium and without concern for their future prospects. But many women who are still single in their late twenties must contend with considerable personal disquietude and social pressure.

Even among those who do marry, the differences in pattern of life followed by men and women are pronounced. The vast majority of women who marry soon become involved in child rearing and running households. After having children, most women, irrespective of desires, interrupt their education or work. If a woman has free time, she may become active in volunteer organizations. Her husband, on the other hand, is focusing most of his energies on getting a start in his career. His life will be affected by his having a wife and children, but his work will be the center of his activities. Not only does his financial future depend on achievement in his occupational pursuits, but the social status of his family will be largely determined by the progress he makes in his career.

The foregoing description, of course, represents the typical. We know that some women, even after marriage and childbirth, keep their ties to the world of work and continue to invest much of their time and energy in their careers. And some young men derive their major satisfaction from their families and are willing to make adjustments in the occupational facet of their lives accordingly.

In outline, and in general, girls from middle-class homes grow up without clear expectations that they will work as adults." During elementary and secondary school they are given much the same type of education as are boys, with the exception that they place more stress on the humanities. In college, they become increasingly preoccupied with the idea of marriage, although some women become deeply involved in their studies. Because of marriage and children, relatively few women go on to graduate school or become heavily involved in careers. They are likely to spend their twenties and thirties primarily in rearing their families. Work has not been central either to their planning for or to their adjustment to adulthood.

This simplified model describes the majority of American middle-class college educated women in the decades following World War II. But the world in which these young women were reared and educated, is undergoing rapid changes. The next generation is being prepared for life differently and the ways in which it will respond to the opportunities and constraints it encounters will probably be different. By drawing on what we have learned from our intensive study, we may be able to discover the direction of the changes that will affect an increasingly large proportion of educated women.

The fact that more and more educated women continue to work after they marry and have children is altering the image that young girls have of their future roles. The expectations of whether they will work are also changing. More and more girls are likely to find models for whom work is important. In former generations, a young woman who decided to work was frequently censured by her family and community. A career was acceptable only for a woman who did not marry and have a family. Today, some men believe that a woman's place is in the home, and some women continue to look with skepticism at other women who are work-oriented. And discrimination against women still prevails in varying degrees in the academic and occupational worlds. But to list these constraints suggests how radical a shift has occurred between the past and the present and how much more conducive the environment has become for educated women to pursue careers.

More and more young women grow up expecting that work will play a significant part in their lives. They seek to realize gratifications from work without reducing their desires for complementary gratifications from other facets of their lives. But because of the many differences that prevail in societal attitudes and behavior patterns, many girls grow up with varying degrees of *ambiguity* in their goals. They do not have the support of a single and unequivocal model.

This lack of clarity may result from early childhood experiences: some mothers do not want their daughters to work, others are ambivalent about it. Sometimes their years in schools do not help young girls to resolve this question; even women teachers are likely to have differing opinions about the proper role for the educated woman.

Nevertheless, the scope for girls to determine the type of lives they will lead in adulthood has been vastly broadened in comparison with conditions that existed a few generations ago. Today, an increasing number of girls realize that if they pursue higher education they will be able to work even after they have children. No longer are family and career mutually exclusive.

Today, the educated woman's scope for self-determination is broad, but if she marries, the element of dependency will still be present. Her plans often hinge on the plans and needs of her husband and family, which take precedence in her life. And the kind of life the family leads and the income at its disposal still rests primarily on her husband's achievements. At most, if a married woman works, she may make it easier for her family to accomplish certain goals. Only in an exceptional case will her career prove determining. In short, the married woman's status remains a *derived* status.

The single woman's status, however, has changed a great deal. At the same time that the occupational opportunities confronting the educated woman have been substantially enlarged, other changes have been occurring which have resulted in broadening the type of life she can lead if she decides to pursue a career and forego marriage and children. While adult society is still structured around the family, modern urban living provides increasingly broad alternatives for single persons. The educated woman who wants to remain in full control and direction of her life now is able to have a home, a circle of friends, and a sexual life without marriage. A considerable number of highly educated women now feel that the margin for satisfaction without marriage may be as great or greater for them than with marriage in light of the nature of their personalities, their career objectives and goals, and the limited number of intellectually compatible partners that may be available.

Nevertheless, the overwhelming majority of educated women seek to find satisfaction within marriage, in a close and continuing relationship with husband and children. Thus, the educated woman perceives that she must make her plans on a *contingency* basis. When she marries and particularly after she has children, her life will be greatly conditioned by a host of circumstances and conditions over which she will have some maneuverability, but little control. Since they realize this, many young women are loath to make long-range educational and occupational plans. In fact, many move in the opposite direction and select their fields and careers with the expectation that they will have to shift after they marry. They therefore plan for this by seeking to acquire occupational flexibility. This search can mean, for example, that an able woman prepares for elementary or secondary teaching on the assumption that she will be able to get a teaching job in almost any community.

There are a great many factors that determine whether an educated woman is able to work after she has children: the nature of her husband's work, the location of the family's residence, the special needs of her children, the availability of suitable work, and her attitude, and her husband's, toward working mothers. These are some of the contingencies which determine whether an educated woman will find it desirable or even feasible to work after marriage and children.

The fact that a college girl understands that her life in the decades ahead will be largely determined by a man she has not yet met and children she has not had does not enable her to plan soundly for the specific contingencies she will meet in the years ahead. There is no way for her to know how she will feel about many of the situations in which she may later find herself. She cannot know how much of a fight she will be willing to make to counter her husband's possible objections to his wife's working. She cannot estimate her physical strength to cope with a growing household and, at the same time, the many strains of a job. She cannot tell in advance whether she will be able to cope with the pull of a young child who wants her to be at home during the day and her own desire to go to work. These are some of the many contingencies she may face and toward which she cannot judge her reaction in advance.

Imbedded in the concept of contingency is a process of confrontation and response. A woman will learn what she wants and what price she is willing to pay only after she has had an opportunity actually to experience different situations and to try out various approaches. As she acquires understanding and insight about her many different needs and desires and about the extent to which reality may facilitate or hinder her from satisfying them, she will need to experiment with the articulation of the two. But she cannot work this out in advance either, for this articulation is more than an intellectual exercise. It requires continual balancing of her conflicting and complementary needs and desires, and those of her husband, her children, and her employer.

The first radical shift in the lives of most educated women comes when they leave school or work for the responsibilities of marriage and child rearing. Some fifteen to twenty years later when their children are grown, they may again find their circumstances vastly altered and may make another substantial change in their pattern of work and life. Educated women must not only cope with many contingencies, but they must be prepared to shift the basic patterning of their lives as their circumstances shift.

The place of work in the lives of educated women can be considered to be the outcome of these three interacting constellations: ambiguous models of an alternative life style, broadened scope for self-determination and the perpetuation of derived status, changes in life circumstances which require contingency planning. Since each of these constellations is constructed in terms of several elements, the number of possible resolutions is indeed substantial. No category scheme or model can do more than order the major elements.

No matter how powerful the influences that are exerted on educated women, the resolutions they reach will vary according to their basic orientations toward themselves and the outside world. Briefly, their underlying orientations are likely to differ in three fundamental ways.

First, these women are likely to differ with respect to their *time perspective*. Some are likely to gear their decisions to the near future while others have long-term objectives and goals. Inherent in this concept of time perspective are such considerations as the need for continuity in work for high achievement, the alternative ways of articulating education, family, and work, the capacity to project oneself and one's family into the future, and above all to know where one would like to be in the future and how to get there.

Second, they are likely to differ with respect to the *fixity* of the occupational goal. Some are set upon entering upon a particular field and working within it in a quite specific manner in the hope of achieving a known objective. Others, at the other end of the distribution, have an orientation which can be described as highly tentative. They may be more or less interested in working, but they have left themselves room to maneuver. They are not wedded to any particular type of work at any particular time.

The third way in which educated women differ from each other with respect to their approach to work is in their *stance*. Some have an active stance. Propelled by strong interests and values, their approach to the world of work is to find a way of making a place for themselves within it. While many of these women face hurdles all along the line, they conduct an active and continuing search for a resolution that will enable them to continue working and to achieve the important satisfactions that work provides them. In contrast are those with a passive stance who have no strong inclinations toward work but who are willing to respond to circumstances and conditions. If they find themselves with time and energy to spare and job opportunities present themselves, they will work, but if they find that their time and energy is taken up with homemaking and child rearing, they are content to leave the world of work to others.

One cannot fail to be impressed with the broadened options of educated women to pattern lives in which work has an important place. As they avail themselves of these opportunities, their life styles will resemble those of men. But physiological or social realities will continue to keep young women anchored in the two worlds of home and work. However, if conventional hours of work decline, men in turn, may increasingly develop a counterpoise to the imperatives of a career. They may seek and find more of their satisfactions off the job. It is no longer simply that more and more women are following the pattern usually followed by men; men are also beginning to enjoy the broadened options that have become available to many women. The place of work in the lives of women is being radically altered, but this change has its counterpart in the lives of men. We are in the midst of a larger revolution.

19. THE NEW WORLD OF WORK

Karl Marx, writing about a century ago, directed his heaviest attacks against the conditions of industrial employment prevailing in capitalist countries. He argued that parents were forced to consider their children primarily as economic instruments and put them out to work just as early as possible, often before they were ten. The factory, according to Marx, was manned by conscripts who worked under the whip of the foreman and were totally dependent on the whim of the employer. Their work was long and hard and repetitious, and the labor market had all the hallmarks of slavery except that employers did not actually own the laborers. Marx did not believe that the nascent trade unions could help the worker; in fact, he expected them to make bad worse, since he felt they would exert power for short periods of time but would not be able to maintain it. As long as capitalism existed, said Marx, the workers had nothing to lose but their chains.

Marx did not make up his indictment out of whole cloth. His principal sources were the British "Blue Books," official reports of government departments and commissions. Yet one need not be a student of economic history to appreciate how very wide of the eventual reality was Marx's appraisal of the future of industrial capitalism. It is not necessary to go back a hundred years or more or to conditions prevailing in England to recognize the great transformations that have been taking place in the world of work.

In fact, if a comparison is made between the conditions of work in the United States toward the end of the last century and those prevailing today, the changes will be found to be startling. Since the new pattern was not introduced suddenly but came about as a result of many small adjustments, relatively few appreciate the cumulative impact of the changes. Every year there are fewer and fewer in the labor market who can personally testify that they went to work in the mines before the age of ten or who remember immigrant families working in their slum apartments from early morning until late into the night to earn enough to buy food. Only a septuagenarian would have even a vague memory of the world of work in 1900. And since the median age of the labor force today is approximately thirty-nine years, considerably less than half of those currently at work had any direct experience in the labor market at the time of the Great Depression of 1929–33.

A review of the important changes which have taken place since the turn of the century will not only help to place them into perspective but will also suggest the direction of changes still under way. At any point in time, the work that a man does, the amount of time he spends at it, the satisfactions and rewards which he derives from it, and the significance of his job for his life are in large measure determined by the conditions prevailing in the larger society to which he belongs. The culture sets the norms. Within the norms, however, there is considerable variability.

While today most Americans work a forty-hour week, the latest reports of the Bureau of the Census show that almost four million workers hold down two jobs. Or to take another example: Some time ago *Fortune* Magazine sketched the work and life of the then president of General Motors, Mr. Curtice. The article pointed out that he frequently spent four nights a week in a special suite in his office to save the time he would otherwise have to spend traveling to and from his suburban home. I recently talked with the male steward on a southern airline who told me that he worked for two days and was off for the next four. In the summer he spent his free time fishing; in the winter, hunting. He was quick to add that many flight personnel have a second job but that he had no need of one since his wife was secretary to a senior executive.

At the turn of the century the majority of the population—46 million out of 76 million—still lived in rural areas. Almost two out of every five workers in the country was a farm owner, tenant, or laborer. The most recent data indicate that the proportion of farm workers decreased to less than one in fifteen. Many of the major alterations in the work and life of millions of Americans are a direct outgrowth of this rapid decline in agricultural employment and the corresponding increase in urban employment. Today few city dwellers rise with the sun and labor until sundown. Yet this schedule is still typical of many farmers during the busy seasons of the year. Accordingly, one of America's great steel companies has made a practice of recruiting engineers for manufacturing positions from the large state universities of the Midwest, where they hope still to find men who grew up on farms and who are accustomed to hard work.

The unhealthy tension which exists in many societies because the younger generations must wait for their fathers to die before they can gain control of the farm or the family business has been avoided in America because youth has been able to strike out on its own. As long as the frontier existed, there was free land for the settler. And millions of young men—and women—could escape from the domination of their parents by finding a place for themselves in the expanding labor markets of the cities.

Over the decades farming, too, has changed radically, and now exceedingly long hours and backbreaking labor are no longer typical. Despite government subsidies however, agriculture cannot yet offer conditions of employment—or wages—that are competitive with work in the cities. Unless a man has been born to farming, he is unlikely to select it as an occupation. If he is wealthy he may be attracted to it as an avocation, especially since it will enable him to take sizable tax deductions. A capitalist, even one who is satisfied with a modest return on his investment, cannot easily make a profit out of a dairy farm if he must depend on hired labor. His best chance is to find one or more families who will work not by the day but by the year, and who are interested not in maximum income but in a way of life.

A further aspect of farming warrants discussion because it helps to explain why so many have escaped from it and why so few have been attracted to it. It is lonesome work. A farmer must be able to enjoy his own company; with tractors replacing horses, he no longer has the companionship even of animals. Some years ago a sociologist wrote a doctor's dissertation at one of America's great universities in which he argued that intellectual work, because of its loneliness, was attractive only to neurotics. Farfetched as this thesis is, the author did understand the important role that social relations play in work. Many who leave the farms do so in search of companionship, just as so many older married women are leaving the stillness of their homes for the activity of the office or the factory. One of the great advantages that urban work offers is the opportunity for social relations which range from the casual to the intimate.

What has been happening to urban employment? At the turn of the century those engaged in manufacturing industries worked approximately sixty hours a week. But this was an average figure. Steel hands still worked a twelve-hour day, seven days a week! Today's average week in manufacturing industries is approximately forty hours. We once had an opportunity to study a group of movie projectionists who worked only three days a week, or an average of twenty-eight hours! Starting with the hypothesis that men who worked so little would find difficulty in making use of their free time, we were proved wrong. As far as we were able to learn, the vast majority were able to keep themselves busy. They spent more time with their children in the park; they helped their wives around the house; they spent additional hours at union headquarters. Apparently so much leisure does not present a problem.

These average work weeks do not include the considerable time spent in traveling to and from work—and allowance must be made for this time in appraising the changes that have taken place. Today most men spend considerably more time in travel than was true of the working population in previous generations. But there are several points worth noting. Many travel together in a car pool or on the train and they enjoy the opportunity to gossip or play cards. Others look forward to the quiet periods in which they can read their morning newspaper or perhaps sleep during the ride back home at the end of the day's work. Many a middle-aged man who has suffered a coronary attack or has had warning of one has been advised by his physician to stop commuting, but few heed the advice. Apparently they like the routine. No one knows how many would agree with the West Coast businessman who lives in Palo Alto and commutes to San Francisco— about an hour each way; he has been doing it for thirty years, and when queried why he continues he replied that those two hours are the most enjoyable in his day, for he is completely free. Many doubtless find commuting a clear loss but probably many others find it at least tolerable, if not pleasurable.

The workday or work week is burdensome when men do not have the time or energy to enjoy the rest of their lives. It is difficult for us to appreciate how exhausted many men used to be when they finished a day's work. They had little interest in anything but the corner saloon. Except for Sundays, many went all week in the winter without seeing the sun; they got to work before it rose and left after it had set. Moreover, American industry lagged seriously in establishing safety devices and in assuming responsibility for workers who were injured. Work was not only arduous, it was dangerous. In 1900 approximately one out of every ten men working on a railroad operating crew was injured during the course of a year!

The extent to which conditions have changed is suggested by the perspicacious remark of Professor R. M. MacIver, who has pointed out that a major cause of family instability today is the fact that many men return home from work with little of their energies spent and look forward to an evening of activity and excitement, while their wives, if they have been caring for young children, are likely to be exhausted and little interested in "stepping out."

Two further changes in the hours of work warrant comment. At the turn of the century, men frequently worked less than a full week, a full month, or a full year. Most industries were unable to operate steadily for twelve months in the year. But this kind of shortened hours was no boon to the worker. He was not paid for the time when the plant was closed and he could seldom enjoy his free time, since he had to find other work to keep him going until his employer called him back. Today, most sectors of the economy operate on a more or less even keel throughout the year. Many workers now enjoy paid holidays and vacations amounting to as much as a full month's working time. And this trend of pay for work not done is not at an end. There have been recent contracts which provide for, among other things, two half-holidays a year with pay for women workers to get a permanent wave!

The United States has had too much need of labor to have ever been tolerant of the idle, even the idle rich. But as long as work was hard or dangerous, it was not proper for women in middle- and upper-class families to seek employment out of the home. However, as the number of safe and clean jobs available for women increased, this attitude changed. Today an unmarried woman is expected to work whether her father is poor or rich. And the same attitude is beginning to obtain for married women who do not have demanding responsibilities in the home. To have a paid job is increasingly viewed as a positive value. A rereading of Veblen's *Theory of the Leisure Class* underscores the rate of change which has occurred in the last half-century. The conspicuous waste of time which was a mark of distinction fifty years ago is no longer sanctioned, even among the rich. Moreover, leisure is now within the reach of all.

There is great variability in the amount of time spent at work among the employed population. While one out of every twenty workers holds down two jobs, others average less than thirty hours per week at one job. Of the 33 million women who work for wages outside the home during the course of the year 1964, less than thirteen million are regular, year-round workers; the rest work part time or part of the year. Millions of young people in high school and college combine study and work and earn their spending money, their out-of-pocket expenses, or, in a minority of cases, their entire expenses. Millions of older persons continue to hold down full-time jobs while others prefer to retire and take advantage of the government or private benefits to which they are entitled.

At the turn of the century it was taken for granted that a man would work from the time he left school, at around fourteen, until he died. There was no forced retirement or pension system. If a man lived beyond the age when he could continue to work, he used his savings or sought help from his relatives. Girls from lower-income families worked after they left school until they married; only a minority—primarily among Negroes, immigrants, textile workers—continued to work after marriage. Women from middle- and upper-income groups were not expected to work either before or after marriage. Today nobody expects a father or a brother to assume responsibility for the support of a young woman who has been suddenly widowed. She is expected to take a job. Only certain married women now have an option about working or not working. And as more of them take jobs new pressures make themselves felt on those who remain at home. Knowing that most of her friends work, a woman may decide that she ought to add to the family's income and her husband may indicate that he, too, wonders why she is not contributing.

Whether a family remains poor or is able to lift itself one or more rungs on the income ladder has long depended on how hard a man works and whether his wife—and his children—are willing and able to help. Today the options that a man and his family have to determine their status by their work are greater than ever before. Most children's start in life is determined by their fathers' income; but, with education increasingly the open sesame to high-level jobs and with college open to the sons of laborers as well as to the sons of bankers, what a young man makes of his future depends increasingly on himself. Although a much higher percentage of young people from rich homes attend college than is true of those from poor backgrounds, over 40 per cent of all college students come from families where the father is a farmer, a laborer, or a clerk.

That American society is open and fluid can be illustrated by the story of a pupil of mine who, after failing his oral examinations for the doctorate, went into a very competitive business. At the end of three years he returned to ask my advice about a round-the-world trip he was planning. I inquired what he had been doing in the interim and he complained bitterly about how hard he had been working and what a difficult business he had been in. In passing he commented that he had earned enough in those three years to be financially independent, if he remained single, for life!

This is an extreme example but only because of the speed with which the young man accumulated his wealth. Consider the opportunities available to a skilled construction worker who went overseas after World War II to work on a foreign base. He earned $3.50 per hour for a forty-hour week, or a base salary of $140 per week. He was usually guaranteed up to thirty hours' overtime—at time and a half for twenty-two hours and double time for the other eight—which brought his total earnings to over $16,000 annually. If he remained overseas for more than eighteen months he was exempt from income tax liability. His living expenses were minimal. Hence, if he did not gamble or drink excessively or squander his money on women, he could accumulate in a two-year period a nest egg of about $30,000!

Less startling, yet very much more pervasive, is the situation which permits any couple at a lower income level to enter the middle class by their own volition if the woman of the house goes out to work. Even if the man earns as little as $5,000 a year, his wife, by holding down a full-time job, can insure the family a combined income of $7,000. At that figure a family can enjoy the essentials of middle-class life—a car, a television set, a home of their own (usually with a mortgage), and an annual vacation. Of course, if there are several young children at home who require supervision, the situation is not nearly so favorable financially. But by thirty-two about half of all married women no longer have preschool children at home, so they are frequently able to return to work. And if the wife's mother or mother-in-law lives with them, she may be able to stay at her job except for short periods just before and after the birth of each child.

Such a pattern is not necessarily a good one for the individual or for society. It may be, as most members of the clergy believe, injurious to the welfare of the younger generation, although the facts available to prove this are by no means conclusive. But the point we want to stress here is that American couples are able to determine, largely for themselves, whether they want more children, more leisure, more income. In almost half of the families with incomes between $6,000 and $10,000 both husband and wife work.

Although most economists have paid little attention to the satisfactions and frustrations that people derive from work, industrial employment has long been under attack by such diverse critics as Karl Marx, John Ruskin, Emile Durkheim, and Charlie Chaplin. To this august company could be added a much longer list of psychologists and reformers who have repeatedly returned to the theme that the modern worker is *alienated* from his work. The term alienation assumes that it is extremely frustrating to require a man to perform repetitive operations in a highly subdivided manufacturing process such as the assembly line. The critics bemoan the disappearance of the skilled craftsman who in earlier centuries engaged in the creative process of transforming raw materials into a finished product.

Admittedly the London silversmith of Adam Smith's day differed greatly from the automotive operative on the Detroit assembly line. But this contrast does not justify the usual conclusion that the former found pleasure in his work while the latter is severely frustrated. In the first place, in the "good old days" most men were farmers, not craftsmen. Now, as we have seen, farming is such an unattractive occupation that many left as soon as they saw an opportunity to support themselves by factory or other types of urban employment. Certainly a man can make a wrong decision and be forced to live with it, and certainly some regretted leaving the farm, even to the extent of swallowing their pride and returning to the land. But it is surely impossible to believe that in generation after generation in Europe, North America, and now in Asia and Africa, men continue to act against their own best interests.

The critics further weaken their arguments by selecting as their contemporary prototype the assembly-line worker who is "chained" to his place. Only a small percentage of the labor force work as assembly-line operators. Moreover, a man does not remain on the "line" for all of his working life. Even if he has little skill and less ambition, the operation of seniority will probably catapult him into a better position after he has been on the assembly line for a relatively few years. If he is determined to find a different type of work, he can probably do so very quickly; in fact, in a full employment economy he need never accept such a job in the first place.

Some years ago I had an opportunity to inquire of Secretary of Labor Mitchell whether in his experience he thought that there were many frustrated workers—men who found their jobs unpleasant and disagreeable, not occasionally but most of the time. His reply was that he could not imagine how this could be possible in periods of reasonably full employment. A man who was frustrated in his work could pick himself up and find a new job. If he hated working indoors, he could get a job in the open. If he found working with a group upsetting, he could get a job as a milk driver, as one rehabilitated veteran did, as reported in our study (*Breakdown and Recovery*). If a young man gets bored in his home town, he can join the Navy and see the world; and when he has had enough traveling, he can get a job on land.

The alienation doctrine has other shortcomings. It ignores the marked improvements that have characterized work during the past half-century—the shorter hours, less physical effort, greater safety. The doctrine also ignores the extent to which the individual worker is secure from arbitrary actions by the employer. In the early nineteen hundreds a Pennsylvania manufacturer decided that his workers were becoming too "uppity" and that he had better teach them a lesson. So one morning, without warning, he dismissed them all. He rehired most of them that same afternoon. Today, an employer who has signed a contract with a union can discharge a regular employee (usually one who has been on the payroll for ninety days) only for cause. If the union and management disagree about whether a particular employee should be discharged, the company may spend up to $20,000, as one large manufacturing enterprise recently did, to get a definite decision from the arbitrator—always with a chance that the judgement will be in favor of the worker.

There are further defects in an approach which sees the typical worker as an automaton, frustrated from the time he starts work until the quitting whistle blows. Most men have a realistic opinion of their strengths and weaknesses, especially after the expectations of youth have been whittled down by circumstances. They know how hard their fathers had to work to support their families, so if their own lot is easier they are likely to be reconciled to it. And they understand that the better jobs are likely to go to those who have trained themselves. Men who dropped out of school early and who are not especially interested in work do not expect to move into the ranks of management. But they are not industrial slaves, as Marx called them, nor are they company serfs, forced to do what the employer wants or suffer blacklisting. The days of blind obedience are gone. There is more than one industry where the employer has practically no disciplinary power left. The union alone keeps rein on the unruly and the inefficient.

The clinching argument against the alienation doctrine is that most men get considerable satisfaction from the money they earn by their work. To be able to support oneself and one's family and put something aside for vacations or an emergency, all as the result of one's own labor, is satisfying. Men know that they are being paid because they are doing something useful, even if their contribution is limited to putting hub caps on automobiles or running an elevator. The industrial psychologists have often argued that many workers fail to see the significance of their work and are therefore frustrated. But that is not so. The man on the assembly line understands just as well as the old-fashioned cobbler that he is making something useful—and that is why he is being paid. It is likely that the workers who are unhappy are experiencing a gap between their training and expectations and their present assignments. This happens, for instance, when an accountant, lawyer, or engineer is turned into a clerk by the Army. But in a peace-time economy where jobs are plentiful, such discrepancies are rare and they need not persist. The worker can bring about his own relief.

If the worker is not alienated from his work, why is management concerned with increasing employee motivation? At the turn of the century, when the employer held the whiphand, he could usually force the pace, and those workers who failed to keep it would find them-selves out of a job. Today the employer's control is much more cir-cumscribed. Workers must now be led, since they can no longer be forced. This helps to explain the constant striving of industry to heighten the identification of the worker with his job and with the company for which he works. For if the worker is to perform efficiently, he must largely discipline himself. Unless American workers are will-ing to do a fair day's work for a fair day's pay, American industry can-not make a profit.

There is constant disagreement between workers and management as to what constitutes a fair day's work or a fair day's pay. The inter-ests of the two, while complementary, are by no means identical. Moreover, any agreement which is reached is bound to be unstable, since our economy is subject to rapid change. Management wants "dedicated" workers, men and women who will do their best. Workers are primarily interested in the security of their jobs and in higher wages and better working conditions.

Management is largely oblivious to the extent to which its own behavior parallels in many regards that of the work force. Many large corporations have been led to codify their rules and regulations govern-ing the selection, training, promotion, and separation of executive personnel. Prevailing practices indicate that management, like the work force, is primarily interested in "job security." Prospective col-lege graduates when interviewed for executive-trainee positions press questions about pension systems from which they can benefit only after forty years! But since these young men are being asked to tie their entire future to one company, their concern may appear less strange.

Another reason why the executive group is interested in a formalized structure for career development is that so few of them are able to accumulate special skills. They acquire a detailed knowledge of the people, problems, and procedures of the company for which they work, and each year sees them add to this capital. But if they leave and must find another job, there is frequently little that they can offer a new employer. More and more, managerial work involves group action. This in turn makes it very difficult to assess objectively the strengths and weaknesses of a man. More frequently than not, an executive who gets along easily with others, who does not fight too hard for his position, who is willing to see the point of view of the other fellow, especially if the other fellow is his superior, gains a reputation of being constructive and co-operative. And that he is. The question remains, what else is he?

It would be an exaggeration to contend that there are no effective methods of judging an executive's contribution to a business. For those engaged in purchasing, manufacturing, selling, reasonable criteria of evaluation exist. But for many functions no reliable measures are available with which to assess a man's contribution. In the large corporation many executives seek and find their satisfactions in their relationships with others—their superiors, peers, and subordinates. They do not have a specific skill the exercise of which brings its own rewards. This has led one incisive industrialist to comment that there is much less difference than most people believe between a career in Tammany Hall and one in a large corporation.

Large organizations are of necessity political. Individuals must make alliances to protect and further their interests. A change at the top may force out of the organization those who have backed the loser. To be on the winning team is as essential in business as in politics. There was at least one outstanding general who had served in the Far East during World War II and who resigned from the Army once he realized that the succession was likely to include, as in fact it has, those who had served under Eisenhower—Bradley, Collins, Ridgway, Taylor.

In a Broadway comedy some years ago a caricature was drawn of a general who is convinced that his superior in the Pentagon is plotting his downfall so that he can inherit his corner office. In point of fact, high-ranking officials must frequently devote hours to adjudicating the distribution of office space. For a man's status and authority are generally reflected by his propinquity to the center of power, and in a literal-minded organization this is best revealed by the location of his office.

How can one reconcile the conventional belief that Americans are aggressive individualists constantly striving to raise their income and living standards with a world of work which sees trade unions stressing job security and corporate executives seeking to minimize their risks? The startling decline in the average hours of work could never have taken place if there had been an unlimited commitment to work. Consider, by contrast, the American worker at the close of the last century who, noting the apathy with which a labor audience responded to the proposal of an eight-hour day, explained to the lecturer that the others did not have enough sense to realize that it would enable them to work two eight-hour shifts every day and earn twice as much! The fact that the American worker has consistently sought a shorter work week emphasizes that he has long been interested in goals other than maximum income.

The community decides what constitutes a reasonable day's work, and while emergencies such as war may suddenly shift the norm, the long-term drift is unmistakably downward. Moreover, at any time there is considerable variation around the norm; witness the independent taxi driver who works twice as long as the office employee—six days of twelve hours each in contrast to a thirty-seven-hour week! The unwillingness of the secretarial staff to work more than a five-day week makes it next to impossible to keep a law office open on Saturday. A partner can come in to work, but he cannot dictate his brief. Fixed hours are sacred in one large manufacturing company which has long prided itself on its research laboratories. A scientist can gain access to the laboratories on weekends and holidays only by going through a tortuous explanation to the personnel and security departments.

In the United States a man is willing to follow his job. The Bureau of the Census reports that in a twelve-month period approximately one out of every six members of the labor force moved to a different county, no fewer than five million to a different state. This willingness to move is deeply rooted in our history, for our ancestors migrated to these shores in the hope of bettering themselves. Except for the South, the various sections of the country are very much alike; a man can quickly feel at home in a new location. How different in Europe, where a Welshman feels lost in Birmingham, only two hundred miles from his native valleys, and a Berliner in Stuttgart may not be able to converse with a farmer who comes into town to market his produce.

In former generations, the Vermont boy knew that if he went west he could find good farmland and would no longer have to work acres strewn with rock. Until recently the migrant in Southern California could earn $100 a week in a defense plant.

But it is the executive group that most thoroughly accepts the obligation of mobility. The many good positions at the top of a large corporation are available only to those who are willing to play the game according to the rules, which include a willingness to go where the company sends them. If a man is asked to move and declines, he knows that he will not be quickly asked again. But even those who accept the need to be mobile do not necessarily accept all the other obligations involved in capturing a top prize. There are many men to whom money, power, prestige are sufficiently important that they will devote themselves unreservedly to getting ahead. But most corporate executives are willing to adjust to the pace, and the pace is determined by the average rather than the exceptional man. Young men soon learn that the "eager beaver" is frowned upon and that if one is determined to get ahead as quickly as possible, he had better mask his intentions to avoid becoming a target. Management is constantly bemoaning the fact that its work force operates considerably below its optimum, never realizing that the same holds true for itself.

But it does not require many who are willing to play hard to create what one busy executive has called a fast track. Intercompany and interindustry competition throws a heavy load on those at the top who have the responsibility for the key decisions. They are in no position to choose a quieter life with smaller profits. Their only choice is whether to play or not.

In the last century when England was the leader in international trade and finance, a four-day weekend for executives was the rule in London. A recent President of the United States was under severe criticism for playing golf twice a week even though exercise was essential for his health. A well-entrenched labor leader, president of a major union, refused to take an overseas trip of three months' duration on the ground that he could not be sure of still being president when he returned. An assistant secretary of one of the armed services who had been in office for two years felt constrained to apologize that he had only recently returned from his first tour of inspection through the Pacific. And so it goes; many at the top are busy, much busier than they would like to be, but they are on a fast track and if they slow down they will be soon out of the race.

Speedier transportation is no help; it is the opposite. A New York executive does not hesitate to leave early in the week for a meeting on the West Coast even if he must be in Paris on the weekend. With American business and government operating on a continental and intercontinental scale, top executives are constantly on the move. The former Secretary of State was only an extreme example of a man who was convinced that his personal presence was required whenever the United States was faced with a serious problem abroad. But the reluctance of Mr. Dulles to act on reports and work through his staff has its counterpart in business, where the top management team is disinclined to reach a final decision on important matters until one of their group has had a talk with the man on the spot.

While most men behave in a manner which proves that they consider their job only *one* important center of their lives, there are some who have made an unlimited commitment. Every facet of their lives is oriented to their work, to their getting ahead, to their success. They make use of their wives, they neglect their children, and they frequently sacrifice their health. Although reliable statistics on the relation between work and morbidity and mortality are scarce, the British have published data which suggests that for the first time in the world's history those with lower incomes may, on the average, live longer than those with higher incomes. Some men are unwittingly trading years off their lives so as to provide a greater inheritance for their wives and children.

There are many who believe that the United States is undergoing a weakening in its national character because men do not work as long or as hard as formerly, and that we must reform or perish. It may be helpful to view in perspective some of the major changes which have occurred in the place of work in modern life in relation to the urgency for action.

It is not necessary for an American worker to push himself in order to improve his position. All he need do is wait for time to pass. He is on a moving escalator, and, even if he stands still, time alone will qualify him for a better job which will eventually pay about three times as much as his first job. And time will see that his labor will be more liberally rewarded even if he remains in the same job. Between

1940 and 1964 such a man would have secured more than an 80 percent increase in wages, measured in stable dollars. In addition, he will be the beneficiary of additional emoluments from his employer, his trade union, and government. He will have to work less to earn the same amount, and the conditions of work will be more pleasant. All of these advantages will be his without special striving.

Those who fear our becoming soft must not overlook the obvious—that a major reason for the spectacular gains in the productivity of the American economy is the quality of the American working population and its high level of performance. As long as our economy is producing as many goods as we require to meet our needs, why should men and women work longer and harder? However, if we should need to raise our defense output or if we decide to give more money to nations in need, a more austere regimen might be indicated.

The American worker who is willing to put forth special effort to advance himself has many opportunities. As was pointed out in *A Policy for Skilled Manpower*, most workers in the United States acquire skill not through a long and arduous apprenticeship but by picking up some training in school and in the armed forces, learning what they can from their fellow workers and their foremen, moving on to new jobs where they can learn more, taking correspondence courses, and attending whatever formal training courses their company makes available to them. They may have to pick themselves up and move from a community where business is relatively stagnant to another where it is booming. In short, they can run up the escalator if they so desire.

Or they can compromise and decide that they will accept what life offers them but try to give their children a better start. They may work a little harder, or even encourage their wives to take a job to insure that their children get such education as they need to qualify them for good jobs. The number of New York taxi drivers who have sons in the professions runs in the hundreds, possibly in the thousands. Although education, guidance, and training facilities are broadly available in larger communities, in the armed services, and in industry, it is not true that anybody with ambition can realize his goals. There are many communities where facilities are totally lacking or grossly inadequate, where members of handicapped groups are blocked from employment, where the American commitment to equal opportunity has not yet been honored.

Since standards of living are rising for most workers without their having to strive too much, their primary concern is to protect their place on the escalator. The question of job security—of a fair chance for training and promotion and, in the case of a decline in employment, of holding on to their jobs as long as possible—is a paramount issue for them. And well it might be. While it is true that industry is constantly searching for competent members of the work force to promote to foremen, there is little that a laborer can aspire to beyond that. Entry into the executive echelons is sharply differentiated in many businesses from entry into the work force and there are few if any ways for a man to bridge the two. Some imaginative concerns, recognizing that college education alone may not make the difference between a good and a poor manager, have sought to identify, encourage the training of, and facilitate the promotion of able people from the ranks.

With a forty-hour week, with physical strain largely eliminated, with jobs for their wives increasingly available on a full- or part-time basis, with their children able to become self-supporting by the time they are twenty if not before, the great majority of American workers have new options facing them, options such as they never had before. If they want to pay off the mortgage, their wives can work for a few years. If they have a hankering to visit Ireland, Italy, or Israel, they can take a long vacation and make up the hole in their savings when they get back. They can start early to prepare for their retirement by getting a little place in the country. The Negro porter who participated in the employees' stock-saving plan of a major mail-order company during the past thirty years now has a stake in it of over $40,000. It is incorrect to compare, as so many do, the attitudes and behavior toward work in previous generations with those prevailing today, without giving full weight to the significant changes that have taken place as a result of greater income and, therefore, greater options for the majority of American families.

For the majority of American men and the overwhelming number of employed women there is no great tension about work. Only the "strivers" continue to push and pull, and for them there can be no peace, for ambition, true ambition, can only be slaked; it can never be satisfied. There is always more work to do than any man, no matter how great his ability, can accomplish. Until recently, as the depression of the nineteen thirties faded into the background, only a minority still worried about jobs. Many have never known fear and those who did had become reassured by the long years of uninterrupted prosperity. Only a depression with large-scale unemployment will alter this perspective. But anxiety remains—witness the widespread uneasiness in 1949–50, 1953–54, 1957–58, 1960–61 when unemployment rose substantially though it did not come near the catastrophic proportions of the nineteen thirties.

Over the decades many alterations have been introduced into the pattern of work as organized labor has sought to achieve particular goals and as employers have sought to increase productivity. The worker's overriding aim is control over his job. Since his life is largely determined by his work and the wages which he earns, he has sought to make his control over his job ever more secure. He has also sought to protect himself from arbitrary employer action. He has wanted to be treated as a man, not as a vassal. Since he knows that he contributes significantly to any increase in profits, he wants his fair share. He is willing to bargain about his share but he is determined to get more as his employer gets more. Revolting against a work schedule that was much too long—twelve hours a day, six days a week—the American worker has pressed for reductions until today he is working an average of only a little more than half as long as a century ago. He apparently desires to see his working time further reduced.

While the worker has succeeded in gaining control over his job, reducing the arbitrary authority of the employer, insuring a fair share of the gains from increased productivity, a shorter number of hours of work, and many other advantages that need not here be detailed, the employer has also been busy bringing about alterations in work. He has sought to increase the efficiency of his employees, recognizing that herein lies the key to his profits. To this end he has been willing to replace old machines with new machines, and to scrap old processes for new ones. He has been strongly committed to technological change and this commitment has paid off. And he has done more. He has recognized that the efficiency of his work force is affected by the quality of supervision and management. Over the past decades American employers have devoted large sums to improving both. And while they could not prevent labor's gaining control over the job, they have protected their other prerogatives so that the center of managerial decision-making has remained in their hands.

These multiple changes have done much to make work a more satisfactory and satisfying activity, surely for the majority of the work force. The transformations that have taken place over the past half century, especially in the United States, have gone far to insure that most men will not be unhappy in their work. They cannot be driven beyond their physical strength, nor will they be abused by their superiors. They will have time for their families and they will usually earn enough to make ends meet. The serious shortcomings which characterized the work situation at the turn of the century have been largely eradicated.

What margins remain for a highly prosperous economy such as ours to make further alterations? Once again, since there are many different types of individuals with different training, values, and expectations, the need is for a broadening of opportunities and options. Some people are willing to work hard in order to go far; others are willing to settle for a modest return. Some are happy only if they have responsibility heaped upon them; others will demonstrate great ingenuity in avoiding even minimum responsibility. There are those who have an urge to keep learning all the time, for unless they do they feel stultified and frustrated. There are others, however, who like nothing better than to be permitted to do today what they did yesterday and the day before.

The world of work was once man's prison from which most men sought to escape. But today escape is no longer essential. The major drawbacks have been eliminated. Only the morrow will tell whether man has the intelligence and the imagination to structure his world of work so that it can provide a much wider range of satisfactions than it now does. Fortunately for our progress and security there is a minority that finds in work the challenge which they seek from life. Unless the Russians press us much harder it will not be necessary for all of us to make an unlimited commitment to work. But if work can be made more meaningful, then all men will be able to gain some of the satisfactions that have always enriched the lives of the fortunate few.

AFTERWORD:
RESEARCH
AND POLICY

The field of human resources is currently attracting a constantly growing number of investigators, but, as we have sought to make clear at the beginning of this book, it is a young discipline. Its inception can be dated from World War II. And a quarter of a century is a brief period indeed in the realm of human ideas. Twenty-five years cover the work of only one generation and the start of another.

Let us briefly assess where we are and where we are likely to go in the period immediately ahead. We have acquired important new understanding about the relations among various stages in the developmental process, between family attitudes and environmental mores, and the attitudes and behavior that children develop with respect to the future, particularly their performance in education and the learning process. We have also developed many new perspectives about the links between a man's education and training and his later performance in the world of work. These have been two of the principal axes along which considerable progress has been made in identifying and assessing the complex factors that affect the acquisition of skill.

During the past years another level of inquiry has been opened up which can be subsumed under the broad heading of "investment in human capital." The economists have taken the lead in adapting their techniques to the problem of the "profitability" of public and private investments on behalf of and for the benefit of individuals and the community measured by increased personal earnings and general economic growth. One major use to which this approach has been put is the delineation of criteria to measure the limits of profitable investments in human resources both in developed and in developing countries. Since very large sums are now being invested in education, health, and welfare in sophisticated economies and since unsophisticated countries are seeking desperately for leverage to speed their development, recent concern with human resources has markedly increased.

Since early research in human resources was concentrated on learning more about the ways in which young people prepare for work and life, it may be helpful to set forth certain critical questions that warrant further study. The United States is belatedly concerned with the problem of poverty, with the reasons that more than 30 million people live below an acceptable minimum level, and particularly with the alternative policies that might be pursued to reduce the proportion of the total population that lives in straitened circumstances.

We know much less than we need to know about who the poor are, whether they were born and bred in poverty, or whether they were precipitated into it by a slow erosion of their strengths or through a calamitous event. Some, probably many, were born and bred in poverty. But that is the beginning not the end of the question. What held them prisoners while others, including siblings and other relatives, managed to escape? Only as our knowledge becomes broader and deeper and we can differentiate between those who have been trapped and those who, also handicapped by birth and upbringing, succeeded in escaping, shall we be able to fashion policies and programs that hold promise of rapidly reducing the poverty population.

Similarly, we need to know much more about those who were precipitated into poverty. Is sickness a major cause, or business failure, or emotional instability, or family disorganization? Each can be a precipitant, but what distinguishes the man who is caught from the man who can extricate himself? The processes that transform a man and his family from being self-supporting at an adequate standard to a marginal existence and dependency must be analyzed in sufficient depth so that the interaction among the strategic variables can be delineated and assessed. We confront here, as in so many other facets of human resources research and policy, the necessity to learn enough about the complex interrelations between people and their environment so that we can find the leverages that may exist to reverse pathological processes. We must learn enough about people in trouble so that we can identify the specific problems that overwhelm them and the specific types of intervention that will help them surmount their difficulties in order to establish adequate policy.

We have set the challenge in terms of poverty, but it can be broadened to cover most of the other key areas in social pathology, for example, crime. We know that many criminals come from low-income homes and have had only a limited amount of schooling. But we also know that many with the same characteristics never have trouble with the law enforcement authorities. Many have a record of one arrest. But many others become deeply involved in the ways of crime until it becomes the pattern of their lives. Despite the horrendous personal and social costs of delinquency and crime, we have only started to learn about the processes which encourage delinquency, and we know even less about the design of effective preventive and rehabilitative programs.

There is no need to extend the discussion of pathology, but we shall list some of the more important areas so that their significance can be kept in mind: alcoholism, mental disease, desertion and divorce, gambling, and drug addiction. Their individual and collective cost in human misery, in dollars, and in wasted individual and national potential can only be approximated; there is no way of calculating it exactly.

We should like to suggest how the new discipline of human resources might prove useful in exploring the dynamics of these areas of pathology and thus point the way to their reduction. The following questions might profitably be pursued. First, what interventions are required to ensure that all young people who are capable of learning can profit from school? This is most important since we know that unless the child can acquire the skills essential for meeting the responsibilities of adulthood, including the requirement that he earn a livelihood, he will not fit into our society. A second line of inquiry would explore the extent to which a society provides employment opportunities for those who need to work. If we expect a man to support himself and his dependents, we must provide the opportunity for him to work.

We hope that in time the educational process will be greatly improved and the scourge of unemployment largely eliminated. Nevertheless, we must anticipate that many of our citizens will stumble. We need much more study about how to help the person in trouble—the mental patient, the prisoner, and the drug addict—so that we do not compound his difficulties either in confinement or when he is released. To keep men idle invites their disorganization and disintegration; yet we have done too little to provide meaningful training and work for most institutionalized persons. Moreover, we discharge many without skill or the prospect of employment, thereby setting the stage for another breakdown.

We can accept the position that even in a much better functioning world—one in which all young people are adequately educated and trained and where there are jobs for all—there would still be significant numbers of individuals who could not meet the prevailing standards and who would run into conflict with family, neighbors, or the larger society. But this conclusion does not weaken the thrust of the foregoing which is to emphasize the need for deeper explorations into the processes of social pathology and for more effectively articulated programs of education and employment which will provide an optimum opportunity for individuals to perform at their best level.

Let us shift for a moment from the pathological to the opposite end of the curve, to the talented—leaders, artists, and scientists. For this sector, too, we are only beginning to acquire knowledge, and we are only beginning to design effective programs to conserve and nurture the most valuable segment of our human resources. Longitudinal studies are difficult to design, hard to carry out, and very costly. We therefore undertake too few. As a consequence, we know much less than we need to know about the paths traveled by people who reach the top or near top of their fields—be it politics, business, the arts, or science. Since the security and progress of the society depend on the accomplishment of the talented few, it is amazing how little effort we have invested in studying those who have demonstrated superior performance. In fact, we do not have even adequate retrospective analyses. All we have are a few statistical analyses and a few exploratory investigations based on interviews and questionnaires.

We act today much as did our ancestors, who believed that the great man was not a subject for study, since his greatness was a gift of the gods and defied systematic analysis. It may be that even after we make much more effort to unravel the determinants of superior performance, we shall still be left with an unknown quality which cannot be measured because it cannot be identified. But we have a long way to go between where we are and that point.

There are several lines along which progress might be made in this illusive but significant area. We must attempt to gather systematically information about the major stages in the lives of talented people. With regard to their developmental experiences, special attention might be focused on the key persons with whom they identified, the time at which they began to delineate their goals, the decisions which they made when confronted with attractive alternatives, the ways in which they handled setbacks and defeat, how they dealt with their sexual drives, the education and training which they acquired and how they strove for balance between learning from their teachers and being overawed and overwhelmed by them, and their approach to marriage and children. These are illustrations of the kinds of questions that it would be worthwhile to explore in considerable depth as they pertain to significant numbers of men who have made their mark upon society.

Another facet of success is the role of structured organizations, such as corporations, trade unions, the church, the armed forces, and even politics. The institutions within which people work, compete, and conflict must be introduced into the equation and studies made of the interactions between those who are striving for power and positions of leadership and the structure and functioning of the organization and of the larger environment. Among the issues that might prove revealing are the acquisition of specialized competences or skills, the capacity to maneuver around blocks, investment of time and energy, the willingness to take risks, the making and breaking of alliances, the building of prestige on the outside, and the element of time in the selection-promotion process.

Another interesting dimension which has significance for private and public policy is the experiences and the results of lateral movements by able and successful people as they leave the field of their primary competence to enter new domains. We live in a democracy where there is more and more mobility of leaders among the universities, business, civilian government, the armed forces, and the foundations. There are many examples of persons who, after making a radical shift, succeed in their new roles and equally many abysmal failures. An effort to collect relevant samples and to study them as intensively as possible would probably shed considerable new light on some of the important determinants, personal and social, of superior performance.

An interesting and important related facet is the process of aging of leaders in various fields and the implications for their productivity and for the effectiveness of the organizations in which they play key roles. A determination of the conditions under which obsolescence is likely to set in early, where it is delayed, and the escape routes that exist both for the individual and the organization to cope with the leader who has been left behind by time—all these are issues that have theoretical and practical importance.

We have considered, at least briefly, the two ends of the spectrum of human potential. We can now consider a few questions that concern the vast middle group that invite study both for the sake of deepening knowledge and for the light that the answers might shed on important issues of policy.

The most important question relates to the proper scale and direction of public investment in the fields in which government is presently engaged, including health, education, welfare, housing, urban development, recreation, and other functions directly related to the development of human potential. Such inquiries should include within their purview such considerations as whether on balance the withdrawal or partial withdrawal of governmental effort in any area might prove beneficial, since this possibility should not be prejudged.

Consideration should also be given to the potentialities of articulating more effectively the efforts of various nongovernmental units—business, trade unions, and corporations—so that the total scale and direction of expenditures might yield a closer approximation to a social optimum.

Other fruitful studies in depth would concern the effectiveness with which key programs are designed and operated. For example, since we now spend for education about 40 billion dollars annually and about the same for health services, we need continuing critical assessments of objectives and implementations, particularly as they bear on the utilization of scarce manpower resources. Many questions arise. Why do we continue to talk about nurse "shortage" if one has existed since 1940? Or, relevant to education, although it may be sound public policy to look to the day when most young people will complete high school and possibly junior college, does it follow that every youngster should be encouraged to continue in school, and if he does, can he succeed? Or, what steps must be taken to give reality to the formulation that in order to avoid skill obsolescence, a man must be engaged in education or training not for one short period of his life, but throughout his entire active years, possibly even after he retires.

To call attention briefly to a few other questions of overriding importance: how can the Negro revolution, so long delayed and now fully under way, be accelerated so that men are no longer kept apart from the rest of American society because of their color? What can be done to enable more women to take advantage of the increasing options that they confront as a consequence of better health and education, smaller families, and increased ease in running their households?

On still another front: we can expect that the average hours of work will soon be reduced again. It is likely that a decade or two hence, the workweek will be closer to thirty hours than to forty. More and more men and women will then be in a position to pursue two lives—one connected with their work, another with their activities off the job. This is, therefore, a good time to study more intensively those who already confront these broadened options.

The moral is clear. Our society is made by and for men. We must learn a great deal more about men in order to build a better society. We have a new and exciting opportunity to seek knowledge at the interface of man and society, to study the processes whereby the infant with potential is transformed into the adult who can perform, often brilliantly. The study of the development of human potential and its later utilization holds promise of yielding much new knowledge, knowledge that will teach us about man in his social and economic habitat and therefore will help us to shape and reshape that habitat so that it can better serve the ends of man. To respond to this opportunity and challenge requires the reknitting of what has been and can again be a basic unity—the pursuit of knowledge for its own sake and the use of knowledge for the betterment of men.

BIBLIOGRAPHY *

† 1   Chapter 3 in **The House of Adam Smith,** by Eli Ginzberg, 1934, re-printed with new Foreword by Octagon Books, New York, 1964.

2   Chapter 3 in **Democratic Values and the Rights of Management,** by Eli Ginzberg, Ivar E. Berg, John L. Herma, and James K. Anderson, 1963.

3   Chapter 11 in **ibid.**

4   Chapter 13 in **Occupational Choice: An Approach to a General Theory,** by Eli Ginzberg and Sol W. Ginsburg, Sidney Axelrad, and John L. Herma, 1951.

5   Chapter 5 in **Talent and Performance,** by Eli Ginzberg and John L. Herma, with Ivar E. Berg, Carol A. Brown, Alice M. Yohalem, James K. Anderson, and Lois Lipper, 1964.

6   Chapter 7 in **ibid.**

7   Pages 131–145 in **About the Kinsey Report,** edited by Donald Porter Geddes and Enid Curie, New American Library of World Literature, Inc., New York, 1948.

8   Chapter IV in **The Optimistic Tradition and American Youth,** by Eli Ginzberg, James K. Anderson, and John L. Herma, 1962.

9   Chapters I and III in **The Labor Leader,** by Eli Ginzberg, The Macmillan Company, New York, 1948.

10   Chapter 13 in **Patterns of Performance,** vol. 3 of **The Ineffective Soldier: Lessons for Management and the Nation,** by Eli Ginzberg, James K. Anderson, Sol W. Ginsburg, John L. Herma, Douglas W. Bray, William Jordan, and Major Francis J. Ryan, 1959.

11   Chapter 7 in **Grass on the Slag Heaps: The Story of the Welsh**

* Except as noted, all books were published by the Columbia University Press, New York City.
† Numbers refer to chapters in this book.

Miners, by Eli Ginzberg, Harper & Row, Publishers, Incorporated, New York, 1942.

12 Chapter VI in **The Unemployed,** by Eli Ginzberg, Ethel L. Ginsburg, Dorothy L. Lynn, L. Mildred Vickers, and Sol W. Ginsburg, Harper & Row, Publishers, Incorporated, New York, 1943.

13 Chapter 4 in **The Uneducated,** by Eli Ginzberg and Douglas W. Bray, 1953.

14 Chapter III in **Human Resources: The Wealth of a Nation,** by Eli Ginzberg, Simon and Schuster, Inc., New York, 1958.

15 Chapter 14 in **Patterns of Performance.**

16 Chapter XII in **The American Worker in the Twentieth Century,** by Eli Ginzberg and Hyman Berman, The Free Press of Glencoe, New York, 1963.

17 Chapter V in **The Negro Potential,** by Eli Ginzberg with the assistance of James K. Anderson, Douglas W. Bray, and Robert W. Smuts, 1956.

18 Chapter XI in **Life Styles of Educated Women,** by Eli Ginzberg, Ivar E. Berg, Carol A. Brown, Sherry Gorelick, John L. Herma, and Alice M. Yohalem, 1966.

19 Chapter V in **Human Resources: The Wealth of a Nation.**

INDEX